WAR, DIPLOMACY AND
INFORMAL EMPIRE

WAR, DIPLOMACY AND INFORMAL EMPIRE

Britain and the Republics of La Plata, 1836–1853

DAVID McLEAN

BLOOMSBURY ACADEMIC
LONDON • NEW YORK • OXFORD • NEW DELHI • SYDNEY

BLOOMSBURY ACADEMIC
Bloomsbury Publishing Plc
50 Bedford Square, London, WC1B 3DP, UK
1385 Broadway, New York, NY 10018, USA
29 Earlsfort Terrace, Dublin 2, Ireland

BLOOMSBURY, BLOOMSBURY ACADEMIC and the Diana logo
are trademarks of Bloomsbury Publishing Plc

First published in 1995 by I. B. Tauris
This paperback edition published by Bloomsbury Academic in 2021

Copyright © David McLean, 1995

David McLean has asserted his right under the Copyright,
Designs and Patents Act, 1988, to be identified as Author of this work.

All rights reserved. No part of this publication may be reproduced or
transmitted in any form or by any means, electronic or mechanical,
including photocopying, recording, or any information storage or retrieval
system, without prior permission in writing from the publishers.

Bloomsbury Publishing Plc does not have any control over, or responsibility for,
any third-party websites referred to or in this book. All internet addresses given
in this book were correct at the time of going to press. The author and publisher
regret any inconvenience caused if addresses have changed or sites have
ceased to exist, but can accept no responsibility for any such changes.

A catalogue record for this book is available from the British Library.

A catalog record for this book is available from the Library of Congress.

ISBN: HB: 978-1-8504-3867-0
PB: 978-1-3501-8451-0

Typeset by Cylinder Graphics London

To find out more about our authors and books visit
www.bloomsbury.com and sign up for our newsletters.

Contents

Introduction   1

1. La Plata and the British before 1836   5
2. War and the Invasion of Uruguay, 1836–43   19
3. The Failure of Diplomacy, 1843   39
4. Britain, France and the Policy of Intervention, 1844   49
5. The Beginning of Hostilities, 1845   66
6. An Expedition into the Paraná, 1845–6   82
7. Hood's Mission to La Plata, 1846   101
8. Ouseley Continues the War, 1846–7   118
9. The Diplomacy of Howden and Walewski, 1847   128
10. Palmerston's Search for a Peace Settlement, 1848   147
11. The Resumption of Relations at Buenos Aires, 1848–9   158
12. The Liberation of Montevideo and the End of the War   172
13. Conclusion   188

Notes   207
Bibliography   227
Index   237

Acknowledgements

This book has been published with the aid of a grant from the bequest of the late Miss Isobel Thornley to the University of London. I am grateful also to Eva Gordon and Andrew Porter, both of whom made valuable contributions to the final text.

Introduction

Perhaps it is inevitable that so much research undertaken into Britain's diplomacy and international relations in the nineteenth century touches on the wider, albeit nebulous, question of whether any model might best explain her relationship with the world's weaker nations and economies. Historians of British expansion have, of course, grappled with that issue for decades. Since Gallagher and Robinson published their article on the Imperialism of Free Trade in 1953 a copious literature has developed, a great deal of which has derived inspiration from their work.[1] Much of this literature has enhanced our understanding of nineteenth-century foreign affairs. At the same time it must be acknowledged that some of it has come to represent little more than self-perpetuating theory.

Theoretical structures may have a place as points of reference for serious investigation but they serve only to be tested and, as necessary, discarded. The purpose of this book is to examine British activity in the lands which bordered the River Plate at a time of war and intense diplomacy between 1836 and 1853 and to measure the findings against some of the arguments and assumptions which have underlain historical debate.

Admittedly this region was not vital to Britain's economy – although commercial opinion was unanimous as to the potential of South American markets. Nor was the region of strategic value for the defence of Britain's empire – although officials in London were certainly concerned that it should not fall prey to colonial rivals. On the surface, then, it would not appear an obvious location for armed intervention by Britain at all. Yet the British were drawn into a conflict there; later, when disillusioned with proceedings, they withdrew from the fighting with such dignity as could be salvaged. Documentary research reveals the reasons for this intervention and, as important, the reasons for the subsequent recoil. Thereafter it became a tortuous process to reestablish relations with the states of La Plata on terms comparable to those which had existed before.

Yet the significance of this study goes beyond establishing why Britain participated in warfare in the region. However they perceived their own interests in the Americas, the British were also players in the complexities of its politics. The River Plate republics, as successors to the old Spanish viceroyalty, were partly nation states and partly the fiefdoms of warlords who fought for and controlled them. The creole elites of their societies were irreconcilably divided as to their polities and as to the extent that economic contact with the world beyond was desirable. Warfare, in fact, became a way of life in the post-independence era. Although the British most wanted to encourage peace and trade in South America, as the global power of the age a strict neutrality in local disputes was both difficult to practise and always likely to be misconstrued by local parties. Statesmen in Buenos Aires and Montevideo naturally had suspicions about European powers and the appetite which they manifested for dominance and empire. The British were respected but never fully trusted; when their sympathy was courted it was usually to gain advantage in parochial struggles.

Without acknowledging this South American dimension and without reference to historical sources of the region, British involvement in La Plata would lack a necessary context. A large body of published documents and the works of many Latin American scholars, however, make that perspective possible. This book makes no pretension to be a study of the politics and economic development of the Argentine and Uruguayan republics but it does attempt to explain Britain's behaviour towards those states with a due appreciation of their histories.

The warfare in La Plata in the 1840s also illustrates a wider historical theme in that it is indicative of the limits of Britain's international authority. That the British wished to stop conflicts between the factions and nations of La Plata was understandable – as perhaps was their belief that they could do so. They had in fact brought peace before and through their trade and diplomacy were familiar with local problems. In the 1840s, too, their actions were coordinated with those of the government in France which, for reasons of its own, was happy to join in an international initiative. In these circumstances success might be thought a foregone conclusion. Yet the difficulties which the two European powers encountered compel a reappraisal of the leverage which the strong could exert upon the weak in international relations in the early Victorian age. By implication this must reflect on an idea beloved by many historians – that of Britain's informal empire.

Informal empire, of which Latin America has always been held to be an integral part,[2] has long been a staple of discussion within the discipline of British imperial history. It has been differently defined and variously identified for both the mid- and late-nineteenth century. Some scholars seem to require little more than contact between industrial and non-industrial economies; others demand an awareness and conscious exploitation of advantage in order to justify the concept. In theory, informal empire gives the dominant power control without responsibility: its attraction might therefore be considered obvious. But if the relationship between the weak and the strong was not as unequal, particularly in the mid-nineteenth century, as has often been assumed, and if the capacity of British governments either to perceive or to exercise advantage was likewise less of a reality, then the idea of informal empire is challenged. In La Plata, where the British made a forceful effort by diplomacy and by naval action to exercise persuasion and to bring the governments of what were prima facie economic satellites to heel, the idea of informal empire may fairly be considered as put to the test.

Impressive as the Royal Navy was, it was of course a blunt and politically unsophisticated instrument. For that reason governments in London were usually reluctant to employ it and, even where its use was deemed appropriate, it was always thought possible that the judgment of commanders on the spot could create more problems than firepower could solve. In the River Plate in the 1840s, the use of the navy was felt to be necessary but the complications which followed exceeded the worst that could have been imagined. In fact, diplomatic agents and a naval squadron ran out of control and interpreted the policy of a far-away government in a manner which they decided best fitted local requirements. This study thus throws light on another controversial aspect of British expansion in the nineteenth century – the role and effectiveness of metropolitan authority when confronted with the individual enterprise of men on distant stations.

To speak of coherent British policy is at times confusing. To speak of the needs of British commerce is likewise so, for the trading houses which operated in the River Plate were at loggerheads in supporting different parties in civil and international strife. Indeed, divisions and inconsistencies among the British undermine routine historical generalizations about identifiable national interest or ambition. That being so, the suggestion that governments in London even recognized, let alone promoted, the fortunes of British trade becomes contentious. The rhetoric of politicians and the anxieties expressed by commercial men need be no guide to their interaction. With respect to La Plata, not only is it hard to discover an official mind but officials even failed to reconcile their differences. For all these reasons, this study, I hope, offers some answers to problems which recur when assessing the process of British expansion in the nineteenth century.

1· La Plata and the British before 1836

The growth of Britain's industrial economy in the eighteenth century led its merchants to the farthest shores of the New World and to the mouths of the great rivers which gave access to a continent still imperfectly explored and only marginally exploited. The disintegration of Spain's empire extended opportunities for commerce between Europe and South America. Indeed, the emergence there of independent states spawned visions in Britain of an El Dorado for her manufacturers. Of the waterways within the old Spanish dominion, the most imposing was the River Plate, which drained a quarter of the continent and led inland to a series of tributaries, the largest among which were the rivers Paraná and Uruguay. From their confluence these rivers were navigable by ocean vessels for hundreds of miles into the interior. Here the British discovered arteries for international trade. Here they found a vast and fertile land which awaited the wakening touch of their global economic order.

Spain had taken little interest in the Atlantic seaboard of South America. The gold and silver of its empire were shipped back to Europe via the Pacific coast of the Peruvian viceroyalty. The lands of La Plata had neither mineral wealth nor concentrations of indigenous population to merit much settlement or enterprise. The only early settlements of note were Corrientes, which was established on the Paraná in 1587, and Buenos Aires, which was founded in 1580 at a point 150 miles from the mouth of the Plate but where the river was still 30 miles wide. Few ships, however, called at Buenos Aires, which was permitted only a small trade exporting cattle products from its hinterland. The town in fact served little economic function. Occasional threats of Dutch or English attack, however, made it a useful outpost which guarded the rear of Spain's position in the Americas.

The development of an Atlantic economy had enormous significance for the region of La Plata. Spain's ability to isolate her imperial territories from contact with the commerce of northern Europe had long been eroded by progress in maritime technology. Then, in the late eighteenth century, Spain's involvement in European warfare left her colonies vulnerable and ultimately severed from metropolitan control. Even before this, administrative reorganization had reflected the growing identity of the eastern coastline. In 1776 a separate viceroyalty of La Plata was created. Old restrictions on trade embodied in mercantilist statutes were either gradually ignored or else superseded by an economic liberalization characterized by greater international connections. The British merchant community established at Buenos Aires prospered from Spain's weakness and from the security which their own navy increasingly afforded by its control of the Atlantic.[1]

Yet in turn these foreign merchants created tensions within the city. While many Spaniards gained from the new freedom in trade, others were threatened by the dismantling of control and monopolies. Such divisions were eventually widened to the point where allegiance to Spain became itself a matter for debate. Inadvertently the British also contributed to the tide of particularism in a more dramatic fashion when, in 1807, a force of 7000 men under General John Whitelocke was compelled to abandon its campaign to capture Buenos Aires.[2] From this defiance of a foreign army the population derived both pride and a shared identity in which their formal status as subjects of a Spanish king played little role. Buenos Aires also drew confidence from expansion and prosperity. Its population grew from 20,000 in 1776 to over 40,000 in 1810 as it attracted migrants from Spain and from other parts of Europe. By the beginning of the nineteenth century, indeed, Buenos Aires boasted many of the trappings and refinements of a Mediterranean city.

The *porteños* of Buenos Aires, however, drew much of their growing wealth from a very different society. Beyond the port and its environs lay the immenseness of the Pampas stretching out for 500 miles in an arc and in all directions from the banks of the Plate. Here the land was flat and featureless, but its rich alluvial soil determined its quality as one of the world's foremost grazing regions. By 1800, 1,400,000 cattle hides were exported from La Plata every year[3] – predominantly through Buenos Aires, where the volume of shipping grew spectacularly. The interior resented the economic dominance which Buenos Aires came to exercise. It resented, too, the influx of largely British manufactured goods which drained money from the land in payment for them. While Buenos Aires formed an ever wider window to the Atlantic economy, those who made their living on the Pampas saw the city more often as a source of exploitation than as one of opportunity.

The Pampas was remote in every sense from the culture of Buenos Aires. Whereas city life displayed a growing sophistication, the countryside was stark in its character of lawlessness and violence. This was the realm of the rootless gaucho, where the staple of life was not the land but the cattle which roamed over it. The gaucho prized skills with horses, knife and bolas above the accumulation of material reward. Unsettled and untamed by the habits of an ordered society, the Pampas conjured images of anarchy which evoked fear among large sections of the urban population. Yet even in the interior a social elite held sway. Control and ownership of land lay with a class of creole *estancieros* whose vast estates contained their peons and their gaucho followers. From this class, whose members lived like feudal magnates among those who owed or gave them loyalty, were drawn the men who vied for the political as well as economic dominance of the emerging states of the region. As Spanish authority collapsed they were to challenge the *porteños* for power in the post-colonial era.

The fragmentation of Spain's empire meant more than a change in sovereign status for the former viceroyalty. Independence was followed by a decade of civil war, widespread economic disruption and collapse of the structure of central government from Buenos Aires. The viceroyalty was effectively dismembered. Paraguay and upper Peru, which in 1825 became Bolivia, established separate political entities, as indeed did the northern shore of the Plate east of the Uruguay river. Loyalty to the kings of Spain was replaced by the rise of *caudillos*, or warlords, in the interior who frequently affected a sovereign autonomy for the regions which they controlled. In the decade after 1810, sentiment hardened around two opposing political visions for the newly independent territories of what the British came to call the Argentine. The *porteños*, and those liberal elements who looked to Europe for both political and economic inspiration, rallied to the unitarian cause. Crucial to their way of thinking was the creation of a unitary Argentine state governed from an administrative capital whose authority would be binding throughout. In opposition to this was the federalist approach. This entailed not a unitary nation but a federation of autonomous states which would devolve only the limited function of external relations upon the government of the state of Buenos Aires. Such a view was favoured by most of the *caudillos*, who saw in this a constitutional structure most suited to protecting both their personal powers and their provinces against central control.

Continuing divergence between the interests of the cattle-based economy of the interior and the needs of the entrepôt which regulated its trade served only to reinforce political divisions. In 1814 delegates from the interior and from Buenos Aires met to consider the future, and from these and subsequent deliberations came a declaration in 1816 of the sovereignty of the United Provinces of the River Plate. These congresses, however, were dominated by unitarian sympathizers; they favoured, therefore, the authority of Buenos Aires at the expense of the inland states. In 1819 the unitarians put forward constitutional proposals for the United Provinces, under the terms of which the government of Buenos Aires would assume the powers of a central administration and would assert the right to appoint local officers and provincial governors.

Any regime in Buenos Aires undoubtedly had substantial means with which to enforce its will. It was by far the most populous state and thus the easiest from which to raise a military force.[4] In addition, it derived large revenues from the prosperity of the port. Above all, perhaps, by virtue of its coastline along the Plate, the state of Buenos Aires effectively controlled access to the interior. In 1819, in support of its constitutional settlement, Buenos Aires closed the Paraná to trade in order to apply an economic sanction against those who opposed it. Its army meanwhile invaded the neighbouring state of Santa Fé. But the unitarian government's attempt to wield the might of Buenos Aires to its advantage foundered on the field of battle. The armies of Santa Fé, Entre Rios and Corrientes, all of which bordered the Paraná and were the most injured by closure of the river, inflicted a decisive defeat on Buenos Aires in 1820 and captured the capital. Most of the governors in the interior declared their territories to be independent and the 1819 proposals for a unitary constitution lapsed. The state of Buenos Aires would henceforth elect its own legislature and Governor, but its institutions would have no powers outside its own borders. 1820 marked, at least temporarily, the triumph of federalism and of the resolve of the *caudillos* to defend their way of life.

The British found the era of independence conducive to business, even though, of course, in terms of Britain's total foreign trade Buenos Aires remained a backwater. By the mid-1820s the British community in the city was near to 1300 and still more were arriving whose search for economic opportunity took them into the countryside to settle as either farmers or labourers as their means allowed. The unitarians, whose party returned to power in Buenos Aires in 1821, encouraged this migration and that from France and Italy, whose nationals arrived in far larger numbers. By 1831 as many as 5000 British immigrants resided in the state of Buenos Aires.[5] But their economic importance was out of all proportion to their number – particularly in the capital. They dominated the import and export trades, provided much of the entrepreneurial activity in the city and emerged as creditors and arms suppliers to the authorities in times of strife. In the period 1822 to 1825, British exports to Buenos Aires ran at an annual figure of about £700,000 – a level maintained, without appreciable increase, throughout the first half of the century.[6] In 1824 there were 39 British trading houses operating in Buenos Aires, constituting about one third of all the trading firms there.[7]

Unitarians favoured free trade and international connections and while they remained the dominant faction in Buenos Aires the British community flourished. In 1822, 50 per cent of Buenos Aires' imports came from Britain; almost all of these were textiles and other manufactured goods which, especially in the case of cottons, also penetrated the markets of the interior. The privilege of the British in Buenos Aires was enshrined in the Anglo-Argentine treaty of 1825, whereby freedom from forced loans was confirmed, religious toleration was acknowledged, freedom from military requisitions and security for property was afforded, and British families were exempted from the compulsory military service required of the native population and of other foreign nationals. The British thus acquired a favoured status in the Argentine, whose economic future appeared to lie increasingly in their hands.

Yet in many ways the 1825 treaty formalized Britain's existing ties rather than opening the door for any extension of them. The value of British exports to the region never exceeded £1 million in any year between 1810 and 1849. Nonetheless, British enterprise continued to contribute significantly to the local economy. In 1824, for instance, 27 per cent of all ships entering Argentine ports flew the British flag. But the 1825 treaty acknowledged not only the position which British traders had established. In addition, it reflected a political affinity which characterized the early years of independence. A variety of British settlers, adventurers and military commanders had played a part in the national struggles in South America and many among the creoles who aspired to independence admired both the liberal values and the tangible assistance which Britain, albeit usually unofficially, had provided. Crucial to the new states of the continent was diplomatic recognition by the British government, which in the case of the United Provinces was granted in 1824. The treaty which followed bore the credentials of nationhood. A treaty signed with the greatest naval and industrial power of the age conferred upon the unitarian authorities at Buenos Aires both a recognition of their cause and a guarantee of Britain's friendship for the future. However, this preeminence of the British in Buenos Aires had implications for business life at large. The British squeezed out both local merchant houses and those owned by other foreigners from the entrepôt trade of the city. Not only did Lancashire textiles and Midlands hardware dominate the markets of the region but gradually the British came to exert control over the trade in hides and economic contact with the interior. Local enterprise concentrated increasingly on cattle ranching and the fast-growing salt meat business of the Pampas, the needs of which could be satisfied in the 1820s by expanding the frontiers of settlement through a series of wars against tribal societies which for 300 years had survived beyond the pale of, and almost untouched by, European influence.

* * *

While Buenos Aires was unquestionably the focus of British interest in La Plata, the far side of the Plate also offered opportunities. To the east of the River Uruguay lay territory which Spain had long disputed with the Portuguese empire in Brazil. Portugal had first established a permanent settlement there at Colonia in 1680 and for a century or more merchants from here had conducted a contraband trade with Buenos Aires. In 1724 the Spaniards founded their own settlement at Montevideo, and eventually the whole region of La Plata became a Spanish domain when the Portuguese finally ceded the area east of the Uruguay in 1777. Montevideo remained in quiet colonial obscurity, however, until in 1811 José Artigas led an uprising in its hinterland against city authorities who were still loyal to the Spanish crown. The Portuguese were quick to interfere and invaded in support of Montevideo. But the British were equally swift to step in to prevent a broader conflict and the Portuguese withdrew their army in 1812 under diplomatic pressure. In 1814 Montevideo fell, not to Artigas, but to a force which had arrived from Buenos Aires. Any hopes that this newly liberated region would join with Buenos Aires, however, were soon dispelled. The defiant Artigas proclaimed the land east of the Uruguay to be independent, owing no allegiance to, or wishing any linkage with, the Argentine states.

Artigas was a radical republican. As such his ideas were anathema to the Portuguese, who feared the spread of democracy, slave emancipation and the overthrow of the imperial order in Brazil. Unable to watch such chaos beyond their frontier, the Portuguese invaded again in 1816 and in January 1817 captured Montevideo. In 1821 Portugal incorporated Montevideo and its hinterland into the Brazilian empire as the Cisplatine province. In the following year it became part of an independent Brazil. But in language and culture the people who had settled east of the Uruguay were Spanish and in April 1825 a revolt began against what was perceived as a foreign occupation. Buenos Aires was still willing to assist those whom it regarded as compatriots across the River Plate and by 1826 the struggle in the Cisplatine region had broadened into a war between Brazil and the United Provinces. An army crossed from Entre Rios and laid siege to the Brazilian garrison at Montevideo. In reply, Brazil's navy blockaded the port at Buenos Aires in an attempt to cripple its economy. It accomplished more than that. The resultant disruption of trade so damaged the British merchant body that Britain once more brought its diplomacy to bear in order to restore peace. Britain's solution to the dispute was that the Cisplatine province should be neither Brazilian nor Argentine but recognized, as Artigas had imagined, as a sovereign state. In August 1828 the British brought the governments at Buenos Aires and Rio de Janeiro to acknowledge in a treaty the independence of the Banda Oriental del Uruguay; thus was Britain midwife at the birth of this, the smallest of the nations of South America. It was one, though, which sat uneasily on the frontiers of two powerful neighbours, both of whom had been reluctant to renounce their claims and both of whom, the British believed, still harboured territorial ambitions.

The creation of the Banda Oriental, or Republic of Uruguay, served the British well. It was the best guarantee available for avoiding war again in La Plata; it also created a separate base for their economic penetration of the continent. But this success for British diplomacy had a most unfortunate corollary. As a result of the war against Brazil, the unitarian regime in Buenos Aires was overthrown in 1826 and Britain's standing in the economic life of the city was consequently weakened. A new period of civil conflict in the Argentine followed, in which the merchant community suffered serious financial losses and several of the British houses were forced to close. After almost three years of struggle, the federalists regained power in Buenos Aires when the last of the unitarian claimants, Juan Lavalle, was defeated and forced to flee to Montevideo. At the head of the new administration, as Governor, was a 36-year-old warlord who in 1829 demanded and acquired unlimited powers with which to restore the rule of law – General Juan Manuel de Rosas.[8]

Rosas was to prove the dominant force in the politics of La Plata until 1852. He remained Governor of the state of Buenos Aires save for an interlude between 1832 and 1835. His era, despite his federalist credentials, was characterized by the growth of centralized authority since Rosas himself was jealous of his dictatorial powers and increasingly came to see the governors of the other Argentine states as potential challengers. His federalist ideals, however, were reflected in the loose constitutional structure of the United Provinces which survived throughout his career. Rosas did dabble briefly in constitutional matters. On 4 January 1831 Buenos Aires signed a treaty with the other three littoral states of Entre Rios, Corrientes and Santa Fé which provided for a regulation of commerce and for an offensive and defensive alliance between them. Other states were invited to join and new provisions were to be made for the conduct of foreign affairs whereby a representative commission was to sit in Santa Fé. But Rosas saw in this a threat to his control. A federal assembly, for which the 1831 treaty had also provided was never called to sanction these arrangements; responsibility for external relations remained therefore in the hands of the Governor of Buenos Aires. Henceforth Rosas rejected suggestions for any specific, even federalist, constitution for the territory.

The 14 states which made up the Confederation of the United Provinces of the River Plate were thus essentially self-governing domains of the *caudillos* who controlled them, subject only to the growing power of Rosas to subdue his rivals through an effective network of henchmen and through the commercial power of his own capital at Buenos Aires. Rosas could, and did, cut access to the Plate estuary for the trade of the littoral states, thereby denying those states opportunities for economic development and the expansion of their own ports. Exports and imports had to pay duties at the port of Buenos Aires, thus providing Rosas with a handsome revenue which he could employ for his own purposes. For many federalists, of course, Rosas' creeping dominance over the interior was a betrayal of their cause. Nonetheless, the size and resources of his native Buenos Aires made

Rosas nigh invincible. The city had grown to house a population of 70,000 by 1832. The state of Buenos Aires had around 200,000 inhabitants in 1840; Entre Rios, Corrientes and Santa Fé between them could not boast even half that total. Indeed, the population of the entire Confederation in 1840 was not above 800,000.[9] The British saw in the Argentine little which resembled a unified nation and little sense of a common nationality among its people. Nor had the British any great respect for those whom they encountered. British merchants, as best they could, kept their own society in Buenos Aires while the general attitude of British officialdom was correct but condescending. So long as the door for trade was kept open, however, British interests, for the most part, were adequately served.[10]

Nowhere were the British more brought face to face with what most of them regarded as the worst abuses of government than at Buenos Aires in the age of Rosas. Here was a military figure with unlimited power who ruled by means of an elected assembly packed with his federalist supporters, a bureaucracy and judiciary over which he exercised the strictest supervision, and all the instruments of popular oppression necessary to eliminate once and for all the enemy within – the unitarians.

Rosas' background was conventional for a political career. He was born to the racial and economic elite of creole landowners and was related through extensive lines of kinship to many of the great *estanciero* families of the Buenos Airean interior. His rise to prominence came not only from his success as a rancher, however, but also from a reputation for command gained in campaigns against the Indian tribes in the 1820s and again in the Indian wars between 1832 and his return to the governorship in 1835. In both 1829 and 1835 he stepped forward as the only man who had adequate support to end political chaos and to prevent the territory from sliding into civil war.

Rosas' concept of government, though, went well beyond the maintenance of order. His crusade against the exponents of unitarist ideas reached its apogee during the reigns of terror on the streets of the capital between 1839 and 1842. Most infamous of Rosas' tools was the *Mazorca* society, consisting of irregular gangs of murderers and sadists who stepped beyond the usual limits of official intimidation. Hundreds, and probably thousands, of Rosas' opponents perished at the hands of his regime: many of his victims were simply discovered at dawn on the streets while even more of his opponents fled abroad to escape the death squads. 'Almost every day we hear of the shooting of respectable people by the Dictator's command or of having their throats cut by some of his assassins,' the British consul reported in 1840. 'I never saw Buenos Aires in such a lamentable condition before and the timidity and terror of all decent persons is increasing more and more.'[11] For many British traders and officials, and for a section of the Press in London, Rosas was indeed the incarnation of political evil.

Yet Rosas was not a complex individual, nor one whom a succession of British diplomats in Buenos Aires found difficult to comprehend. Rosas fitted easily into their experience of a world comprising peoples and societies which, for reasons obvious to them, were less fortunate and less developed than their own. Rosas was regarded by the British as a curiosity. He kept odd hours, his moods were unpredictable, he gave his personal attention to the humblest details of administration and he cared as much about the outward symbols of his power as for matters of political substance. In appearance and lifestyle he clearly identified with the gaucho culture of so many of his supporters. Rosas controlled the spread of information through a rigid censorship of publication; he was also secretive, distrustful and incapable of delegation. Fascinating, too, for all foreign observers was his dependence on his daughter, Manuelita, who, by the 1840s, had become the dictator's main channel of contact in all public affairs. Manuelita Rosas interceded to arrange audience with her father. She was the 'high priestess' of his regime who seemed to lend it a human and even elegant facade.[12] Manuelita was totally loyal: she was felt, by many, to be the only person whom the Governor fully trusted. Few really believed that Rosas was popular. The force of his authority was terror for most of his time in power; he was, as one British diplomat remarked, 'everywhere detested, but implicitly obeyed.' 'We live here,' he wrote from Buenos Aires, 'as if it were in a great prison.'[13]

There was less consensus, however, on whether Rosas served or hindered Britain's broad interests in the region. Some diplomats and members of the merchant body saw him as a conservative and isolationist leader, hostile to liberal commercial thinking and determined to minimize all foreign economic penetration of the Argentine. Others set great store by his maintenance of order, however brutal, and foresaw only a disruption of trade in the anarchy which would surely replace him were he ever overthrown. Such views were not incompatible. Despite his differences with the British in the 1830s and 1840s, Rosas never manifested overtly anti-British policies. In fact, the United States' chargé d'affaires in Buenos Aires found Rosas exasperatingly sympathetic to the British. For all their arrogance and interference in La Plata, the British were much admired in Buenos Aires, he wrote to Washington.[14] The reason for this should have been obvious to anyone who dealt with the Argentine dictator. Rosas respected power: the British were unquestionably powerful and contributed much to his nation's prosperity. While Rosas purged his capital of political opponents, the British community went discreetly about the streets and about their business with only minimal inconvenience.

Quarrels with the British, nonetheless, proved a feature of Rosas' era. One dispute was over debt default. In 1824 a loan for £1 million had been arranged through the London finance house of Baring, the annual charges arising from which were £65,000. These payments were in arrears after 1828 and, although the British government never pressed the claims of the bondholders as a matter of priority, the issue was a constant source of complaint. In 1838 the British envoy wrote stiffly to the long-serving Argentine Foreign Minister, Felipe Arana,[15] of his nation's 'long-continued indifference to its engagements towards its British creditors,' and added that measures should promptly be put in hand to meet the repayments due.[16] But the main contention was political, not financial. In 1833 the British occupied the Falkland Islands, about 300 miles off the coast of Patagonia, to enforce a claim which dated from the 1770s. This clashed directly with an assertion from Buenos Aires that these islands belonged to the United Provinces by virtue of a former Spanish claim. Henceforth Rosas complained about the occupation every year in his address to the Hall of Representatives in Buenos Aires and looked to the day when Britain would return the islands to their rightful sovereignty. The British government dismissed such presumption and deemed the issue unworthy even of negotiation. The subject would die of exhaustion, the British Minister in Buenos Aires informed the Foreign Office in 1838. It would never be of any importance in Argentine politics 'unless some unworthy motive should induce the government to reproduce it and take shelter under its cover to screen themselves from the stigma of injustice.'[17]

Close as Britain's ties with the Argentine Confederation had become by the 1840s, its connection with the Banda Oriental del Uruguay was in some respects even closer. The little state had prospered since 1828; its inherent problem of defence made it naturally more receptive to cordial relations with great powers from beyond the region. Under the terms of the 1828 treaty between Brazil and the United Provinces, both parties were obliged to give Britain six months' notice of any renewal of hostilities. On paper, this offered Uruguay some security – assuming that the country could avoid entanglement in the politics of its neighbours. After Rosas' rise to power in Buenos Aires this was no longer possible. Driven from their homeland, the unitarian opposition to Rosas sought refuge in Montevideo, which throughout the 1830s and 1840s developed as a political base for thousands of Argentine exiles. By 1839 Montevideo had a population of about 40,000, of whom roughly 2000 were thought to be Argentine emigrés. Thereafter the pace of migration quickened. A further 2500 *porteños* were reported as settling in Montevideo and the other towns of Uruguay between 1840 and 1842. On top of this, immigration from Europe, especially from Italy and the Basque regions of France and Spain, swelled the foreign population further. For Uruguay as a whole, the total population in 1839 was about 200,000, of whom half were thought to be foreign nationals.[18] As in the Argentine, ranching formed the backbone of economic life: as at Buenos Aires, so in Montevideo British merchant houses formed a crucial linkage with the wider world. Of the 87 commercial houses which operated there, 36 were British. In 1840 the British community in Montevideo numbered over a thousand. They owned assets in the city to the value of over £1 million, much of it in the form of hides, horns and other produce from the interior, stored in warehouses and awaiting shipment. Most of the exports from Montevideo, in fact, went to British ports. Over £180,000-worth of produce was exported to Britain in 1836 – more than the £150,000-worth to neighbouring Brazil, and far more than the £80,000-worth to France and approximately £55,000-worth to Uruguay's other main export markets in Cuba, the United States and Holland. The British also dominated the import trade of Montevideo. In 1836 British produce entering the port was valued at £215,000, that of Brazil at £130,000 and of France at £106,000. All told, Montevideo's foreign trade in 1836 was worth about £650,000 in each direction.[19]

After 1828 Montevideo developed quickly as a competitor to Buenos Aires. Civil war and disturbance within the Argentine Confederation made Montevideo an attractive alternative for some of the foreign merchant houses who either moved their operations to the Banda Oriental or at least established premises on both sides of the

Plate. This threat to the monopoly of Buenos Aires as the great emporium of the region had, inevitably, a political dimension. By the mid-1830s it was apparent that the revenues which the government of Buenos Aires derived from trade were being, and would continue to be, adversely affected by commercial changes. This was particularly galling for Rosas since his opponents not only found sanctuary across the river but the assets and enterprise which many refugees took with them played no small part in the growth of Montevideo as a rival to his own capital. Britain's Consul-General in Montevideo in 1836, Thomas Hood, warned the Foreign Office that the Argentine dictator would not tolerate this indefinitely. Once Rosas felt assured in his control of Buenos Aires he would have to move against the Banda Oriental. Already in March 1836 Rosas had introduced a discriminatory tariff which placed merchandise entering Buenos Aires from Montevideo on a worse footing than that from any other port of origin and he had simply ignored the protests of the Uruguayan government. A conflict, Hood concluded, was not far away.

Hood's pessimism was noted in London. The 1828 treaty, however, had given Britain adequate safeguards for the protection of the Banda Oriental. If the worst occurred and a war did develop between Uruguay and the Argentine, the Royal Navy had contingencies. Towards the end of 1837 the Minister at Buenos Aires asked the captain of a British warship to make discreet surveys of the harbours of Colonia and Maldonado on the Uruguayan coast. Colonia was the key to La Plata, the navy surmised, since it stood directly opposite to Rosas' capital. But all this really was peripheral when viewed from London. La Plata was geographically removed and, whatever its commercial potential, it remained as yet economically as well as politically insignificant. British traders were indeed important in Buenos Aires and Montevideo and British trade was vital to the economies of the region. But it was valued, at both ports, at only a few hundred thousand pounds. By contrast, Britain's total export trade in 1840 was worth £116 million and her total imports £67 million; by 1845 those figures had increased dramatically to £150 million and £85 million respectively.[20] Diplomatically, relations with France and other European powers preoccupied British governments in the 1830s and 1840s, while beyond the horizon of Europe attention turned predominantly to the security and problems of a global empire. Politicians in London, and the civil servants who administered their departments of state, presided over the fortunes of the world's first industrial economy and of its foremost political and military power. Such men seldom thought of Buenos Aires or of the Banda Oriental. In the late 1830s it seemed but fantasy to dwell on circumstances which might draw the British into war in the Argentine. The seeds of such a conflict, however, were already sown in the tubulence which by then was engulfing La Plata.

2· War and the Invasion of Uruguay, 1836–43

The complexity of politics within and between the states of La Plata obscured the origins of the warfare which dominated the region between 1836 and 1852. One of its roots, however, was a struggle for power in the Banda Oriental between two military leaders, Generals Fructuoso Rivera and Manuel Oribe, whose rivalry in fact predated the founding of the state in 1828. The charisma of these men rested in part on their participation in the movement for independence. Fructuoso Rivera was elected the first President of Uruguay in 1830 and served out his constitutional term until October 1834. He was a populist politician, by origin and temperament a gaucho leader. Never happier than when campaigning with his troops and sharing the rigours of military life, Rivera struck most foreigners as a greathearted and generous commander, albeit politically untrustworthy and often lacking in judgment when selecting those who surrounded him.[1] The growth of Montevideo as a trading centre and the prosperity generated there in the early 1830s masked the growing debts of his administration, which were eventually bequeathed to his presidential successor – Manuel Oribe.

Oribe's accession to office on 1 March 1835 ushered in a period of financial retrenchment. Oribe's stance in politics was as a figure of discipline and unbending integrity. He and his principal supporters were from patrician families and men of substance in Montevideo. Visitors to Uruguay wrote of Oribe's quiet and urbane character. He was a man of dignity, conscientious and open to persuasion, though equally of limited intellectual vision and prone to indecision.[2] In an effort to contain public spending, Oribe's government began to reduce the number of surplus officers on the military payroll, one of whom was the ex-President, whose post as Commander-in-Chief of the Army of the Interior was abolished. Discontented with this diminution of his power, Rivera in 1836 led an unsuccessful revolt against the government, after which he was forced to seek refuge in the Brazilian province of Rio Grande do Sul. From there, in 1837, he conducted guerrilla excursions into Uruguay. Alone, Rivera was a containable threat to Oribe's regime in Montevideo. But Rivera found allies whose interest in his struggle went far beyond the bounds of a civil war in the Banda Oriental.

Rivera had been encouraged and aided in his revolt by supporters of the exiled Argentine General Lavalle. Lavalle, having escaped the dictatorship at Buenos Aires, organized political opposition from Montevideo and planned a military expedition against Rosas. Helped by recruits, money and propaganda skills from the Argentine exiles, and by supplies from across the Brazilian frontier, Rivera kept up his insurgency in the Uruguayan countryside and in June 1838 defeated an army which the government had sent against him. Rivera's ascendancy on the field of battle was now matched crucially by the arrival of another ally. In 1838 a quite separate conflict had developed between France and the government at Buenos Aires: a European power thus sought assistance from anyone in the region who was hostile to General Rosas.

Lavalle and his unitarians in Montevideo were naturally pro-French. For Rivera, the French offered an opportunity to get back into office. France's involvement in La Plata arose from a dispute about the rights of French subjects who had settled in Buenos Aires. By March 1838 this had reached the point where the French consul was threatening a naval blockade of the port of Buenos Aires if his demands remained unsatisfied. France claimed for her nationals the same exemptions from military service as were accorded British subjects under the terms of the Anglo-Argentine treaty of 1825. Rosas refused to continue negotiations under threat of naval force; on 28 March a French admiral, with six warships in the Plate, announced a blockade.[3] Britain was not a party to this quarrel and her Minister Plenipotentiary at Buenos Aires, John Mandeville, judged the dispute to have got quite out of hand. Mandeville did what little he could to try to repair the diplomatic damage, aware as he was that the blockade would inflict considerable damage on the British trading houses, but by June he gloomily reported to London the hardships suffered by all classes of the population as the blockade gradually brought the economy of the city to a halt.

Privations in Buenos Aires brought a renewed prosperity across the river in Montevideo. It was there that the French navy took its prizes to be sold and to there that the trade of foreign nations was now diverted. But this was not to the taste of Manuel Oribe, who considered that the use of Montevideo as a base for the blockading squadron was incompatible with the neutrality which he wished Uruguay to maintain in the conflict between France and the government of Buenos Aires. Oribe forbade the entry of captured Argentine vessels into the port, and this at a time when the French navy was becoming increasingly frustrated at its inability to bring Rosas to his knees. The French turned their attention to Oribe's opponents. Lavalle was entertained aboard one of the warships in the river and Rivera's men in the interior were supplied with arms. Pressure was applied against Oribe's government by a blockade imposed on Montevideo, so as to prevent the Uruguayan navy from taking any measures against Rivera's campaign. By October 1838 Rivera's insurgents had laid siege to the city and the government's forces were cut off from the military supplies which were essential for its defence. On 24 October, with Rivera, the French and the Argentine exiles all against him, Oribe fled with about 300 of his supporters and loyal soldiers to Buenos Aires. He had just over four months of his presidential tenure still to run.

On 11 November Rivera entered Montevideo and was greeted as a conqueror by the city authorities and by officers from the French naval squadron. His first act was to declare the constitution suspended and proclaim his own authority to be the basis of government in a new epoch which had dawned. Then, in return for French assistance into power, Rivera declared war against Rosas in March 1839. What had begun as a dispute between two Uruguayan generals had thus become at length a war with the Argentine Confederation.

In London all this was viewed with considerable unease. It mattered little to the British which factions in local politics governed these faraway lands so long as commerce flourished and was open without impediment to the traders of all nations. Warfare was inimical to this objective, as the merchant houses in South America and their associations in Britain were quick to complain. There was widespread condemnation of the French blockade at Buenos Aires since France had little trade there and her actions damaged only British interests. It was for this reason that in 1838 the Foreign Secretary, Lord Palmerston, offered his government's good offices to try to resolve the differences which had led to the blockade. When this proved to be of no avail, Palmerston tried next to persuade Rosas to accept the French demands, though in this he was equally unsuccessful. In the meantime war had spread into Argentine territory. Lavalle raised an army from among his followers and Uruguayan volunteers and, with French naval support, launched an expedition intent on the capture of Buenos Aires and the overthrow of Rosas. He was aided by revolts among the governors of the Argentine states and in particular that of Corrientes, who put an army of 5000 men in the field. For a while the Argentine Confederation was embroiled in civil war between those states which accepted Rosas' brand of federalism and the governors of others who either harboured unitarian sympathies or else were disillusioned and alarmed by Rosas' accretion of personal power.

Rosas had two allies in his struggle to maintain control within the Confederation. One was General Pascual Echagüe, Governor of the strategically located state of Entre Rios, who engaged and destroyed the army of Corrientes at the end of March 1839. The other was Manuel Oribe, now of course an Uruguayan exile in Buenos Aires, to whom Rosas entrusted command of his forces in the tacit agreement that if Oribe could quell dissent in the Argentine, then Rosas would send troops from Buenos Aires into Uruguay to enable Oribe to regain his rightful place as President. Yet throughout 1839 neither side was able to gain a decisive advantage. The French blockade continued at Buenos Aires, whose inhabitants awaited with apprehension the advance of Lavalle's invading army. Meanwhile Rosas was forced to divert loyal troops south of the city to put down a rebellion within his own state. Only from Entre Rios was there good news for Rosas. Not only had the threat from Corrientes been crushed but in August 1839 Echagüe crossed into Uruguay with a force of 5000 Argentines and Oribist Uruguayans and marched swiftly towards the capital. In September about 400 sailors and marines were landed from the French navy to help defend Montevideo. Then, on 29 December 1839, Rivera achieved a spectacular victory over the Argentine forces at the battle of Cagancha, after which he returned to Montevideo once again as a national hero. At the height of his career as soldier and statesman, Rivera somewhat rashly took the view that the war was over and that Uruguay had escaped from its entanglement both with internal Argentine upheavals and with French ambitions. But neither the French nor the unitarians, and certainly not Rosas or Oribe, would allow that.

Rivera's victory at Cagancha seemed to harden attitudes on all sides. Rosas could not accept defeat for fear of the danger to his own position. The French remained adamant that they could never honourably make a peace settlement with Rosas which gave them less than they demanded. In the meantime Mandeville continued his forlorn efforts to bring the adversaries together, hampered as he was by dissensions among the French political agents and also disputes between them and their admiral. In Buenos Aires Mandeville found a tiresome obsession with national dignity and a refusal even to discuss French demands when accompanied by naval blockade and by military support for Rosas' enemies. In June 1840 Palmerston urged Mandeville once again to represent the opinion of the British government to the Argentine authorities that the French were asking for so little that no loss of national honour was entailed in simply agreeing.

By the time that Palmerston's advice reached Mandeville, events seemed to have turned in favour of Rosas. Lavalle had been repulsed during an incursion into Entre Rios in April 1840 and the governors of several more states loyal to Rosas had raised troops with which to crush those of separatist leanings. On 16 July Lavalle's campaign in Entre Rios came to a sudden end when his army was dispersed by Echagüe and he was rescued from capture only by French warships in the Paraná River. But that was not the end of Lavalle's efforts to topple Rosas. He was equipped by the French for another expedition and on 4 August was landed with 3000 men on the coast within a short march of Buenos Aires. Rosas quickly raised a force sufficient to bar his progress but dared not risk a battle. Lavalle, however, was disappointed to find no spontaneous uprising to greet his landing and, realizing that his army was not adequate to take the city, retired back along the shoreline and then towards the town of Rosario. At this point an unexpected, but for the British by no means unwelcome, event brought the prospect of an end to this relentless warfare. On 12 October 1840 a new French admiral, Baron René Armand de Makau, arrived off Buenos Aires with instructions from Paris to negotiate an end to the blockade and to disengage the French navy from the struggle to depose Rosas.

Makau signed a treaty with the government at Buenos Aires and lifted the naval blockade on 29 October. The terms agreed as to the status of French subjects and their military obligations were only little modified from those which previous admirals and diplomats had requested. However, with the threat from Lavalle receding, Rosas had clearly felt confident enough to settle with the French and thereby to remove their interference from Argentine affairs without too great a loss of face. Makau, too, had helped the process of reconciliation. His sense of tact and his genuine wish for peace distinguished him, in

Mandeville's opinion, from all other French officials in La Plata since 1838; he had proved adept at recognizing Rosas' sensitivities and had made concessions in matters of form in order to gain acquiescence in matters of substance. Makau's treaty naturally found no favour with Lavalle or Rivera, nor with the large numbers of French residents in Montevideo who had both gained materially and derived security from French naval operations. The admiral ignored such considerations, however, and returned to France convinced, quite rightly, that he had done his duty by his own government.

The revolt against Rosas within the Confederation continued despite the French withdrawal. By the end of 1840 Corrientes had once more proclaimed its independence and was joined in this by Jujuy, Tucumán, Salta, Catamarca and La Rioja. Gradually, however, the armies of Oribe pushed back the tide of insurrection, defeating Lavalle in November 1840, and then in the first half of 1841 pursuing the rebel forces into the northernmost regions of the Confederation and towards the borders with Chile and Bolivia. But a decisive victory eluded Oribe and the war was no nearer a resolution in September 1841 when Mandeville reported to London the appalling damage which it was inflicting throughout the Argentine. In the state of Buenos Aires, where Rosas recruited most of his soldiers, forced levies of men, horses and cattle had left the land untended and had produced a chronic scarcity of labour in the towns. Such spoliation would go on until Rosas and his federalist supporters had crushed Lavalle and all other opposition, Mandeville predicted with an air of resignation. Neither he nor any other foreign diplomat, of course, could properly offer to mediate in a civil war. The British government, nonetheless, remained determined to contain the fighting within the Confederation if possible and, more particularly, to arrange a peace with Uruguay which would effectively insulate that country from the conflict. By now, with his French supporters gone and with Lavalle's forces in retreat, Rivera was more than willing to accept any British offer of mediation with Buenos Aires.

Palmerston's instructions to Mandeville were precise on this point. Having been requested by the government in Uruguay to use his good offices to arrange a peace treaty, Palmerston was happy to comply. On 5 May 1841 he asked Mandeville to tell the Argentine Foreign Minister, Arana, that Britain was most anxious to bring to an end all differences between Buenos Aires and Montevideo and to offer diplomatic mediation for that purpose. Mandeville made the offer to Arana on 28

July but held out no hope of success. He reminded Palmerston that he had already made one such offer in July 1839, which had been rejected, and in his judgment there was even less likelihood of it being accepted now. For one thing, Rosas had recently issued a decree in January 1841 which closed both the rivers Paraná and Uruguay to the navigation of all vessels unlicensed by the authorities at Buenos Aires. This was a response to Uruguay's declaration of war against the Argentine republic and, when pressed on the subject, Arana told Mandeville that even British property found on board ships flying the Uruguayan flag would be considered a legitimate prize. Furthermore, in January 1841 Rosas had also ordered a blockade of the port of Montevideo. The Buenos Aires fleet had then appeared off Montevideo on 29 March and had, on 24 May, inflicted heavy damage on the six vessels which made up the Uruguayan navy in a valiant but rather one-sided skirmish.[4] Such were not the actions of a government willing to compromise.

Equally important in determining Rosas' attitude towards Rivera's government was the support which Lavalle, and indeed all the enemies of Rosas, had received from Montevideo and the danger into which his own regime at Buenos Aires had been plunged. Civil war in the Confederation had been a consequence of Lavalle's ability to raise men, equipment, and to organize from a safe haven in Uruguay, and this, Mandeville told Palmerston, would never be forgotten. Furthermore, Oribe's steady success in the field against his enemies had deepened Rosas' sense of obligation. For Rosas, the war against Uruguay had become but a logical extension of his campaign to assert his authority within the Argentine Confederation. He would not rest until his adversaries in exile, and Rivera, had been driven from Montevideo and until therefore his ally, Manuel Oribe, was restored to his position as legal President of the Uruguayan republic.

Arana's eventual reply on 3 September to Mandeville's offer of mediation reflected this unyielding attitude. It was not just a rejection of what had been offered but, to the British diplomat's surprise, set out terms which Mandeville might propose to Rivera's government as the only possible basis for peace. Arana listed four demands. Oribe was to be restored as President in Uruguay. Rivera was to leave for exile in Europe. Argentine refugees and other persons listed as undesirable by the Argentine authorities were also to leave Montevideo and, finally, compensation would be paid by the Uruguayans for Rivera's actions. Mandeville responded indignantly at an interview that no power offering itself as a mediator could convey such proposals and that he must therefore decline to receive them; such terms were scarcely less than the Argentine government might require were its troops already occupying Montevideo. Mandeville continued his rebuke by expressing the opinion that Oribe was not the legal President of Uruguay. He had resigned and left the country in October 1838: in any case, his constitutional term would have ended on 1 March 1839. Rivera now held the presidency, having since been accepted by the necessary constitutional forms. But Arana was not prepared to make any worthwhile concessions. Mandeville later summed up his conversation with the Foreign Minister by forecasting that there would be no peace while Rivera and Rosas were in power.

By the time Mandeville's dispatch reached London the government had changed. The new Foreign Secretary in Sir Robert Peel's Conservative administration was the Earl of Aberdeen. There was no immediate change of attitude at the Foreign Office, however. Aberdeen approved all that Mandeville had said and in January 1842 requested that the latter should remind Arana, whenever circumstances might make the Argentine government more receptive, that Britain's offer of mediation was still open. Developments in the war within the Confederation, however, made such circumstances ever less likely. In September 1841 Oribe at last delivered the telling blows which crowned his military campaign when, in two battles near Tucumán and Mendoza, his forces destroyed Lavalle's remaining armies. In October Lavalle was killed while trying to escape into Bolivia. The only region now left as serious resistance to Rosas' power was Corrientes, where its military *supremo*, José María Paz, conducted a spirited defence against another invasion by Echagüe from Entre Rios.[5]

On 28 November 1841, to the delight of the inhabitants of Montevideo, Paz threw back the Entre Rean army with a brilliant display of generalship at Caaguazú and thereby gave encouragement to the state of Santa Fé to defect from the Argentine Confederation. This was seized upon by Rivera as an opportunity to intervene in the Argentine civil war and, allying himself with General Paz in Corrientes, he led an Uruguayan army across the border and occupied Entre Rios. Success, though, proved to be short lived. Within weeks disputes had broken out between Paz and Rivera: in Mandeville's opinion, because the two leaders could not agree on a division of the spoils which they had plundered in Entre Rios. In March 1842 Rivera had sent back across the Uruguay River about 200,000 head of cattle and perhaps as many as 40,000 horses from the occupied territory. The British Minister could not conceal his disgust at this opportunist incursion: Paz and Rivera between them had devastated one of the finest states of the Confederation, he observed. But retribution for this pillage, it seemed, was at hand. The Entre Reans regrouped across the Paraná in Santa Fé where the rebellious Governor was soon defeated. For Rosas' commanders in the field the plan of operation was first the submission of Corrientes and then onwards to Montevideo and the overthrow of those who had usurped Oribe's power.

While frustrated by its failure to secure Argentine agreement to British mediation, the Foreign Office in London nonetheless seemed at a loss to devise any other policy. The only alternative suggested to stop the war was that mooted by the Uruguayan government, whereby Britain would declare the entire Banda Oriental to be under its protection. When the British consul at Montevideo had first been approached with this idea in 1838 he had been able officially to ignore it. In March 1841, however, the Uruguayans pressed for a response and Mandeville, uncertain what to say, referred the matter home. Palmerston was horrified by the prospect. British protection, such as requested, would commit Britain to repelling all attacks against Uruguayan territory without giving the British government any capacity to influence the nation's external affairs. Worse than that, any invitation to assume the status of protector would come only from the faction currently in power in Montevideo, which thereafter would call on Britain to act against its enemies even in a civil war. The British had no wish to incur responsibilities in Uruguay beyond the commitment to its independence implicit in the 1828 treaty, nor any desire to be drawn into the intrigues of local politicians and military *caudillos*. Aberdeen agreed. But he also had a better idea: the way to stop the carnage in La Plata was by cooperating with the French.

*   *   *

By the norm of party division in England, a will to work with France was a trait of Whig, not Tory, politics. By inclining towards cooperation with the French on a variety of international issues after 1842, Aberdeen was a lonely figure in Peel's Cabinet. By tradition, Tories were suspicious of France. It was an old rival for dominance in Europe and, since 1789, had proved the font both of dangerous ideology and of military adventurism. To the Tory mind, legitimist autocracies in Central and Eastern Europe seemed safer fellows in diplomacy. Aberdeen however had inherited, somewhat awkwardly, the Foxite legacy to nineteenth-century Whiggery. By this interpretation the French people had cast off the yoke of oppression in their revolution and had emerged from years of political trauma as that model on the continent of Europe which resembled most closely Britain's greatest gift to civilization – a liberal society and a constitutional democracy which was soundly based on the privilege of property. France, therefore, was a natural ally in support of liberal causes against the anachronistic forces of Prussian, Russian and Austrian despotism.

Anglo-French relations during the Whig governments of the previous decade had shown signs of this more optimistic attitude. Palmerston, though by instinct no friend of France, had in the early 1830s spoken of 'a cordial good understanding' with the Orleanist regime, especially after the French government accepted the principle of Belgian sovereignty in 1831 and joined with Britain in overcoming resistance to the idea elsewhere.[6] In 1833–4 a sharp deterioration in relations with Russia on the Eastern Question once more led Palmerston to place his faith in *entente*. In 1834 Britain again joined France in a diplomatic alliance to bring an end to a civil war in Portugal and to try to limit a potential conflict in Spain. But underlying these common measures lurked Palmerston's belief that British and French interests, both in Europe and in the wider world, remained fundamentally irreconcilable. France was politically unstable and discontent with her status in the post-1815 international order. Palmerston, like most of his Tory opponents, did not believe that cooperation with short-lived and usually hostile administrations in Paris was a proper basis for Britain's security.

Even at the height of *entente* Palmerston had pointed to what was surely the writing on the wall. Despite his persistent pressure in 1833 and 1834, the French government refused to reduce its tariffs on trade and to negotiate a free-trade treaty. Political opinion in Paris made any economic concessions to Britain impossible; Palmerston took this as vindication of his view that, even if French governments were inclined to work with him, their domestic and staunchly Anglophobe opponents would render all efforts fruitless. By 1835 any illusions about the French had evaporated as far as Palmerston was concerned. In Spain, British and French policies had clearly diverged and as the country lapsed into civil war the two powers were obviously backing different claimants to the Spanish throne. By 1836 the *entente* of the Whig governments with France was finished.

After May 1838, relations with the French deteriorated further when France refused to join with Britain in upholding the integrity of the Turkish empire in the face of Mehemet Ali's rebellion in Egypt and his subsequent invasion of Syria. Palmerston's resolute defence of Turkey and his apparent intent to isolate the French led to an agreement with the Tsar of Russia in January 1840 and to a four-power convention, concluded additionally with Prussia and Austria in July, which brought Britain and France to the verge of war. The French demonstrably could not stand alone. In October 1840 the government in Paris collapsed when confronted with an overwhelming diplomatic failure as Mehemet Ali accepted the four powers' terms for a settlement. Palmerston thus emerged from this Near East crisis with his reputation for diplomacy immeasurably enhanced. In this his moment of glory, though, Palmerston saw his party swept away in a general election at home. Aberdeen entered the Foreign Office in September 1841 with Britain's standing seldom higher.

The Tories' efforts to revive the spirit of *entente* owed much to Aberdeen's pacific inclinations and a little to Peel's willingness, at least initially, to support him. It owed a little, too, to the poor state of Britain's relations with the United States in 1841 and the general expectation in London that war in North America would not be long delayed. To Aberdeen's way of thinking, this gave a greater urgency to improving relations with France. If this was not done then the French would likely take whatever advantage they could of Britain's preoccupation with the United States and British interests would come under pressure the world over. Aberdeen's vision of Britain's international preeminence required cordial ties with both Paris and Washington, though in both cases he acknowledged that some price would have to be paid. But any concessions made to lesser powers invariably drew forth cries of weakness from his opponents – particularly, of course, from Palmerston, who believed that Aberdeen was a timid man, ill-suited to uphold Britain's global ascendancy.

Aberdeen was certainly not like Palmerston: he preferred making diplomatic friends to humiliating diplomatic rivals. He neither possessed nor aspired to Palmerston's great qualities of bluff and brinkmanship in international affairs and he did not believe, as Palmerston appeared to do, that history had ordained Britain and France as implacable enemies. He did, however, lack one of Palmerston's virtues – attention to detail. Aberdeen trusted his skill with the political compass to compensate for his neglect of the diplomatic tiller. His understanding of international issues could be insufficiently precise and his instructions to British envoys abroad were occasionally couched in rather vague and even ambiguous terms. This problem was exaggerated after 1841 by his deteriorating health. Aberdeen endured headaches of blinding intensity and increasing frequency while at the Foreign Office. In May 1842 he wrote of his inability to carry on. For weeks at a time he was 'tormented with a continual noise and confusion in the head' and suffered 'sensations which chiefly affect the power of application'.[7] But Peel would not hear of resignation when Aberdeen offered it. Infirm or not, Aberdeen was too important a figure to lose from the government and too valuable in its conduct of foreign policy because of his earlier experience as Foreign Secretary between 1828 and 1830.

Aberdeen's forbearance in international politics did not reflect an essential naivity. He was perfectly aware that in seeking to repair relations with Paris he was holding out a lifeline to the weak administration of François Guizot which had come into office in the wake of humiliation for French diplomacy in the Near East. 'The unpopularity of Guizot seems to be so great in all quarters that it would not surprise me if he were to be sacrificed,' Aberdeen reflected in July 1842.[8] Not only did he risk association with a French ministry of questionable duration but also with a politician who was more renowned for his Anglophile sentiments than for their practical application. In fact, Guizot shared Aberdeen's dream of an Anglo-French alignment in international politics and recognized the need for trust and understanding in working towards it.[9] He saw the political value of being able to claim in Paris that his government had influence, through co-operation, with the British; the previous administration of Adolphe Thiers had, after all, come to grief as a consequence of its futile clash with Palmerston, the likes of which might be avoided by working with Peel and Aberdeen. Aberdeen was also happy to extend his hand to an old friend. Guizot had been French ambassador in London during Aberdeen's earlier spell at the Foreign Office and the two men had developed a good personal accord. A fresh start in Anglo-French relations would be to the benefit of both.

La Plata was not, of course, an area where the two powers had comparable interests at stake. The British predominated in terms of trade and property; French contact and enterprise were at best a poor second. France sold wines, silks, woollens and cottons in the region to the value of £110,000 in 1825, rising over the years to £500,000 by 1850.[10] In Montevideo by the mid-1840s, French nationals owned £500,000 worth of merchandise and real estate; the comparable figure for the British was £2.2 million. Yet while the French lacked capital assets in Latin America they did provide a stream of migrants in the decades after independence, mostly to Mexico, Uruguay and the Argentine. By 1830 about 3000 French had settled in the vicinity of Buenos Aires. By 1839 even the conservative official emigration statistics cited 4500 French nationals as having settled in the Banda Oriental. This emigration increased markedly in the early 1840s. In July 1842 the French consul at Montevideo had the names of over 7000 adult Frenchmen on his register as being resident in or near the city. Women and children were not included in this figure, nor were the many Frenchmen who had settled in the interior. By 1844 an estimated 17,000 French nationals lived in the Banda Oriental.[11] This movement of population provided a basis for the political aspirations of French diplomats in South America and for those officials in Paris who promoted policies designed to give their country a wider and more active international profile. Although Algeria and the Pacific were the chief areas of French expansion under the Orleanist monarchy, Mexico and La Plata were seen as valuable regions for the spread of French culture and for a long-term economic connection which might one day enable France to challenge the supremacy in trade and commerce which the British enjoyed. It was French policy to erode the instinctive nativism of the Spanish in the Americas and to foster those regimes or political movements which welcomed settlers from Europe and which were eager to extend economic contact through legal and institutional liberalization.

France had a record of diplomatic and naval activity in Latin America which reflected such aspirations. In 1829 a French admiral had first demanded equality of status between French and British nationals in the Argentine and the French had returned to this issue in 1838 with their blockade of Buenos Aires. In the interim the French navy had blockaded the Mexican gulf ports of Vera Cruz, Tampico and Matamoros in 1838 to support the claims of French subjects for compensation arising from a civil war and for freedom from forced loans imposed by the Mexican government. In November 1838 French forces stormed the castle of San Juan d'Ulúa in the harbour at Vera Cruz, thereby conveying to the world France's readiness to assert her rights by action if need be.[12] For men of Palmerston's persuasion, all this was typical of the French: it showed nothing other than the aggressive nature of French policy and how admirals and diplomatic agents sought out pretexts for cheap military victories in order to bolster the prestige of Louis-Philippe among his own people. The obvious conclusion was that cooperation with France was impossible. But Aberdeen did not agree. In any case, Palmerston's diplomacy at Buenos Aires since 1839 had achieved next to nothing on its own to bring peace to La Plata. No doubt the French had shortcomings as potential allies but, Aberdeen concluded, Britain's diplomacy would be much strengthened if supported by that of France.

In March 1842 Aberdeen informed Mandeville of the new Anglo-French initiative to mediate in the war between the governments of Buenos Aires and Montevideo. The British embassy in Paris had invited the French to join in this attempt at reconciliation; Guizot had agreed and would be sending a French diplomat to Buenos Aires to work with Mandeville. On his arrival, Aberdeen continued, the two men should call on Arana and formally present the joint offer from their governments. They were also to urge acceptance and to point out that the Uruguayan authorities had already agreed. If Arana still insisted that the Montevidean government should accept Oribe's presidency, then Mandeville and his French colleague were to reply at once that mediating powers could not with propriety carry such demands from one party to the other since one essential quality of international mediation was to convey only such terms as were consistent with the sovereignty of states. Moreover, they might point out that it was impossible for them to uphold Oribe's claim at Montevideo since demonstrably the ex-President was no longer acceptable to the majority of his own people.

Assuming that the Argentine government accepted this offer of mediation, Mandeville was next to propose that it should submit 'moderate and honourable terms of peace' to Uruguay. All this, Mandeville should explain to Arana, was urged only on account of Britain's warm interest in the prosperity of both nations. Naturally, he should add, Britain and France expected that an offer of mediation 'by two such powerful states' would receive the most mature consideration. Aberdeen thought it inconceivable that this offer, so firmly pressed and made from such worthy motives, should be declined, but if it were then Mandeville was not to leave the matter there. The British government had 'a just regard for the commercial interests of Her

Majesty's subjects in the river Plate,' he should declare, and then add that Lord Aberdeen might find that he had a duty imposed on him to resort to 'other measures for the purpose of removing the obstacles which at present interrupt the peaceful navigation of those waters'.[13] Aberdeen's dispatch was not specific. In March 1842 there were no other measures contemplated.

There was nothing, however, that Mandeville could do until the French envoy, Comte Alexandre de Lurde, arrived at Buenos Aires. That did not happen until August and only on 24th did the two diplomats gain an interview with Arana and officially present the Anglo-French offer of mediation. Even beforehand Mandeville was pessimistic as to the success of this joint venture. When speaking informally with Rosas several weeks earlier, he had thought it best to warn the Governor that such an initiative was coming. Rosas' response had been far from encouraging: as great naval powers, Britain and France could no doubt capture and destroy his capital, Rosas declared, but even this would do the cause of peace no good. His fanatical supporters would withdraw into the countryside and conduct a guerrilla struggle against the invaders before they would ever compromise. With this, Rosas headed off any veiled threat which Mandeville and de Lurde might plan to deliver. Feeling now that the warfare endemic in La Plata since 1838 had at last turned in his favour, Rosas, it seemed, was not prepared to settle for anything less than a political as well as a military triumph.

De Lurde was only too willing to cooperate in any presentation to the Argentine government: 'even to back it with acts which I should have great difficulty to join him in the sanction of,' Mandeville reported to Aberdeen.[14] De Lurde assured his British colleague that he had authority to call upon the French navy for anything which might assist their joint effort to stop the war. That seemed of little use, however, given the confidence which Rosas had in his ultimate victory. The initial problem was to get any response at all to the mediation offer of 24 August. After six weeks Arana asked what terms the two European powers were offering, to which Mandeville brusquely replied that, in such a diplomatic procedure, terms for peace could not be discussed until the offer of mediation had been formally accepted.

On 18 October, as Mandeville had long anticipated, the mediation was politely declined. Arana explained that the Argentine government felt its own security to be endangered by its enemies who were allied with Rivera in Montevideo; it had no option, therefore, but to continue hostilities. Mandeville made plain that this was not a satisfactory answer; when it was confirmed a month later that no further representations could induce Rosas to change his mind, Mandeville formally gave notice that the British government might feel obliged to resort to other measures.

News of this did not reach London until well into the new year. In the meantime, on 7 December 1842, Aberdeen approved the manner in which Mandeville had presented the mediation offer and indeed, with de Lurde, had worked out terms for a six month armistice which it was hoped both the Argentine and Uruguayan authorities might observe. Even a temporary lull in the war would probably be sufficient to produce a treaty of peace, Aberdeen remarked, 'and will spare the governments of Great Britain and France the disagreeable alternative of resorting to any ulterior measures, should such be thought necessary'. Nonetheless, he reminded Mandeville, 'the possible adoption of such measures is still under the consideration of the two governments.'[15]

While diplomats and politicians refined their arguments at Buenos Aires, Oribe in Entre Rios gathered one of the largest, best equipped armies ever seen on Argentine soil. Mandeville estimated in June 1842 that the supply ships leaving Buenos Aires and destined to meet Oribe on the Paraná River contained sufficient horses, ammunition and provisions for eleven or twelve thousand men. In an attempt to interrupt Oribe's communications, the three seaworthy vessels of the Uruguayan navy entered the Paraná, where they were engaged and destroyed by an Argentine squadron. When all was ready, Oribe moved against the combined troops from Corrientes and Uruguay commanded by Rivera and on 6 December 1842 routed them at the battle of Arroyo Grande. Rivera escaped with a handful of cavalry back into Uruguay where the government, understandably, was seized with panic. By the end of the month Oribe was moving his army across the River Uruguay near the town of Salto, secure in the knowledge that there was no force between him and the outskirts of Montevideo. Arroyo Grande had dramatically changed the balance in the war and for the British and French diplomats at Buenos Aires this had serious political consequences. Until now they had offered mediation to belligerents each undefeated in the field. After the battle, their mediation offer took on the appearance of being more a mechanism for staving off a Uruguayan surrender than an impartial intervention. With Oribe now campaigning in his own country to regain his presidential seat, Rosas could and did describe the conflict as a civil war in Uruguay and not an Argentine invasion. The troops from Buenos Aires who accompanied Oribe into the Banda Oriental served merely as auxiliaries, Rosas insisted, and were lent to him by a faithful ally solely to achieve his just purpose.

The response of Mandeville and de Lurde to these developments was as much a point of departure in their diplomacy as Oribe's victory was in the course of the war. After hearing of Rivera's disaster at Arroyo Grande, and believing that the navy of Buenos Aires was about to sail for a seaborne attack against Montevideo, the two envoys decided that they should at once request an armistice. On 16 December 1842 Mandeville and de Lurde formally demanded of Arana a cessation of hostilities and the withdrawal of all forces back within their own territory. It was, they stated, the intention of their respective governments to prevent a continuation of the war both in the interest of humanity and, more specifically, of their countrymen resident in Uruguay. At the same time, the two Ministers ordered the commanders of their warships in the Plate to take steps to arrange for an evacuation of British and French nationals from Montevideo should lives be placed in danger. Mandeville hoped that the Foreign Office would approve these measures. He had, as he confessed, no instructions which covered the steps taken but he had felt it essential to act immediately. 'I passed the line of my generally cautious conduct,' he observed.[16] Aberdeen received the news without enthusiasm. He did not disapprove of the demand for an armistice and troop withdrawal, though he made it plain that such a step had certainly not been requested from London. As for the future, Aberdeen replied, 'You will understand that Her Majesty's Government are unwilling that the officers in command of any of Her Majesty's ships in the river Plate should interfere in the contest between Buenos Aires and Montevideo unless force should be necessary for the protection of the lives or property of Her Majesty's subjects residing in either of those ports.'[17] De Lurde was sent the same reminder from Paris.

The vanguard of Oribe's army came within sight of Montevideo on 16 February 1843. As the General well knew, however, the city was not the same as when he had fled it nearly five years earlier. Its population had grown significantly on account of the waves of immigrants since 1838. In the single year of 1841, Mandeville reported, 6000 Basques alone had settled in the capital. These migrants had considerable military value. Many of them were 'ready made soldiers', as Hood described the Basques arriving in 1839, who had fought with Don Carlos in the civil war in Spain; after 1839, indeed, all Basques, Catalans and other Spanish men settling in Uruguay were obliged to render military service after three years of residence.[18] The city had expanded during the prosperity brought to it by the two years of French blockade at Buenos Aires. Its old walls had been pulled down, Mandeville observed in 1842: to withstand a siege new fortifications would need to be constructed.

However, there was no doubting the will to defend the city. Most inhabitants believed that its conquest by Oribe's Argentine auxiliaries would lead to the same scenes of bloodshed on the streets as had been so evident in Buenos Aires during Rosas' reign of terror in 1840. By the end of December 1842, 4000 men had volunteered for a militia force within Montevideo and about 1500 newly liberated slaves were also undergoing military training. By January 1843 extensive earthworks formed an outer line of defence across the top of the peninsula on which Montevideo was located. A ditch three yards wide had been cut and behind it two brick walls, each five feet high and three yards apart, had been built and the space between them filled in with earth. On this rampart were sited, at intervals, batteries containing 30 pieces of cannon. An inner line of defence was also constructed along the edge of the densely built-up area of the city.[19] Out in the countryside Rivera was at work to raise another army. He was thought to have nearly 6000 horsemen under his command – not sufficient to engage Oribe's army but enough to harass his supplies and to conduct guerrilla raids. On 1 March 1843 Rivera assumed the title of General-in-Chief when his presidential term expired. Since, clearly, no election could be held to find a successor, the headship of state passed, under the restored constitution, to the leader of the Senate. By this means Joaquín Suárez was declared acting President of the republic in this moment of national crisis.[20] The comet which lit up the night sky at the time was taken as a poor omen for his survival.

The British who watched these developments were less guided by the heavens. For some of the diplomats and naval officers in La Plata a rapid victory for Oribe did not seem likely. When the commander of the Brazil naval station, Commodore John Purvis, arrived in the Plate in February 1843, he gave his professional opinion of the situation. Oribe had brought 20 pieces of artillery, 3000 artillerymen and infantry and 5000 cavalry to Montevideo, Purvis estimated. Against him there were about 6000 soldiers inside the city, cannon on the ramparts and Rivera with his cavalry to Oribe's rear.[21] Barring treachery or cowardice, Purvis concluded, the defenders should be able to withstand an assault. As long as the port remained open, supplies of food should be plentiful and, with the southern winter season approaching, the shortage of grazing for the besiegers' horses might force Oribe to retire. John Dale, the new British counsul in Montevideo, shared this view. Undoubtedly, he informed the Foreign Office, Oribe had advanced upon Montevideo in the confident expectation that there would be an uprising in his favour from within and he had been greatly surprised to find on arrival defensive preparations conducted with such enthusiasm. No one doubted that Oribe's soldiers were superior in quality: most had recent experience of battle in the Argentine and those from Buenos Aires were considered to be among Rosas' best troops. But in small numbers even they were not invincible, as Rivera proved on 18 June 1843 when a body of his horsemen dispersed a crack unit of 1000 Argentine cavalry. Oribe established as his headquarters a strongly fortified encampment at the Cerrito, just north of Montevideo, and reconciled himself to a siege of the city.

Crucial to the fate of Montevideo, as both besieged and besiegers soon recognized, were the large foreign communities inside. Even before Oribe's arrival the Uruguayan government had asked Mandeville to sanction arming the British residents in Montevideo so that they could participate in its defence. Mandeville had replied, however, that he had no authority to give such approval. But it was not the relatively small numbers of British in the city who mattered – rather the thousands of French and Basques, and it was with respect to these that Oribe made an appalling miscalculation on 1 April 1843. Hoping to intimidate the immigrants into neutrality, Oribe sent a circular message to all the foreign consuls in which he announced that, on his entry into the city, anyone found to have fought for, or in any other way supported, the Montevidean regime would be regarded as a unitarian and dealt with accordingly by his Argentine allies.[22] The effect of this on the foreigners, as Purvis recorded, was 'the same effect as fire upon gunpowder'.[23] Basques and Frenchmen formed volunteer legions and pledged to fight for their liberty, and that of the city, against the tyrant Oribe and his regiments of Argentine cutthroats. The Italians in Montevideo did so too, inspired by a political dreamer and adventurer, Giuseppe Garibaldi, who a year previously had drifted into Uruguay after years of combat in republican insurrection in Brazil.

Dale reported on 3 April that hundreds of French Basques had spent the last two days demonstrating and parading in the streets while singing revolutionary songs from Europe and waving the tricolour. By 25 April he was able to record that around 3000 men had enrolled in the French legion alone and that most of them possessed muskets in good condition. These legions served guard duty on the lines and might even be capable of counter-attack against sections of Oribe's forces. Oribe was later to retract his threat, but not before irrevocable damage to his cause had been done. Dale astutely advised the Foreign Office that 'the decided part now taken by so large a body of the French inhabitants of this city has caused the war to assume a different character.'[24]

3· The Failure of Diplomacy, 1843

In the weeks which followed Oribe's encampment at the Cerrito, Mandeville and de Lurde renewed their efforts to stop the fighting and to protect the large numbers of foreigners now trapped in Montevideo. On 16 March 1843 they proposed to Arana certain limits within which the struggle might be conducted: principally that the Argentine forces should make no attempt to take the city by direct assault. Montevideo was not a fortress, the two diplomats argued. Indeed its lines of defence were so close to the city that any bombardment and fighting would be a disaster for the civilian population. Instead of a siege by land, the Argentine operation against Montevideo should be by means of a naval blockade. Arana gave no immediate response; within days, however, the proposal was firmly rejected at Buenos Aires. Mandeville rebuked the Argentine government for its apparent indifference to his humanitarian concern but, realistically, he could scarcely have expected Rosas and Oribe to relinquish their advantage.

After March 1843 relations between the British and French legations and the Foreign Ministry in Buenos Aires deteriorated steadily. This was in part because the representations of Mandeville and de Lurde were all rejected, but equally on account of the arrival of Commodore Purvis to command the British naval squadron in the Plate. By 1843 the Royal Navy's presence in the river was no longer inconsiderable. In addition to his 50-gun flagship, HMS *Alfred*, Purvis had three warships each carrying approximately 20 guns and two shallow draught steamers and a surveying vessel, each with about five guns. With this force at his disposal, Purvis' instinct was to come to the aid of Montevideo and to resist the tide of Argentine tyranny which he saw engulfing the Banda Oriental. Zealous in his duty and conscious of his standing as head of a naval station, Purvis saw his task as implementing that which all agreed were his country's true interest and wishes – an end to the fighting and an Argentine evacuation of Uruguay. Dale, in Montevideo, merely confirmed Purvis' interpretation. Encouraged thus, Purvis was not much interested in Mandeville's opinions; nor, indeed, did he regard the Minister at Buenos Aires as having an authority above his own. The first sign of trouble caused by this came on 12 April, when both Mandeville and de Lurde were summoned to see Arana.

In support of its army outside Montevideo, the Argentine navy had reimposed a blockade of the port, not as an alternative to a land-based siege, as the British and French envoys had requested, but as an additional form of pressure. In deference to British and French anxieties, this was not to be a strict blockade against all foreign shipping but a partial blockade whereby the government at Buenos Aires could intercept any coastal vessels which it suspected of supplying provisions or munitions for the garrison. Arana's forceful complaint to Mandeville and de Lurde was that Purvis, and the commander of the small French naval squadron in the Plate, had refused to recognize any Argentine right of blockade and had threatened to intervene in order to lift it. Rosas attached an importance to this blockade of Montevideo which went beyond its military value. Poor as his navy might appear to the British and French commanders, it was nonetheless the navy of a sovereign state with as much right to announce and to enforce a blockade against enemy shipping as any other. To deny the blockade was thus to insult Argentine honour and to mock its rights in international law. Britain had respected the French blockade at Buenos Aires between 1838 and 1840 even when the French had encountered difficulties of enforcement. Rosas was not prepared to be treated differently.[1]

The response of the two Ministers to Arana was distinctly unsympathetic. Mandeville told Arana bluntly that neither he or de Lurde had any control over the actions of their naval commanders and he regretted therefore that he was unable to assist the government of Buenos Aires in enforcing its declaration of blockade. Arana refused to believe this and raised the matter again a month later, during which time Purvis continued to obstruct the movements of the Argentine commander, Admiral William Brown.[2] Such evident hostility shown by Purvis, Arana insisted, might well lead to a rupture between Britain and the Argentine Confederation and perhaps place in jeopardy the security and property of the British community resident in Buenos Aires. Mandeville retorted sharply that responsibility for the safety of all foreign nationals in Argentine territory lay exclusively with the Argentine authorities, as was understood by the laws of all civilized states and indeed specifically covered in the Anglo-Argentine treaty of

1825. As for Purvis, his orders came from the Admiralty and, as Arana well knew, Purvis had remained deaf to any suggestions which Mandeville had made to him in recent weeks. All complaints, therefore, against the Commodore's conduct should be raised with the British government through the Argentine Minister in London.

By the middle of 1843, Mandeville's position at Buenos Aires had become an embarrassing one. First of all, Rosas knew that the British government had not authorized Mandeville to present the ultimatum of 16 December 1842 and that Aberdeen was not inclined to follow it up.[3] On 21 April Aberdeen informed Manuel Moreno, the Argentine envoy in London, that Mandeville had acted independently. Arana learned soon after, therefore, that he need not fashion his diplomacy to meet the protests of the agents of the European powers. Secondly, Mandeville's statement to Arana that he had no control over Purvis was no diplomatic ruse but a candid admission of the rift which had developed. Purvis not only publicly contested the Argentine right of blockade but, on 17 February 1843, addressed a letter to Admiral Brown in which he disparagingly informed the latter that, having been born in Britain, he was legally a British subject and that he, and other British subjects in the Argentine service, should abstain from any part in naval conflict.[4] Contrary to Mandeville's inclinations, Purvis also repeatedly made it clear that he favoured an active British involvement in the defence of Montevideo. Mandeville's preference for a diplomatic resolution of the conflict, despite his failures to date, made him appear pro-Argentine in the eyes of the Montevidean population who, understandably, were more impressed with Purvis' robust tones and his measures of practical support.

Mandeville's initial communications with Purvis had been reserved. On 14 February 1843 the Minister explained how the Argentine government had rejected the Anglo-French offer of mediation and that consequently he and de Lurde were now awaiting further instructions from Europe. As for the use of naval force in order to apply pressure on the Argentine government to change its mind and to accept the mediation offer, this was still being considered by the British and French governments and until he received word from London he had no authority to sanction any action. This included the landing of marines to defend the foreign residents in Montevideo which, he told Purvis, he was pleased had not yet happened. However, Mandeville considerably weakened his authority with respect to Purvis when he passed the responsibility for the safety of the British community at

Montevideo to the navy and agreed to defer to Purvis' judgment. In making a decision, though, Purvis was to bear in mind that putting men ashore could not be construed as an act consistent with neutrality. Britain had told the Uruguayan authorities that it was they who were responsible for the safety of British subjects inside the capital: to land marines would be for Britain implicitly to assume that responsibility and thereby free Montevidean troops for other duties.

On 19 February 1843 Purvis landed 120 marines. The French admiral ordered ashore an identical number. The joint force took up quarters in the buildings around the Customs House so as to provide a safe line of retreat from there to the water's edge in the event of an evacuation of British and French nationals from Montevideo. The main body of the Argentine army was, by this date, no more than a mile from the outer lines of the city and a general assault was widely expected. Purvis placed two of his warships at anchor close by in case covering fire from their guns should prove necessary. 'A more prudent and well arranged plan for securing and defending the lives and property of British subjects could not, under the circumstances, have been devised than that adopted by Commodore Purvis,' Dale wrote enthusiastically to Aberdeen.[5] The Foreign Office confirmed that Purvis' move was 'prudent and judicious'.[6] Purvis, however, was soon indicating that measures simply to provide for a safe evacuation were not sufficient. On 14 March he told Mandeville that a larger contingent of marines should be landed in order to assist in the defence of Montevideo itself and that in doing so he would be acting in accordance with the wishes of the British government. Mandeville hurriedly consulted his French colleague and concluded the opposite. On 18 March he replied to Purvis that, by the terms of his dispatches from London, there could be no question of the British government sanctioning an armed intervention for the defence of the city. At the end of March Mandeville thought it best to write privately to the Foreign Office of the gulf between his own and Purvis' policies. The latter, despite having been fully informed by Mandeville of the point reached by Anglo-French diplomacy at Buenos Aires, and the need to await fresh instructions, appeared intent on using the fleet to intervene in the war on behalf of Montevideo and thereby risk a political rupture with the Argentine government.

The uproar caused by Oribe's warning to the foreign population of Montevideo on 1 April 1843 gave Purvis an unexpected opportunity to take matters into his own hands. Even Mandeville, reluctant as he was to do anything which might cause friction at Buenos Aires, conceded to Purvis that the diplomatic and consular communities in La Plata could not allow a declaration to stand which placed in danger almost every foreigner in Montevideo. Purvis had already requested Oribe to revoke his threat. To this he had received an answer which he judged both ambiguous and unsatisfactory. The crucial point, of course, in Mandeville's approval for further measures was to decide just what was necessary for the protection of British subjects. For Purvis, this meant anything which would force Oribe to back down and he decided that the most effective action would be to constrain the Argentine squadron off Montevideo. Purvis therefore informed Brown that Argentine vessels would not be allowed to move from their present positions until Oribe both retracted his circular and issued a guarantee that the lives and property of all British subjects would be respected should he enter Montevideo.[7] When Brown ordered two of his ships to strike sail, Purvis opened fire from *Alfred* and caused the Argentine ships to drop anchor.

Mandeville and de Lurde were immediately summoned to the Foreign Ministry in Buenos Aires, where they found Arana on the verge of hysteria and equipped with a list of complaints against Purvis. He demanded to know if the two diplomats had given prior approval for Purvis' action and also for the way in which British vessels frustrated Brown's attempts to communicate with Oribe on land and with Argentine supply ships at sea. After two days of conference de Lurde declared that he, at least, had not sanctioned any French naval action. He and Arana then prevailed upon Mandeville to write to Purvis officially disclaiming what had been done. On 17 April Mandeville informed Purvis of his disapproval and pointed out the grave political consequences which might result from any repetition of such acts against the fleet of a nation with which Britain was at peace. Purvis later enquired of the Admiralty how a naval officer could be expected to carry out his duties 'when Her Majesty's Minister shrinks from the defence of those acts he partly recommended.'[8]

The differing perceptions of duty held by Mandeville and Purvis were, inevitably, referred back to London. In the meantime the Minister and naval commander continued their uneasy relationship. Mandeville consistently stressed the need to abide by the principle of neutrality while Purvis barely concealed his Uruguayan sympathies. Not until October 1843 did dispatches arrive at Buenos Aires restating the government's policy and thus resolving the conflict of authority between Mandeville and Purvis. In London there had been no hesitation in backing Mandeville's judgment. The Foreign Office wrote to the Admiralty on 3 July 1843 pointing out that Aberdeen 'has entirely approved the determination of Mr. Mandeville not to sanction the measures of forcible intervention in favour of Montevideo proposed by Commodore Purvis'.[9] Aberdeen referred the question of the legality of the Argentine blockade of Montevideo to the office of the Advocate General, which returned the opinion that, as a belligerent in a war against Uruguay, the government of Buenos Aires had every right to impose and enforce a naval blockade which would restrict the supply of war provisions to the enemy; this right, indeed, 'cannot be interfered with or controlled by any third state professing neutrality between the contending parties'.[10] Again then, Purvis was overruled and Mandeville's more cautious interpretation of Britain's responsibilities was upheld. On 5 July Aberdeen assured Mandeville that he approved of all the latter's recent efforts to coordinate his diplomacy with that of de Lurde and that he also approved the manner in which Mandeville had refused to countenance the suggestion by Purvis that British forces should help defend the city of Montevideo in the event of an attack.

Nothing, however, could diminish Purvis' enthusiasm for the Montevidean cause or his dislike of Oribe and the Argentines. In December 1843 the Commodore's patience appeared to snap after Oribe declared the port of Maldonado to be closed to shipping and in the process trapped within it some British merchandise awaiting transit. Purvis informed Mandeville that he proposed, in retaliation, to raise the Argentine blockade of Montevideo and to throw a blockade of British warships around Oribe's main supply port on the Uruguayan coast at Buceo. Mandeville, as usual, consulted his French colleague. Afterwards he responded that, since Oribe controlled the town of Maldonado, his forces were entitled to close its port to foreign commerce if they so chose. Purvis was obliged to drop his plans for further action, but by this time his future was in some doubt. Arana's resentment of his anti-Argentine behaviour throughout 1843 led to a request from the Foreign Ministry at Buenos Aires on 13 December that Purvis should be recalled from his command. Soon after this, the Commodore caused offence again when he complained directly to Arana about attacks made on him in the Argentine Press, rather than having his views submitted through the proper diplomatic channel. On 2 April 1844 the Foreign Office finally asked the Admiralty to order Purvis back to his base at Rio de Janeiro and to send the officer second-in-command on the Brazil station to direct the squadron in the River Plate.

* * *

Throughout his dispute with Purvis, Mandeville had justified his conduct on the grounds that he preserved Britain's neutrality in the war while Purvis, conversely, risked incurring a commitment to the regime at Montevideo. Yet, less publicly, Mandeville had himself allowed the British government to be drawn into a position where it became involved both with the fate of the city and the survival of the government inside it. Even by 1843 neutrality was becoming an untenable position in the war in La Plata and Purvis at times did little more than highlight contradictions and compromises which Mandeville had already brought about.

The diplomacy with the Uruguayan government in 1842 over signing a treaty of amity, commerce and navigation with Britain proved to be one source of embarrassment. The British had first proposed such a treaty in 1834.[11] Years of intermittent negotiation had borne no fruit, however, until in January 1842 Mandeville recognized the opportunity which Uruguay's need for international support presented and found the government in Montevideo ready and willing to sign. Mandeville had been happy to let the Uruguayans believe that a treaty with Britain would enhance the likelihood of assistance in their conflict with Buenos Aires. Indeed, after signing in July 1842, Mandeville continued to encourage such expectations. On 26 October he wrote privately to the Uruguayan Foreign Minister, Francisco Vidal, that 'the sentiments of the British government (and as you say Lord Aberdeen himself declares) towards the Banda Oriental will be very different after the conclusion of the treaty between this country and Great Britain to what they were before.'[12] The Uruguayans, not unreasonably, expected British assistance after the treaty was ratified. Vidal's successor as Foreign Minister, Santiago Vázquez, reminded Mandeville in March 1843 of a promise of support given in the previous June. The correspondence from 1842 clearly showed that the only reason why Vidal had accepted the proposed bases for a treaty was 'the assurance given both publicly and privately by Your Excellency that Her Majesty's Government would shield the republic from the attacks of General Rosas'. 'The treaty being made,' Vázquez now insisted, 'it conferred upon the republic the *right to demand* the fulfilment of the condition upon which it was founded.'[13]

Yet it was not only in his conduct of the negotiations for the 1842 treaty that Mandeville appeared to compromise Britain's neutrality in the war. Confusion also seemed to surround the offer of mediation made by Britain and France in August 1842. This offer was naturally welcomed by the Uruguayans once the tide of war had turned against them. Mandeville, however, in private correspondence, held out hopes for more than simply diplomatic mediation when he informed Vidal, in September 1842, that 'I perfectly agree with you that Her Majesty's Government would not make a second offer of its mediation without being resolved to support it.'[14] More significant still in raising expectations in Montevideo was the spontaneous note which Mandeville and de Lurde addressed to the Argentine government on 16 December 1842, requesting an end to hostilities and the withdrawal of Argentine troops from Uruguayan soil. Dale also believed that this was the turning point in relations between London and Buenos Aires and that it constituted a clear warning to Rosas that Britain would resort to naval action if its representations for peace remained unheeded. Mandeville had, of course, stepped beyond the bounds of his authority in making his demand of 16 December – sufficiently so that, in August 1843, Aberdeen felt it prudent to tell the Uruguayan government that 'Mr. Mandeville acted under some misapprehension of the instructions which he had received.'[15]

But Mandeville's indiscretion did not stop there. On 6 January 1843 he wrote to the Uruguayan government of an Anglo-French fleet which had already sailed from Europe and which would on arrival put an end to the war. He wrote again on 12 January: 'What has prevented the British and French naval forces from coming long before this to the river Plate, I can have no conception,' he confessed. 'Before the end of December I would have sworn that they would have been here.'[16] Dale was delighted to hear that help for the beleaguered city was on its way and in his dispatches to London he informed the Foreign Office of the calming effect that this news had produced among the population. On 19 January Dale wrote that the mood of the city was, however, tinged with some anxiety because of the non-appearance of the expedition, despite Mandeville's repeated assurances that it had set sail in the previous October. Aberdeen learned of all this in disbelief. 'I have no knowledge of the authority upon which you entertained any such expectation,' the Foreign Secretary chided

Mandeville on 3 May, 'and I am compelled to observe that in the absence of any information or instructions on the subject from this office, you did wrong in making that expectation the ground of an assurance to the Montevidean government.'[17]

Unfortunately for Aberdeen it was too late to undo the diplomatic damage. The Uruguayan Minister in Paris, José Ellauri, was heading for London intent on holding the British government to the commitments which Mandeville had made on its behalf. Ellauri came to remind Aberdeen not only of the assistance which Mandeville had held out to Vidal in 1842, but also of the clear statement of support implicit in the ultimatum given to the Argentine authorities on 16 December. In May 1843 he was also badgering both the French and British governments to send the naval force which Mandeville had promised four months earlier. If this were not done at once it might be too late, he warned. Ellauri found the reactions from both British and French governments disturbing: 'Always the same response,' he wrote despairingly to Vázquez. 'The same protests of sympathy and of concerns for our cause; but nothing of written engagements.'[18] Early in July 1843 Ellauri was admitted to the Foreign Office for an interview with Aberdeen. Ellauri pleaded the case of his government and expanded as to its expectations. Aberdeen listened, but his answer was most explicit: it never had been, nor was, nor would be the policy of the British government to enter an armed intervention.[19]

Unquestionably, the erratic manner in which Mandeville conducted matters from Buenos Aires put Aberdeen under growing pressure with respect to events in La Plata. So too did the swelling number of British merchants, at home and in South America, whose livelihoods were jeopardized by the interruption to trade caused by the warfare, siege and blockade at Montevideo. The British merchant community there had sought assurances from Mandeville in the summer of 1842 that their welfare would not be endangered. Mandeville's reply, according to the merchant body, 'gave the strongest assurances to many of his countrymen that, notwithstanding the threatening attitude of the Buenos Airean army in the province of Entre Rios, it would not be permitted to invade the territory of this republic'. 'Relying implicitly on assurances derived from such high authority,' the merchants of Montevideo continued, 'most of the British merchants here, instead of limiting their transactions as they would otherwise have done, extended them considerably.'[20] Dale, as always, was an enthusiastic supporter of the merchant interest at Montevideo. He forwarded their views and petitions to Mandeville and to Purvis. He encouraged the Foreign Office, too, to give more thought to the value of Britain's economic ties with Uruguay. 'Montevideo is well worth some sacrifice to save from the dominance of Rosas,' he advised in October 1842, 'even selfishly viewed, as a market for our manufacturers.'[21]

In Britain, too, commercial groups began to draw attention in the Press and by direct representation at the Foreign Office to the unsatisfactory state of the disturbances in La Plata and to the British government's continued inability to restore tranquillity. From Liverpool, the Association of Mexican and South American Merchants complained in July 1843 that it was impossible to discern any consistent strand in foreign policy. The public rift between Mandeville and Purvis, and the alternating assurances and disavowals of forceful action, added to the confusion felt among commercial men. A clear policy was needed, preferably one where the navy was employed to back up Mandeville's demand to the Argentine authorities of 16 December 1842. A number of other Liverpool traders and shipowners complained in similar vein. In reply the Foreign Office still insisted that 'it is not the intention by Her Majesty's Government to undertake an armed interference in the war.'[22] Returning to the charge, the Mexican and South American Association wrote in October, and yet again in December 1843, pointing out that all efforts by the British government to bring an end to hostilities had proved utterly useless and repeating its demand for an energetic intervention. On 30 November the Prime Minister forwarded to Aberdeen some correspondence which he had received from one of the Liverpool trading houses. Peel made no written comment, but the content of the letters could have been nothing but embarrassing for the Foreign Secretary. Not only was Mandeville labelled 'pusillanimous' and 'imbecile', but the entire policy of the government was dismissed as 'the most contemptible and the most ruinous that could possibly have been pursued.'[23] The burden of doing something to salvage credibility began to weigh on Aberdeen's shoulders.

4· Britain, France and the Policy of Intervention, 1844

It was only natural that vested interests in Britain should voice their grievances whenever and wherever in the world turmoil threatened profitable commerce. The Foreign Office in the nineteenth century was accustomed to pressure from organized lobbies and from individual traders and was usually adept at dealing with both. Diplomatic or naval intervention was widely regarded by the Press and public, as well as by businessmen, as the solution to most international problems; historians, understandably, have long been concerned to illustrate the role of such clamour in the direction of official policy and to establish or refute a causal association. As politicians, Peel and Aberdeen could not be indifferent to domestic popularity. As statesmen, however, they shared many of the reservations which were common within the political establishment as to the propriety, and indeed the effectiveness, of government intervention abroad either in support of economic enterprise or more broadly in the regulation of international affairs. But by 1843 Aberdeen had to face the fact that his failure to stop the war in Uruguay posed difficulties for him which seemed likely only to intensify. Beyond the disquiet of British merchants and manufacturers, Aberdeen's supervision of diplomacy and his grasp of the problem in La Plata were in danger of ridicule. He had come to accept that more than diplomacy might now be needed.

This suspicion that diplomatic procedures had already been exhausted was reflected in an exchange of views with the Prime Minister late in November 1843, when Aberdeen explained, as best he could, the state of play in the region. 'This war which has lasted so long, is perfectly unintelligible and appears to have no object,' he concluded. Aberdeen made plain where he believed blame lay. 'Montevideo desires nothing but peace and makes no conditions,' he informed Peel on 25 November, 'while nothing but entire conquest will satisfy the other party.'[1] Peel at once remarked that any use of force carried risks. 'Interference, when we have no ground for quarrel or complaint, between two states carrying on war, is opposed to principle and is dangerous as a precedent,' he replied. 'Still, there are occasions when it is necessary for great objects to disregard the principles which ought to govern ordinary transactions,' the Prime Minister continued, 'and to incur the danger of a bad precedent for the purpose of avoiding a great present evil.' Peel agreed entirely with Aberdeen's assessment of the war and he clearly held Rosas responsible for its prolongation. 'Here is a power, or rather a *man* wielding the force of a power, waging war on personal grounds against a small state with friendly dispositions to us, listening to no terms of compromise, refusing offers of mediation, disturbing our lawful commerce, and seriously affecting the interests of the Queen's subjects.' Britain, nonetheless, would not intervene in the war to favour one side or the other, Peel insisted. But if Aberdeen did wish to act then he must not leave it too late. If Montevideo fell to Oribe after the British government had announced that it was determined to put an end to the war before that eventuality, Britain would be humiliated and made a laughing stock in Europe as at Buenos Aires. 'Remember also our own domestic position,' he warned the Foreign Secretary. 'The complaints of our apathy already made by the commercial interests connected with Montevideo; the sentence of condemnation on the past which *ore nostro* we shall pronounce if we now resolve on forcible intervention but it comes *too late*. We have had ample warnings.'[2]

Despite this guarded blessing for firmer action from Downing Street, Aberdeen delayed any decision, and when the Uruguayans again pressed him for help he repeated the refusal given earlier to Ellauri. In Montevideo it had been assumed that Ellauri himself had displayed diplomatic shortcomings in Paris and London and that, though his experience as a former Foreign Minister was useful in many areas, the task of enlisting assistance in Uruguay's struggle for survival was best entrusted to a more dynamic man.

For this reason Florencio Varela left for London in August 1843 to plead with Aberdeen anew.[3] He stressed the justice of his government's resistance to Oribe and the importance of Montevideo as an open port for British commercial enterprise in the future. He also spoke of vague plans for a new state which might be formed by the secession of Entre Rios and Corrientes from the Argentine Confederation, and which would be allied in politics and in its economic liberalism with a free and prosperous Uruguay. But Aberdeen was not interested in any of this. He told Varela towards the end of 1843, and wrote officially on 2 January 1844, that the British government would not depart from its declared policy of neutrality. Varela had seen the British mind at work and wrote dejectedly that there was little point prolonging his mission. Aberdeen's thinking was this, he advised his government in Montevideo: 'if abandoned to ourselves, we shall expire sooner and the war will end; while if helped to resist, the war will continue. There is no human exertion that will persuade them of the error of this calculation; commerce, the Cabinet, everyone thinks in that way.'[4]

Varela's frustration was understandable. Aberdeen, however, still looked on international affairs with a keen eye for opportunities to cooperate with France and, whatever might eventually be decided about La Plata, it was important for him first to know the views of the French government. Aberdeen had no reason to doubt that Guizot would encourage him in an initiative. The French navy had been active in the Americas in recent years – too active, many of Aberdeen's Tory colleagues believed. Aberdeen had sounded Guizot on the subject in the summer of 1842 when, after receiving reports of atrocities in the fighting at Montevideo, he had suggested the possibility of 'some immediate and energetic steps'. Guizot's initial response was perhaps more than Aberdeen had bargained for. In September 1842 Guizot replied that the River Plate might provide an excellent opportunity for a demonstration of Anglo-French cooperation and that he favoured sending to the region 'an imposing force'. At this point, however, both Aberdeen and Guizot recoiled. Although officials at the Quai d'Orsay cited such successful precedents for Anglo-French collaboration as the Greco–Turkish war in 1827 and the war of Belgian independence in 1831, Guizot was persuaded by Admiral Makau that the French naval actions at Vera Cruz in 1838 and at Buenos Aires between 1838 and 1840 had been modest successes in terms of achieving political objectives. A venture now, albeit with the British, would be unlikely to end in éclat. On 4 October 1842 Aberdeen had confided his doubts to Peel in that he was 'rather shy of French cooperation, to such an extent as they would probably desire'. That being so, he concluded, 'I propose not to give immediate effect to the proposal of active or coercive measures.'[5]

By the end of 1843 Aberdeen obviously felt greater confidence in working alongside the French than he had felt a year earlier. The past twelve months had seen a steady, even spectacular, improvement in relations between the two countries and a personal trust and mutual appreciation had developed between Guizot and Aberdeen which led them both to consider that they stood at the dawn of a new age in Anglo-French diplomacy. In 1843 Guizot had spoken openly in Paris of his sympathy with Britain and appeared to have cowed those elements in the Chamber of Deputies which were implacably hostile to any *rapprochement*. 1843 saw a fisheries convention, a postal convention and an extradition treaty all concluded between Britain and France; both Aberdeen and Guizot could therefore present their domestic critics with firm evidence that *entente* was capable of tangible rewards. The only small cloud on the horizon were different perceptions of events in Spain. 'Upon all other questions,' Lord Cowley, the British ambassador to France, observed in August 1843, 'a perfectly good understanding subsists between the two governments.'[6]

The highlight of the year was the visit of Victoria to the Chateau d'Eu where, in September, Louis-Philippe played host at a most successful demonstration of royal affinity and where, behind the scenes, Guizot and Aberdeen haggled, with some purpose, about the issues of the day. Foremost among those was Spain, where the young queen, Isabella, and her sister, the Infanta Louisa, were both in need of husbands. Successful suitors would carry political influence in Spain: it mattered, therefore, which of the grandees of Europe were favoured, for upon them might rest the leanings of Spain in international affairs. The French position was clear: Isabella should take her consort from among the descendants of Philip V of Spain, thus guaranteeing a Bourbon candidate, although in deference to the British it should not be one of the sons of Louis-Philippe. At the Chateau d'Eu conference Aberdeen accepted this solution. Guizot was delighted that French diplomatic dominance at Madrid was effectively conceded and he told Aberdeen of the immense value of their political understanding. In Greece, too, British and French diplomats seemed to be working in harmony to establish stable government after the revolution in Athens in September 1843.

Amid such optimism it seemed right that Aberdeen should turn once more for help to Paris in his efforts to restore peace in La Plata. On 27 November 1843 he wrote to Peel to say that he awaited word from Guizot. He made plain to the Prime Minister the dilemma which affairs at Montevideo posed for the Foreign Office and for the French government. Both had frequently stressed their neutrality and both had seen their offers of mediation refused at Buenos Aires. 'Our Ministers then take part virtually with Montevideo and declare an armistice,' Aberdeen admitted. 'Our naval commanders also take measures in favour of Montevideo and go beyond our Ministers. We disapprove of the first step of our Ministers and support them in their subsequent conduct against the naval commanders.' 'Thus,' Aberdeen concluded, 'we shall be guilty of some inconsistency in now abandoning our neutrality.' Like Peel, he was well aware of the pitfalls which lay along the path of naval action. 'Although the desire for our interference is almost universal here we must not let ourselves be carried away by individual interests, or even by feelings of humanity, unless we have a fair prospect of acting with success.'[7] Such commendable wisdom, of course, required a careful survey of what was practicable. Yet there still appeared no signs of urgency. For one thing, Guizot was not prepared at the end of 1843 for the use of force. For another, as the months passed, a distinct cooling in relations with France meant that Aberdeen could do nothing beyond bemoan the continuing hostilities and acknowledge the injury which this inflicted upon foreign commerce. In March, and again in May 1844, Peel spoke discouragingly in the House of Commons about any prospect of a European intervention.

At Montevideo, however, time did not stand still. In the early months of 1844 the legions of foreign nationals which had formed for the city's defence began to exert a growing influence and to assume an identity of their own. Embarrassed by as many as 3000 Frenchmen demonstrating in the streets wearing their national colours and cockades, and fearing that this might develop rapidly into a commitment to defend the town at all costs, the French government instructed the French admiral and the Consul-General in Montevideo to disarm the French legion. In January 1844 the admiral, Lainé, appealed to Frenchmen in the city to lay down arms. The response was one of derision. Powerless to do more, and fearful of the consequences of even trying, Lainé abandoned his effort. Dale confirmed that any attempt to disarm the legionnaires 'would, in the present temper of these men, most assuredly cause them to revolt. They know their own strength and they are not to be trifled with.'[8] Lainé changed his tactics and later announced that he would require the Montevidean governmentto disband the French legion, but this was no more feasible than acting directly. In April 1844 the morale of all the foreign volunteers was greatly lifted when about 1500 French and Italians launched a surprise attack against one of Oribe's fortified outposts and overran it while inflicting heavy losses on the enemy. At this point Lainé made it known that his orders were to disband the French legion by force if necessary, and that he would land the armed crews from his ships as a last resort to ensure compliance.

Purvis witnessed all this and was astonished at the ineptness of his French counterpart. All that Lainé had done, Purvis noted, was to arouse such disgust and a sense of betrayal among the Frenchmen in Montevideo that they were now willing to renounce their nationality and to register as Uruguayan citizens. Recognizing this, Lainé declared that he would now be satisfied if the Montevidean authorities issued a decree officially disbanding the legion, thus enabling him to report to Paris that his orders were fulfilled. Britain's new chargé d'affaires and Consul-General at Montevideo, Adolphus Turner, advised the Uruguayan Foreign Minister to issue such a decree; it was the only way to reconcile the needs of the Uruguayan government with the duties of the French admiral. This was done on 11 April, whereupon the entire legion laid down their arms as Frenchmen and within a few hours took them up again as citizens of the Banda Oriental. Pride had been restored to all parties; the French legion was no longer, technically, comprised of Frenchmen. That, however, as Lainé undoubtedly knew, was not how the Press, nationalist opinion or opposition politicians in Paris would regard the matter. On 29 May Guizot predictably came under pressure from his adversaries in the Chamber of Deputies. Thiers took up the cause of Uruguayan liberty in an impressive speech and rounded on the government both for its failure to defend a democratic regime in its hour of peril and for its blatant failure to protect the true interests of France – and, more particularly, Frenchmen – in a time of great danger.[9]

Although it was easy for the diplomatic corps to discover what was taking place in and around Montevideo, it was much more difficult to know how the war was progressing in the interior. Turner reported to Aberdeen that Rivera appeared to hold much of the country beyond the coast, leaving Oribe only in possession of the ports and, of course, besieging the capital. At this stage, Turner surmised, neither Rivera nor Oribe were prepared to risk an engagement. Montevideo had been under siege for over a year; Turner's impression was that Oribe would not take it in the near future. Oribe had new worries too. To his rear, Corrientes was no longer reliable. In November 1844, indeed, Mandeville reported that Corrientes had again declared war on Buenos Aires and would impound all shipping flying the flag of Buenos Aires in the Paraná and Uruguay rivers. Once again the entire region of La Plata seemed about to be seized by political convulsions.

The merchant lobby in Britain, inevitably, was alert to this. In May 1844 the Mexican and South American Association implored Aberdeen to bring the war in Uruguay to an end – particularly now that renewed rifts within the Argentine Confederation would make it impossible for Rosas to ensure a quick victory for Oribe. But the Foreign Secretary still preferred to wait. In reply, he dismissed the merchants' appeal with the terse expression of opinion that the British government 'do not consider that they would be justified in resorting to force in order to compel the belligerents to make peace'.[10] In July he informed Mandeville that he saw no end to the conflict. Montevideo could hold out for the foreseeable future and all that the British government could do was to ensure the safety of its citizens who were caught up in the fighting.

It was not until November 1844 that the tenor of Aberdeen's correspondence revealed a different policy and that his actions demonstrated a new resolve. The first casualty of this was Mandeville, whose ineffectiveness at Buenos Aires in recent years had, as Aberdeen realized, made it impossible for him to remain there as the exponent of a tougher line. The dilemma which the British government now faced, in fact, was partly the consequence of Mandeville's spontaneous and contradictory diplomacy. 'I have hitherto afforded you all the support in my power,' Aberdeen assured the elderly envoy, 'but I cannot conceal from myself that circumstances have placed you in a position by which you are necessarily deprived of due weight and influence.'[11] Mandeville's long career, which had begun in 1801 with a visit to Paris to negotiate exchanges of prisoners of war, ended with his recall from the Argentine on 6 August 1845. For the 'fresh efforts' which were to be employed to end the war in Uruguay, the new British Minister appointed to Buenos Aires was William Gore Ouseley.

* * *

Aberdeen's plan, long in maturing, was for a three-power intervention. This would involve working not only with France but, critically, with Brazil. As for the French, Aberdeen had been embarrassed in recent months by a succession of incidents which had both overshadowed developments in the River Plate and had reignited the passions of those in London and in Paris who sought to wreck his relationship with Guizot. In February 1844 news reached London that a French admiral at loose in the Pacific had deposed the Queen of Tahiti and had declared the island a French possession. Five months later Britain's consul returned from Tahiti with an account of his arrest, imprisonment and expulsion by the French authorities. Public and political opinion was incensed by such an outrage and by the affront to British dignity which it represented. The Press in England bayed for war while patriots in France rallied behind this welcome display of national assertiveness. Throughout the summer of 1844 the prospect of cooperation with the French looked bleaker than for many years. On top of these events in the Pacific, it became apparent in July that the understanding which had existed between the British and French Ministers in Athens in 1843 had collapsed and that the overthrow of the liberal government which had been established in Greece owed much to a French intrigue with local politicians. Aberdeen refused to believe that Guizot had betrayed him, but there was no escape from the conclusion that Guizot could not be relied upon to control his agents abroad – even assuming that he always wished to do so. When, in August 1844, the British government learnt that the French navy had bombarded the Moroccan port of Tangier, contrary to an assurance which Guizot had given to Aberdeen a few weeks earlier, the credibility of Anglo-French *entente* sank to an unprecedented low.

No one was more distressed at these developments than José Ellauri in Paris, since a rift between the two European powers put paid to any joint expedition to assist his government in Montevideo. All he could do was watch and wait, he wrote to Vázquez on 1 September 1844.[12] Meanwhile, in London the crisis was worsening. Peel distanced himself from the concept of *entente* and sided with Aberdeen's critics in the Cabinet who favoured higher defence spending, and not diplomacy, as the proper way to deal with so unscrupulous a people as the French. On 21 August Peel urged Aberdeen: 'let us be prepared for war.'[13] Yet Guizot and Aberdeen did contrive to settle their differences without a rupture in the relationship. In September 1844 the French government agreed to withdraw its troops from Morocco and to make peace with the Sultan. In the same month Guizot went as far as he dared in Paris when he accepted that France should pay financial compensation to the British consul so ignominiously ejected from Tahiti. In October 1844 Louis-Philippe did his best to restore something of the spirit of *entente* with a royal visit to Windsor. As at the Chateau d'Eu, Aberdeen and Guizot had the opportunity for lengthy discussions and a chance to apply their friendship once more to the realm of active diplomacy. Much of 1844, nonetheless, had been lost to any thought of collaboration in South America. In fact, not until the autumn did any project for a joint initiative in La Plata return within the bounds of political feasibility.

The prospect of cooperation with Brazil was, of course, a different matter and one evaluated by quite separate criteria. The Brazilian government had an obvious concern for the fate of the Banda Oriental; it was a small and weak neighbour but it served the invaluable function of preventing the spread of Argentine influence along the northern shore of the Plate. Disorder there, and the presence of an Argentine army, could scarcely fail either to alarm the Brazilian government or to lead to a rift in its relations with the government at Buenos Aires – as indeed it had done by the end of 1843. From 1844 onwards the Brazilian government concentrated on improving diplomatic ties with its neighbours, and particularly with Paraguay, which had declared itself to be a sovereign state free from any links with the Argentine Confederation in November 1842 and which Brazil recognized as such in September 1844.

But Brazil's anxiety about events in the Banda Oriental had another dimension. Not only did the state of affairs after March 1843 bring Argentine troops to within striking distance of Brazilian territory but, more immediately, it provided encouragement and potentially material assistance for the insurgents in the southernmost province of Rio Grande do Sul, who for the last ten years had been fighting a guerrilla campaign to establish an independent republic. Britain's envoy at Rio de Janeiro, Hamilton Charles Hamilton, confirmed in 1843 that the central administration there held but a 'precarious dominion' in the south which might be weakened further by any involvement in a foreign war.[14] The dilemma which faced the Brazilian government was starkly illustrated by its about turn in policy between 1842 and 1843. When rumours of an Anglo-French expedition to La Plata were rife in the summer and autumn of 1842, Brazil was emboldened to give assurances of support to Uruguay in the war against Rosas. By September 1843, with Britain and France still emphasizing their strict neutrality in the conflict and with Oribe in possession of most of the Banda Oriental, Brazil offered merely its services as mediator in the struggle.[15] Hamilton summed up the thinking of Brazilian politicians quite succinctly. On the one hand they were convinced that Rosas was invincible and that Brazil dare not engage in a war to save its southern neighbour; on the other, they had no doubt that, when Oribe was installed as President in Montevideo,

Rosas would then turn his attention northward and launch an incursion into Rio Grande. Brazil, however, could do nothing on her own and needed help from abroad if she was to make a stand to save Uruguay and thereby defend her southern frontier.

The actions of its navy in the Plate gave the best indication of Brazil's sympathy with the defenders of Montevideo. Like the British and French naval commanders, Brazilian officers had refused to acknowledge the Argentine blockade of the port. To Purvis, this coincidence of interest and an apparent willingness to cooperate on the spot made Brazil a natural ally in any intervention to stop the fighting. Aberdeen shared this view. In his letter to Peel of 25 November 1843 he stated clearly that if the British and French governments did resolve to put an end to the war by an armed intervention, they should certainly take Brazil into partnership. The Prime Minister was in favour of the three nations acting together to propose and, if necessary, to enforce an international mediation. In August 1844 Turner informed the Foreign Office from Montevideo that Brazil, indeed, appeared to be ready to play a more decisive role. Her naval squadron off Montevideo had recently been increased to nine ships with a complement of 900 men while a Brazilian warship had conveyed General Paz back to Corrientes to command its army in the war with Buenos Aires.

Turner was quite right: by mid-1844 Brazil was sufficiently worried about the fighting in Uruguay to be contemplating a diplomatic and even military initiative. Early in July, Hamilton was summoned to the Foreign Ministry in Rio de Janeiro to discuss the state of affairs in La Plata. Hamilton's response, initially, was cautious. When asked about his government's intentions he stated blandly that he had no instructions on the matter. However, as the interview progressed Hamilton's message became more encouraging. 'In no case was it to be conceived,' he assured the Brazilian government, 'Her Majesty's Government would permit the independence of the Republic of the Uruguay to be encroached upon and compromised.'[16] The essential question was then asked: what would be the attitude of Britain and France towards supporting Brazil should the latter try to intervene to save the republic? Hamilton delivered the desired response. If the government in Rio felt matters at Montevideo to be so pressing, he concluded the interview, then he recommended that Brazil should raise the matter directly in London and Paris without delay. On 24 August he wrote privately to Aberdeen that he had just been informed by the head of the Brazilian government that a prominent diplomat, Count D'Abrantes, while on a special mission to Europe, would call upon the Foreign Secretary in London to discuss what might be done. Effectively, Hamilton assured his chief, D'Abrantes would call upon the British government 'for their assistance in the war which appears so imminent between Brazil and Buenos Aires'.[17]

On arrival in London D'Abrantes wrote to Aberdeen and on 18 November the two men met at the Foreign Office. It was soon agreed that their common interest was to preserve the sovereignty of Uruguay, to recognize the independence of Paraguay and to take appropriate steps to stop the fighting around Montevideo. On the following day D'Abrantes formally proposed a combined action by Britain and Brazil. Aberdeen replied that, in order to give effect to the views which had been expressed at the interview, Britain was prepared to act in concert with Brazil, on the specific understanding that France would join with them. 'Without that cooperation,' Aberdeen was adamant, 'it would not be desirable for us to act.' 'Every measure, be it what it may, must be adopted in the name of the three powers.'[18] Aberdeen still believed, however, that a tactful approach to Rosas was essential, as the latter would judge his pride to be slighted by any semblance of an ultimatum. Only if friendly remonstrance should fail, Aberdeen insisted, would it be right 'to make some more decisive demonstration'. Just what this might be would depend on the extent of Rosas' obstinacy. It might depend, too, on the vulnerability of the British community resident in Buenos Aires which Aberdeen did not wish to expose to reprisals. But one thing that Aberdeen fully understood was that great powers needed to support their words with actions. 'If the three powers once take the matter in hand,' he informed Hamilton, 'they must be prepared to follow whatever course may be really necessary to ensure its accomplishment.'[19]

Aberdeen turned his attention to the details of what might be required by way of forceful action as a last resort. On this he saw eye to eye with Guizot: neither Britain nor France contemplated military operations on land against Rosas – under any circumstances. 'All that Her Majesty's Government have in view is to act against the recusant power by a combined naval demonstration,' Aberdeen confirmed in a dispatch to the British ambassador in Paris on 17 December 1844, 'which, if disregarded, may be extended to a blockade and an occupation of the various rivers passing through the territories of such power.'[20] If, in support of this Anglo-French naval action, a military incursion into Uruguay was required to compel Oribe to withdraw, then this could be done only by Brazil who would, thereby, have played a full part in the triple intervention. Whatever came to pass, Aberdeen stressed that Britain had no intention to interfere with the political institutions, or the individuals or factions which controlled them, either at Buenos Aires or elsewhere in the region.

With these developments under way, Aberdeen called William Ouseley to the Foreign Office to explain at length the purpose of his appointment to Buenos Aires and the expectations of the government. Ouseley afterwards recorded his impressions of the conversation and of the ends which, for Britain, the three-power intervention was designed to serve. First, to pacify the republics of La Plata. Second, to secure the independence of Uruguay by bringing about a definitive settlement of its differences with Rosas. Thirdly, to place Britain's commercial and diplomatic relations with all the states of the region on as good a footing as possible and perhaps even, if the opportunity arose, to recognize and establish contacts with the secluded nation of Paraguay. Mediation would be offered once more to Rosas before armed intervention was invoked. But if armed intervention was 'forced upon us', Ouseley concluded, then the methods adopted and the means provided must be adequate for the purpose. The island of Martín García, which lay 130 miles up river from Buenos Aires, would need to be occupied since it was a strategic point which commanded the entrance to the rivers Uruguay and Paraná. The Argentine navy would then need to be seized and Oribe's main supply port at Buceo would have to be blockaded, as would the port of Buenos Aires. Ouseley noted too the importance of an envoy on the spot who was capable and prepared to take responsibility within the broad guidelines of government policy: 'there must be no hesitation,' he insisted, 'no reference home at every step for instructions.'[21] Assured of Aberdeen's commitment, Ouseley left for Paris where his task was to establish the means of implementation with the French government.

Guizot saw Ouseley on 8 January 1845. Ouseley later reported to London that what Guizot said to him very much coincided with Aberdeen's earlier remarks. Like Britain, France was a neutral observer of the conflict in Uruguay but by now the extent of the warfare was proving so injurious to the commercial interests of both European nations and so much endangered the safety of their subjects that the two powers were faced with 'a position which could no longer be tolerated'.[22]

Now that Britain had proposed an international intervention to stop hostilities, France willingly responded and accepted the suggestion of Brazil's involvement. France, too, had no wish to meddle in any nation's internal politics, Guizot emphasized; there was no enmity towards Rosas nor any belief in Paris that even if he fell from power a better form of government would emerge at Buenos Aires. Ouseley concurred. The scene was thus set for a meeting of representatives from all three mediating powers which should settle a common policy and the method of enforcing it. Guizot arranged that this should be held at his house on 13 January.

Among those present there was unquestionably considerable experience of the problems of La Plata. D'Abrantes' expertise was taken for granted. De Lurde was invited to attend following his recent return from the Argentine. Makau was there not merely as the admiral who had conducted the earlier blockade at Buenos Aires, nor as a personal adviser to Guizot, but now, since 1843, as Minister for the Navy and Colonies. Guizot had with him, too, Emile Desages, the political director and permanent head of the Foreign Ministry, upon whose briefings and judgment he was especially dependent. Desages was among those officials in Paris who favoured both a bolder South American policy and a greater cooperation with the British where French interests made it worthwhile. Unlike Guizot, who found no time for such things, Desages conducted private correspondence with diplomats in South America and had a detailed understanding of local events which made his opinions difficult to refute. In recent years only Makau's cautious advice to Guizot had countered the influence of Desages within the Quai d'Orsay. Makau was still wary of a naval action in the Plate, but by January 1845 Desages had managed to persuade Guizot of its political advantages. Guizot, like Louis-Philippe, who also took a special interest in foreign policy, regarded the affairs of South America as an opportunity to improve relations with the British and was prepared to disregard Makau for the sake of wider progress in Anglo-French understanding.'[23] This seemed all the more important by the beginning of 1845 since the dangers to the French nationals at Montevideo had attracted considerable attention in the Press and in the Chamber. By demonstrating a working *entente* with the British, and by supporting French settlers and French aspirations in Uruguay, a joint intervention might serve a double purpose. It would even help his critics to forget his recent climb-down over Britain's insistence on compensation for its displaced consul from Tahiti.

The British government was represented at the meeting on 13 January by Ouseley and Lord Cowley, who witnessed throughout a preoccupying debate about strategy between the French and Brazilian diplomats.

De Lurde argued, and Makau confirmed, that Martín García would have to be seized. This would give control over the movement of all shipping up-river of Buenos Aires. The port of Buenos Aires should also be blockaded with a small naval force. Guizot accepted this advice and took the opportunity to reaffirm that naval action was the limit of his intentions. Cowley informed Aberdeen of what then passed: Guizot had been emphatic 'that the armed mediation would be confined to the navy, and that no land forces should be employed,' Cowley wrote approvingly, 'and upon his appealing to me I answered that Her Majesty's Government entirely concurred in that opinion.' Having heard from his own officials, Guizot invited D'Abrantes to speak. The Brazilian diplomat's response was more adventurous. Contrary to what he had told Aberdeen in London a few weeks earlier, D'Abrantes did not think that Rosas could be cowed by mere naval demonstration and was now convinced that if the three powers really wished to show that their intervention was in earnest then they would need to act by land and that British and French, as well as Brazilian, troops would be required. The French and British representatives said nothing. Cowley explained to Aberdeen that D'Abrantes' plan 'had so much the appearance of being exclusively a Brazilian object that it put an end to all further discussion respecting the employment of land forces'. It was settled, though, that an offer of amicable mediation was the essential first step. If Rosas refused this then a blockade could be imposed on Buenos Aires and the rivers Uruguay and Paraná occupied by warships in order to prevent the movement of troops and supplies. 'All these measures would, in the opinion of Admiral Makau, who is well acquainted with the localities, be quite practicable,' Cowley wrote confidently to London.[24] The notion that naval power alone would be insufficient was conveniently dismissed.

D'Abrantes had upset Guizot at the meeting and on 20 January 1845 Cowley informed Aberdeen that Guizot now attached no importance to Brazil's participation in the mediation attempt. Albeit for different reasons, Aberdeen also came to the conclusion that Brazil should be excluded. His final instructions to Ouseley, on the latter's departure for South America, recalled two conditions on which Britain had agreed to work with Brazil to restore peace in Uruguay –

neither of which, Aberdeen complained, had been met. More than ten weeks after Aberdeen had told D'Abrantes that Britain would require the completion of new treaties concerning commercial relations and the suppression of the slave trade, there was no indication of the slightest progress in the negotiations at Rio de Janeiro.[25] Ouseley was therefore no longer to cooperate with Brazilian diplomats in the conduct of his mission nor, indeed, when he touched at Rio on his journey south was he to discuss the issue of international collaboration.

By setting aside Brazil's assistance, Aberdeen and Guizot now had a chance to display their capacity for bilateral action. Despite their considerable problems of the previous year, the start of 1845 presented not only the chance for cooperation in La Plata but another opportunity in North America, where the British and French governments proved able to form a common stance in support of Texan independence and to offer their joint mediation in the dispute with Mexico. Aberdeen sensed a modest recovery of confidence in the efficacy of combined diplomacy, particularly when the decision had been made to back it with force if necessary. It was hard to believe that naval firepower would not prove decisive. The British had opened the China coast to trade in 1842 after wreaking devastation at Canton and in 1843 they had put a blockade on the Nicaraguan coast in support of British subjects denied their legal rights by the local authorities. Content, then, that all this augured well for an Anglo-French success, Aberdeen informed Turner of the plan now under way and asked that Ouseley should be given whatever assistance was possible from Montevideo. Ouseley had 'full instructions' which reflected the wishes of his government, Aberdeen advised; however, 'the mode in which he is to carry out that measure must depend upon the position in which he may find affairs on his arrival in the river Plate.'[26]

Guizot's choice as the new French Minister to Buenos Aries was Baron Anton Deffaudis. He had served as head of the commercial section at the Quai d'Orsay between 1825 and 1832 and was a known advocate of the extension of French ties and commerce with Latin America and an enthusiast for French emigration. Deffaudis had recent experience in American affairs as Minister to Mexico between 1832 and 1839. It was he who had imposed the blockade at Vera Cruz in 1838, having beforehand presented an ultimatum to the Mexican government which exceeded in its demands the terms for a settlement required by his own government.[27] This had led to his recall and a few months in Frankfurt to cool his heels. Now Guizot recommended him to Cowley as a man of 'conciliatory disposition'. Cowley was impressed by the widespread approval of Deffaudis' appointment which he encountered in political circles in Paris. By the time Deffaudis sailed from France at the end of March 1845, Cowley was convinced that 'a better selection for the important mission with which he is charged could not have been made.'[28]

In his final directions on 20 February 1845, Aberdeen once more reminded Ouseley that it was his great hope that Rosas would recognize the virtue in the Anglo-French initiative and would accept this last offer of mediation. Ouseley was to do all in his power to persuade and flatter the Argentine dictator and to convince him that no loss of face or national honour could result from his doing so. Indeed Aberdeen seemed sure that, if presented properly, this mediation offer could not fail to have the desired effect. 'It is hardly possible to conceive that when the consequences which must follow from a refusal to listen to the advice of the two powers shall have been made evident to him, he will allow it to pass unheeded,' he reflected. 'The point, however, to be principally kept in view,' Aberdeen reminded Ouseley, 'and the one which is of most importance to the mediating parties, is the preservation of the independence of Montevideo . . . It is one upon which no compromise can be admitted.' If Rosas proved obdurate and would not hear of negotiations, then the British and French Ministers would deliver an ultimatum to the Argentine government for the removal of its troops from Uruguay. 'It is needless to say that this declaration, when once made, must be adhered to,' Aberdeen stressed. The British and French naval squadrons must then implement the measures which were agreed at Paris in January. In all matters the British and French envoys were to act strictly together, as, of course, would the naval commanders. Aberdeen ended his official instructions with an expression of his confidence in Ouseley's judgment. The latter's meetings with Aberdeen and Guizot before he left Europe had given him a most intimate knowledge of the intentions of both men. Of course, 'incidents may occur for which these instructions do not specifically provide,' he added, 'and upon which, being far removed from home, it will be necessary for you to act under your own responsibility.'[29] Ouseley and Deffaudis, it appeared, had considerable discretion.

The state of affairs in Uruguay was indeed to be different by the time Ouseley arrived. On 16 January 1845 the Argentine navy off Montevideo upgraded its limited blockade of war provisions which had operated since March 1843 into a rigorous blockade against all shipping entering the port. Turner noted how the years of siege and warfare had taken their toll on Montevideo. He estimated that its population had declined from about 50,000 in 1842 to little more than 20,000 by the beginning of 1845. Many of its former inhabitants had taken refuge in the countryside, or elsewhere, to escape the fighting. A determined intervention to end the war and save the city was welcome news for Turner; his only reservation was that it may have come too late. On 27 March 1845 Rivera's army suffered a crushing defeat near Maldonado at the battle of India Muerta. Certainly this was the most significant engagement in the war since Rivera's previous humiliation at Arroyo Grande. In effect, the military capability of the Uruguayan government now amounted to little more than the garrison of Montevideo. Turner cast some doubts on the estimates which had been made previously of the fighting force within the city. He thought that the garrison comprised about 2200 native soldiers with about 2800 legionnaires of foreign origin. The truth was that no one really knew how many men were armed and prepared to fight. The Uruguayan government tended to exaggerate its military strength, which was hardly surprising since it was obvious to all that Oribe had between eight and ten thousand men camped outside the capital. However, all such calculation seemed less important than in the past. It was the known intention of the British and French governments which now held out the prospect of deliverance.

5· The Beginning of Hostilities, 1845

The appointment of Ouseley to succeed Mandeville at Buenos Aires appeared to be a sensible choice. He was a career diplomat whose family was well-known in political circles. He was first attached to the legation at Stockholm in 1817 and then transferred to Washington in 1825. From there he was moved, after a brief spell in Brussels, to Rio de Janeiro in 1828, where he had the opportunity to act as chargé d'affaires on three separate occasions between 1833 and 1841. His time in the New World established him as an American expert within the service although he was no admirer of the local cultures, north or south, and was particularly scathing of the political structures of Latin America, which he judged to be incapable of producing anything other than bloody civil strife.

By the beginning of April 1845 Ouseley had reached Rio de Janeiro where, in his meetings with Brazilian officials, he scrupulously followed instructions and did not raise the subject of his mission. His impression was that Brazil now appeared eager to distance herself from an international intervention. Fear of a conflict with the Argentine states probably accounted for this, Ouseley concluded; perhaps also pique that Britain and France had decided to act alone. Ouseley's stop at Rio was only of consequence in that he met with the old Argentine diplomat, General Tomás Guido, whom he tried to impress by his use of conciliatory language. Britain proposed friendly mediation and not armed intervention, Ouseley assured him, and an initiative for peace from Rosas would be just as acceptable as any from the mediating powers. Confident that every word he had said to Guido would reach Buenos Aires long before he could, Ouseley sailed on from Rio and arrived off Montevideo on 26 April. Still sensitive to Rosas' feelings, he declined to go ashore and gathered news about the state of the city's defences from Turner while on board ship, before pressing on to Buenos Aires.

Ideally Ouseley would have waited for the arrival of Deffaudis. He was well aware that the obvious tactic of Argentine officials would be to drive a wedge between the British and French representatives by sowing distrust and that a single approach by him to the Argentine authorities might prove a bad start to the mission. Aberdeen's instructions, however, did give him licence to establish separate contact at Buenos Aires should he be the first to arrive, and Ouseley himself now realized that there was no time to lose. Turner's account of the perilous state of the garrison in Montevideo had made a great impression on him. Only a few days' supply of gunpowder was left in the city, after which time the defenders would be compelled to abandon the outer lines and to destroy the batteries as they retreated into the city centre. Given that Britain and France had embarked on an official intervention to end the war, Ouseley immediately wrote back to the Foreign Office, 'it would be a most embarrassing complication if the town was *now* to be taken.'[1] On 10 May, therefore, Ouseley presented himself to Felipe Arana and handed him a memorandum containing the views of the British government.

Ouseley stressed Britain's neutrality in the war and how her effort to find peace was for the good of all concerned. Britain and France were pledged to uphold the independence of Uruguay, however, which was prejudiced by an Argentine army on its soil. Moreover, the losses sustained by European commerce also compelled the two governments to take measures to end the war. This should now be done either by the withdrawal of Argentine troops back across the River Uruguay or else by a suspension of hostilities on terms which Britain and France could guarantee. All this was urged in advance of any formal joint declaration, Ouseley told Arana; the government at Buenos Aires would therefore do well to accept the advantage of friendly mediation 'before it is too late to do so with dignity'.[2] Although Ouseley had conducted these preliminary contacts with the utmost secrecy, Rosas was furious at what he regarded as their threatening tone and sent no answer. Arana later informed Ouseley that his government had been offered services of mediation also by the United States legation.

Rosas was well pleased with this chance to muddy the waters: any alternative offer of mediation gave him a useful diplomatic staff with which to try to keep the British and French at bay. The United States government was not, though, an obvious source of assistance. North Americans had little interest in the distant waters of the River Plate. Save for a few years in the 1820s, when supplying flour boosted their trade with the Argentine, they had nothing much at stake there. Nor did United States traders feel in conflict with British enterprise. Britain's predominance was obvious and accepted. Rivalry naturally occurred between the various merchant houses both at Buenos Aires and at Montevideo, but in broad terms a community of interests existed whereby an open door and commercial freedoms were all that either British or United States nationals aspired to.[3] Politically, relations between Buenos Aires and Washington had been a disaster for years. Diplomatic ties had been broken off in 1832 until, in 1838, Carlos de Alvear was sent to Washington to repair the damage. It was not until November 1844, though, that proper contacts were restored at Buenos Aires with the arrival of William Brent as chargé d'affaires.[4]

Brent was an old Democrat who had been sent abroad knowing nothing of diplomacy or international affairs. He was an Anglophobe and instinctively took the side of anyone in disagreement with the British. Rosas had quickly seized upon his good fortune and through flattery and false friendship had soon fashioned the gullible Brent into a useful tool. Ouseley described Brent as a dupe of Rosas who had even been so crass as to assure Arana that his mediation offer had been fully authorized from Washington. Rosas would use Brent to gain as much time as he could, Ouseley rightly inferred, but in the long run, Ouseley informed the Foreign Office, this personal initiative by the United States envoy was of no consequence.[5] Emboldened nonetheless, on 24 May 1845 Arana spelt out his government's position with respect to the war in the Banda Oriental: the Argentine Confederation, like the British government, Arana added, wished for peace and in no way questioned Uruguay's independence. But the war was not of its making; its troops and its navy merely assisted as auxiliaries the legal President, General Oribe, who had requested them but who, Arana conceded, would also doubtless dismiss them when they were no longer required. Until such time as Oribe had pacified the country where he was the sole legal authority, Arana continued, the British navy should unequivocally recognize the Argentine naval blockade of Montevideo. On his own, Ouseley realized that he had achieved nothing. The pressures on him, however, were mounting.

These pressures were from two sources. The first was from across the river in Montevideo, where Turner continued to make the case for naval action in defence of the town.[6] It was no longer any use for the British government or its diplomats to utter bland statements about the navy being offshore to protect British subjects in the event of

Oribe's forces overrunning the lines, or about requiring guarantees from Oribe as to the safety of life and property. Amid the chaos of battle, communication with Oribe would be impossible and any guarantee given would probably be worthless. Turner wanted to know whether he had licence to use the fleet or not, and he argued repeatedly that Oribe should be openly informed that the city would ultimately be defended by the British and French squadrons. Only such firm measures could preserve morale inside the city and prevent a collapse of authority and outbreaks of pillaging and violence which would endanger all the foreign nationals.

Ouseley, of course, could not be both mediator and participant in the war. Any act which helped the defenders of Montevideo would at once destroy all chance of a diplomatic success at Buenos Aires and he therefore had to distance himself, at least officially, from whatever Turner or the navy might do. His correspondence to the new admiral on the Brazil station, Samuel Inglefield, spoke of nothing more than ensuring the safety of foreign residents and allowing further time for negotiation. Turner soon learnt of this and sprang into action. There was only one way, he decided, to ensure the safety of the foreigners and to gain time for negotiation and that was to supply the garrison with the materials required to continue the city's defence. The British and French admirals agreed and, in mid-June 1845, 540 pounds of gunpowder was supplied by each squadron – discreetly rowed ashore in the dead of night. 'I have judged it expedient to refrain from communicating to Mr. Ouseley the circumstances,' Turner informed Aberdeen, 'in order that, if any information relative to this supply of gunpowder should reach the Buenos Airean government, Mr Ouseley may be able to assert that not only had he not given any authorization on the subject but that he was perfectly ignorant of the transaction in question.'[7] At the same time Admiral Inglefield reminded Admiral Brown that he would not allow any Argentine naval bombardment of Montevideo as British lives would certainly be endangered by indiscriminate fire.

The second pressure on Ouseley for more decisive action came from his colleague, Deffaudis, who arrived off Buenos Aires in the middle of June. Ouseley's initial impression of the man did not presage well. The Frenchman seemed impatient and almost looking for a pretext for coercion. Immediately he wanted to compel a ceasefire at Montevideo and only Ouseley's strong objection talked him out of it. Deffaudis next declared that the attitude of the Argentine government offended him: its language and procrastination were a studied insult not just to the two diplomats personally but to the great powers which they represented. Again Ouseley calmed him, but it seemed all too clear what lay ahead. He wrote to Aberdeen on 26 June that 'there is, since the arrival of my French colleague, little hope of gaining our point with General Rosas without a resort to force. I fear that hostilities must be prepared for.'[8]

Three weeks after their first formal meeting with Arana, which had taken place on 16 June, the two diplomats had to acknowledge that they had made no progress. Arana refused even to discuss the subject of a ceasefire at Montevideo until Britain and France recognized the strict Argentine naval blockade of the port, and he clung to his acceptance of United States mediation as being an obstacle to future negotiations. Ouseley had asked Inglefield to bring all the ships on his station into the River Plate in order to create as imposing a naval display as possible during the negotiations. This, though, had not had any impact on Rosas, nor was there any apparent line of argument which could do so either. The next stage, according to instructions, was to issue a formal demand for the withdrawal of Argentine troops from Uruguay – a step from which both Aberdeen and Guizot had acknowledged there was no turning back.

Ouseley was still wary when he discussed the options available with Deffaudis early in July. 'There is much to be lost and risked by resorting to coercive measures,' he reminded him, and 'very little at present to be gained.' Both Britain and France had large numbers of their nationals in the city of Buenos Aires and still more settled in the countryside. Deffaudis accepted the point, though he claimed to be quite confident that good Frenchmen and Basques were accustomed to the use of firearms and could look after themselves if necessary. Ouseley then stressed, rather surprisingly, that it was not at all clear what was to be gained by naval action. Admittedly the Argentine blockade of Montevideo could easily be lifted but, since the city would still be besieged, its contact with the interior could not be reestablished. Even if British and French warships opened up the rivers Paraná and Uruguay to foreign trade, and a diplomatic and commercial contact was established with Paraguay, this was more of a long term benefit and contributed nothing to solving the pressing problem in the Banda Oriental. Ouseley even told Deffaudis that he doubted frankly whether an Anglo-French naval blockade of Buenos Aires would have much impact. In the middle of this conversation Ouseley slipped in some thoughts on the politics of Montevideo: 'Will it not then be better that Oribe should be reinstated, under certain conditions, and by a "transaction" or compromise with the present government of Montevideo?'[9] Deffaudis rightly objected that this was contrary to their instructions. Those instructions, however, Ouseley replied, had been drawn up in February 1845 before Oribe's victory at India Muerta. Oribe now controlled the entire country except for its capital; Rivera's cause was surely lost. But Deffaudis insisted that the instructions still stood. His government would not see Oribe reinstated as President and he would never yield on this point. With the Argentine government adamant and its army on the brink of victory, a resolute French colleague with whom he was instructed to work closely, and a consul in Montevideo imploring him to use all means at his disposal to prevent a blood-bath when the city fell, Ouseley's room for manoeuvre had simply disappeared.

Ironically, in the time that had passed since Ouseley's arrival in La Plata, the naval build-up which had taken place there had increased not his confidence in, but his doubts about, success through coercion. At first he had thought the French to have 'sufficient force if we require it'.[10] By the end of June, however, he was informing Aberdeen that force would meet an 'obstinate and protracted resistance'.[11] He warned Inglefield, too, that in taking the crucial step beyond diplomacy 'we must prepare for a state of warfare for two or three years to come.' The admiral had no words of reassurance. Given what any armed intervention was intended to achieve, he replied, 'You cannot have been aware of the limited resources of the squadron as regards *men*. I have no men at all available for landing to defend positions.'[12] Overcoming his misgivings nonetheless, Ouseley agreed with Deffaudis that they should proceed according to their instructions and prepare for stronger measures. 'I have urged my objections to such a line at present and conceive that the discretionary power with which we are invested would be well employed in modifying our instructions *quoad* Oribe,' he told Aberdeen, 'but I hold it of so much more importance that no serious difference of opinion should arise between the French and English plenipotentiaries that I might be induced to adopt the view of my colleague.'[13] On 8 July the two diplomats addressed an official note to the government at Buenos Aires demanding the withdrawal of its forces on land and sea from the siege of Montevideo while at the same time formally offering their mediation in the war to the government of Uruguay, which at once accepted it. When Arana ignored the note the two men wrote again, but they succeeded only in eliciting a firm refusal. Ouseley warned Arana of the gravity of the matter and of the possible consequences which might follow from this. From his flagship, HMS *Eagle*, Inglefield realized that these exchanges had finally brought matters to a head. 'Pray send me some small steamers,' he wrote privately to the Admiralty, 'we shall I think soon know what we are about and have to do.'[14]

The first function of the naval squadrons was to make it clear that they would not permit the capture of Montevideo. This was done by means of a letter of 21 July 1845 which the diplomats requested should be sent from admirals Inglefield and Lainé to General Oribe. Since the Argentine government was required to withdraw its army from the Banda Oriental, Oribe was informed, the British and French navies could not allow any assault by that army to proceed without doing their utmost to resist it. Not only would the fleets assist in the defence of the city but they would, if necessary, blockade the supply ports for Oribe's army along the Uruguayan coast. The following day, and again on diplomatic instruction, the two admirals intimated to Brown that they would not sanction any Argentine warships to leave their present anchorage, thus effectively ending the blockade of Montevideo.

By this point, of course, relations between the British and French envoys and the government in Buenos Aires barely existed. As a matter of form, rather than in anticipation of success, Ouseley and Deffaudis delivered an ultimatum that if orders for a troop withdrawal from Uruguay were not sent by 31 July they would have no option but to demand their passports. Arana pointedly sent the passports on 30 July and the Ministers prepared to depart for their warships in the river. Both sides, though, gave tokens of conciliation at the end. Britain and France, for the time being, left chargés d'affaires in Buenos Aires to indicate that they did not wish a complete rupture. The Argentines, for their part, indicated that Brown's navy, now useless off Montevideo anyway, would be recalled. On essentials, however, the differences remained unbridgeable. Ouseley had a final private meeting with Rosas, arranged on the pretext of taking leave of Manuelita, but found the Governor utterly intractable on the question of Oribe's army. More worryingly, perhaps, he found Rosas quite confident about any armed conflict which lay ahead.

Having left Buenos Aires and transferred their residences to Montevideo, the British and French Ministers now began consultations with the two admirals about the deployment of their vessels and the goals to be achieved. An immediate problem was what to do about the five Argentine warships still at anchor and under surveillance off Montevideo. Massively outgunned by the British and French squadrons they were not much of a threat to naval operations. In any case, they had been ordered back to Buenos Aires and in these circumstances, Ouseley told Inglefield, the British and French had no right to interfere with their movements. However, like most fighting forces in South America, the navy of Buenos Aires was an amalgam of foreigners with nearly half its total crews of European and North American origin. In the light of imminent hostilities Ouseley and Deffaudis decided that it would be intolerable if British and French subjects should be fighting the forces of their own nations. Admiral Brown was therefore informed that before sailing he should first hand over all foreign nationals to the British and French squadrons. On 2 August 1845 Brown's ships weighed anchor and tried to win a hopeless race 100 miles back up and across the Plate to Buenos Aires. Within half an hour HMS *Comus* had overtaken them and fired a broadside across their bows. After a few desultory shots Brown surrendered his ships to boarding parties, who sailed them into the harbour at Montevideo.[15] Of the 515 crew aboard, 147 were found to be British subjects and 23 French. Ouseley and Deffaudis were well pleased, since the five captured ships could now be joined to their own fleets of ten British and eight French vessels in the river.

Next, the ports of Buceo, Santa Lucia and Maldonado were to be blockaded by one vessel from each of the squadrons. Martín García was to be captured and then protected by another two ships. Colonia was to be taken, if Oribe would not surrender it, and two warships left there to defend it. Following that, the River Uruguay was to be cleared of all armed Argentine shipping, any fortifications on its west bank were to be destroyed and the towns of Mercedes, Paysandu and Salto on the river were to be blockaded. In some operations there would be assistance from the ten small armed boats of the Montevidean navy, but these would nearly always need to be accompanied and certainly supported in any attacks. After these steps along the coast and rivers of the Banda Oriental had been completed, a blockade was to be put on Buenos Aires as the only realistic hope of applying political pressure on Rosas. For such a campaign, Ouseley urged Aberdeen on 13 August, he needed steam powered ships of shallow draught drawing eight or ten feet of water for work in the rivers. Most of the ships in the

Plate were too big and too slow to do what was required of them; some could not get to within four or five miles of Buenos Aires and would therefore find it very difficult to enforce a strict blockade against small coastal vessels. More small firearms and ammunition would be required, too, if there was serious fighting to be done. Contemplating what he described as the 'utter inapplicability' of the British and French squadrons, Ouseley concluded that, contrary to what Aberdeen had written in his instructions, the two governments had never really intended more than a mere demonstration of force in support of diplomacy on the erroneous assumption that this would induce Rosas to comply with their demands.[16]

The blockades of Buceo, Santa Lucia and Maldonado were quickly put in place and Martín García was easily occupied by a landing from the Montevidean flotilla. The first real engagement came at Colonia, which had to be taken and held in order to serve as a port of refuge for the ships to be employed in the blockade of Buenos Aires. Colonia, which had over 12,000 inhabitants, had been strongly fortified in the colonial era and, to the landward side, its crumbling walls still presented an imposing barrier.[17] It was defended from the sea by a few batteries both in the town and on the hill above it, and these would have to be silenced before men could be landed.

Four British and four French warships began a bombardment of these positions on the evening of 30 August 1845. By midnight much of the town was ablaze, but the guns were still returning fire and continued to do so until abandoned the following morning. When a combined landing party came ashore, British and French sailors and marines marched to the central square and took up positions from which to repel any counter attack, while Montevidean soldiers skirmished with the enemy on the outskirts of the town. By noon on 31 August Colonia was under the control of the Uruguayan army, whose supplies and artillery pieces brought from Montevideo for the town's future defence were now landed by British and French seamen. The ships kept up their fire to disperse the enemy outside the town while the marines remained ashore constructing lines of defence. On 3 September they drove off a brief Argentine attack during which one of the British officers was wounded. In the following two days all the British and French were reembarked. By 6 September Colonia was considered sufficiently secure to allow the last of the vessels to return to anchorage at Martín García.[18]

Rosas' response to the outbreak of hostilities, though scarcely unpredictable, added to the problems of the naval squadrons and emphasized his determination to resist them. Early in September he decreed that all communication between Argentine territory and the foreign warships was illegal. This posed problems of acquiring food and fuel and meant that supply vessels had to make trips to the coast of Brazil or to the Falkland Islands. Rosas also instituted what Ouseley described as a *levée en masse* among the citizens of the state of Buenos Aires and was preparing the population both by propaganda and by military training for a struggle of national survival. Nonetheless, Ouseley and Deffaudis began the blockade of Buenos Aires on 24 September 1845 and announced that the last date for shipping to leave the port was to be 31 October. The remaining diplomats would then gather up the legation archives and withdraw, leaving British and French interests and the protection of residents in the hands of the Sardinian Consul-General. The rupture, then, was complete. By November the entire coastline of Buenos Aires as well as the port itself was declared under blockade, regardless of persistent doubts about strict enforcement. Confidence had, however, been boosted by a remarkable piece of good fortune which Ouseley was quick to seize upon. An Atlantic storm had forced a military transport ship *en route* for South Africa to take shelter in the harbour at Rio de Janeiro, from where Hamilton had immediately ordered it south to the River Plate. On board was the second battalion of the 45th regiment, which was disembarked and posted on the inner defences of Montevideo.

The landing of these 626 officers and men in Montevideo at the end of October 1845 freed many of the 300 British and French sailors and marines already there for other duties. It also meant that the warships anchored off the city in case of an emergency could now be moved. With Montevideo more secure, at least for the time being, Ouseley and Deffaudis could devote themselves to broader tactics. The expedition up the Uruguay river had gone well, with no Argentine resistance on its west bank and Montevidean troops capturing Salto from Oribe's soldiers. A landing at the mouth of the Río Negro had beaten off Argentine forces and constructed a fortified position to command its entrance. Ouseley was encouraged by the splendid spirit of co-operation between the British and French fleets and, forgetting his earlier reservations, now spoke in glowing terms of Deffaudis as a colleague. Rumour had it that morale at the Cerrito was falling now that Oribe's assault on Montevideo had been thwarted and desertions from among the ranks of his Uruguayan soldiers were becoming commonplace. All this was not enough, however. The next step was to carry the fight to Rosas, for only by that means could Britain and France achieve a decisive victory. Blockade alone would not be sufficient.

The plan to enlarge the conflict had as its ultimate objective the overthrow of Rosas' regime. For this, three things were necessary. First, a formal declaration of war by both Britain and France against the government of Buenos Aires. Ouseley wrote to Aberdeen as early as September 1845 that the two powers were already engaged in a 'quasi-war';[19] six weeks later he urged once more that 'we are carrying on war *de facto* even now' and that great advantages would follow from making it official.[20] It would show to all the opponents of Rosas that Britain and France were in earnest and it would encourage rebellion within the Argentine Confederation, particularly when the extra troops for which Ouseley now asked arrived from Europe. Second, the opposition to Rosas which was known to exist among the other Argentine state governors had to be supported and contacts with these chiefs established. Santa Fé had already seen rebellion by forces under General Juan López. Entre Rios and Corrientes might perhaps be recognized as sovereign nations in order to support the separatist inclinations of their military leaders – particularly General Paz in Corrientes, who might be supplied with money and weapons. Paraguay, which Ouseley believed to be already at war with Rosas in order to assert its independence, should also be aided with recognition and materials. 'We must not now mince matters,' Ouseley exclaimed, 'intervention must be complete to be useful in the Rio de la Plata.'[21]

Thirdly, to overthrow Rosas the war must be carried deep into Argentine territory by means of a naval expedition into the River Paraná. This would serve the dual purpose of freeing the river to merchant shipping and in making an impressive demonstration of firepower. Furthermore, it would give the opportunity for naval commanders to make unofficial contacts with the states of the interior. Here, then, was a grand strategy laid before the British government for a decisive outcome to the intervention. What had started as an attempt to find a diplomatic settlement between the governments of Montevideo and Buenos Aires had become, in Ouseley's mind, by the end of 1845, a campaign to remove Rosas at any cost. Looking back over his months in La Plata, Ouseley admitted his complete misjudgment of Rosas. 'I thought that with all his faults and enemies his was in some respects a good government for us – that he had some nobility of character and a sort of bastard chivalry about him, and a half savage sort of patriotism.' Now, he wrote to Aberdeen, 'there never was a greater butcher... thus policy, justice, and humanity are all served by opposing him.'[22]

Rosas had become isolated in Buenos Aires and certainly looked vulnerable in the face of Ouseley's onslaught. He had been misled on two accounts and his earlier confidence was undoubtedly shaken. First, Tomás Guido's judgment was proving uncommonly faulty. Guido had met both Ouseley and Deffaudis as they put in to Rio de Janeiro. After two hours of conversation with the former he had written to Arana that the deep distrust which the British held for French ambitions at Montevideo would make any cooperation between the two powers ineffective and shortlived. Guido's meeting with Deffaudis a fortnight later merely confirmed this impression.[23] Yet the rift anticipated had not occurred and in the course of their joint negotiations and subsequent actions Ouseley and Deffaudis had drawn closer together and developed an excellent understanding. Worse, Rosas lost his only hope of any outside assistance when on 26 July William Brent withdrew his offer of mediation and the United States government subsequently confirmed its neutrality.

In order to ensure that neutrality, Aberdeen applied a gentle pressure. On 2 October 1845 he spoke with Louis McLane, the United States Minister in London, and explained that Brent's unauthorized diplomacy at Buenos Aires had been a hindrance to Britain and France in settling their dispute with Rosas. Aberdeen was at pains to show that the two European powers acted only to put an end to a war which had long damaged the interests of all the world's commercial nations.[24] Aberdeen's prudence, however, was quite unnecessary. The United States government was wary of being drawn into difficulties in a region where it knew it was powerless. The President, James Polk, took the view that Brent had indeed displayed 'little discretion and judgment' in offering Rosas mediation.[25] His Secretary of State, James Buchanan, already had sufficient problems with the British and French and events in Buenos Aires were viewed as an unwelcome complication. Neutrality was the only option in South America and on 13 October Buchanan informed the British government that the United States had no intention of interfering with the allied intervention in La Plata. Rosas sensed that the conflict was not developing as he had foreseen and sent an overture to Ouseley and Deffaudis on 26 October, at least indicating that he still believed discussions possible. But the message contained nothing new and certainly no Argentine concessions. On that basis, the two Ministers were resolute that the time for talking was well past.

*   *   *

The Plate was at least eight weeks' sailing from London. French diplomatic dispatches took between three and five months to reach Paris. It was therefore October 1845 before the Foreign Office knew that Ouseley and Deffaudis had been sent their passports and had left Buenos Aires. 'I therefore regard coercive measures as having now become indispensable,' Aberdeen replied. 'It seems to me that you have acted with moderation and prudence.' As for the coercive measures which Ouseley would adopt, 'I trust they will have been executed with vigour.' The objective remained to force Oribe's Argentine army out of the Banda Oriental; nothing short of this would have any lasting effect on restoring peace. When he read of Ouseley's suggestion to Deffaudis, made in July, that the two powers might arrange a last minute deal among the political factions in Uruguay to restore Oribe to the presidency, Aberdeen was greatly relieved that nothing had come of it. 'I confess that I think we are indebted to the Baron Deffaudis for his opposition to your idea,' Ouseley was reproached, 'and I am very glad that you did not press this further.'[26] Early in November three small steamers, such as Ouseley wanted, were assigned: in Paris, Guizot expressed himself equally satisfied with developments and assured Cowley that the French fleet would be reinforced with six vessels of light draught. On 5 November Aberdeen sent Ouseley a long dispatch approving the manner in which instructions had been carried out.

The first worry for Aberdeen came with the news from Rio de Janeiro that the 45th regiment had been diverted. There seemed no justification for this step, Aberdeen wrote to Ouseley. Since it had always been made clear that land operations were never contemplated, it was the government's hope that these troops had not been detained but had been sent on to their original destination. Only a 'real and pressing emergency, such as Her Majesty's Government cannot now contemplate, should render their stay in the river Plate indispensable.'[27] By December 1845 the tone of Aberdeen's correspondence had fundamentally altered from what it had been just a month before. Far from hoping now that coercive measures were being executed with vigour, he suggested to Ouseley that the decision to throw the blockade on Buenos Aires 'appears somewhat rapid'.

Aberdeen also now prescribed a more conciliatory tone towards Rosas and, amazingly, towards Oribe's pretensions to the presidency of the Banda Oriental. 'His establishment at Montevideo will be quite consistent with its independence,' Ouseley was informed. 'It will be a most desirable object to terminate the present state of affairs by promoting, rather than impeding, his settlement in the town.' Once Oribe was assured of his return to office, which unofficially Ouseley and Deffaudis should now try to arrange, there would be no need for any Argentine troops across the River Uruguay and Rosas would presumably simply withdraw them. 'In truth, it becomes a matter of form and propriety rather than anything else. If we can declare that Montevideo is independent and that the Argentine troops are withdrawn, we need not require more.'[28] Oribe should be required to grant a general amnesty which guaranteed the safety of his opponents and their property inside the city. But no other conditions need be attached. Aberdeen admitted that peace restored by this means might not inspire lasting confidence: in particular, 'it will fall short of what we had contemplated.' 'But it will be sufficient to satisfy our honour,' he affirmed.[29] Moreover, Guizot shared his sentiments and would be writing to Deffaudis accordingly.

All this indicated a quite remarkable *volte-face* in Aberdeen's thinking. This could scarcely be due to Ouseley's reports from Montevideo, for nothing had happened there which had not been either foreseen or indeed provided for by the British and French governments as long ago as December 1844. There were, however, pressures mounting on the British government by the end of 1845 which led Aberdeen to the conclusion that he should abandon the armed intervention. One source of protest, predictably, was Manuel Moreno who, despite the diplomatic breach at Buenos Aires, had remained in London, being neither recalled by Rosas nor required to leave by the Foreign Office. On 3 December Moreno presented a note insisting that Ouseley should be recalled and stating that his government would demand reparation for damage inflicted by the British navy against Argentine property. Far more compelling was the pressure from commercial and public opinion, and this at a time when Peel's government was weakened by the differences which had emerged within Tory ranks. Aberdeen had assumed that a vigorous intervention to bring an end to the war in Uruguay would be popular with mercantile opinion, since peace would bring renewed prosperity and freedom of opportunity for British traders. This was not an unreasonable assumption given the vociferous outcry on behalf of the trading houses whose cargoes and property were besieged in Montevideo, and who believed that they stood to lose everything if Oribe's army overran the town. Aberdeen had taken these expressions of concern and the accompanying entreaties to intervene by force as broadly accepted commercial views.

By November, though, there was no doubt in Aberdeen's mind that something was going wrong. Letters from trading houses, chambers of commerce and merchants' associations began arriving at the Foreign Office and deputations of City worthies were begging, and were granted, interviews in order to put the record straight. 'The fact is,' Aberdeen concluded, 'we have been a good deal misled with respect to the nature of this contest and the condition of the two parties. The agents of Montevideo have been indefatigable and have greatly exaggerated the importance of our interests in that place while the merchants of Buenos Aires have been quiescent.'[30] Now that the blockade was on Buenos Aires, the latter group were up in arms against the interruption to their trade. They were protesting too that the government in London had been utterly deceived if it believed the propaganda from Montevideo that Rosas was opposed to all trading links with Europe as part of an exclusive *sistema Americano*. While an active and self-seeking minority had pushed the British government over the brink of war in defence of Montevideo, the bulk of Britain's commercial interest in La Plata could only be the loser by such a policy. Caught now between conflicting strands of commercial opinion, Aberdeen at least showed some consistency in taking the side of those who complained the loudest. 'You may perhaps recollect my great reluctance to engage actively in the affairs of the river Plate,' he wrote despairingly to the Prime Minister, 'and how long I resisted all the representations upon the subject made both by the merchants and in Parliament. I now regret that I had not been still more obstinate.'[31] A policy initially popular had rather badly backfired.

Beyond these difficulties with commercial opinion, Aberdeen had also lost confidence in the ability of Britain and France to see a conflict in the Argentine through to a successful conclusion. When deciding in December 1845 to call a halt to Ouseley's belligerence, this perhaps was the greatest influence of all. The blockade at Buenos Aires had been the limit of the coercive measures specified in Ouseley's instructions; on 3 December Aberdeen wrote bluntly that, 'I should be very sorry if this blockade were to degenerate into actual war.'[32] Three weeks later he exhorted Ouseley that he objected to the latter's proposal of declaring war against Rosas and emphatically stated that 'you are not *to make war* against him.'[33] Again Aberdeen claimed that he had been misled. 'We have been greatly misinformed by all the officers professing to have local knowledge, as well as by those more directly interested, with respect to the effect of a naval demonstration and a blockade,' he complained to Peel.[34] Since the naval squadrons could not force Oribe's army out of the Banda Oriental, a compromise with Oribe would have to be reached.

Ouseley had suspected back in August 1845 that the British government had always believed that naval demonstration and blockade would be adequate to get the Argentine troops out of Uruguay and that there was no appetite in London for any serious fighting. Now this was confirmed by Aberdeen. Furthermore, the plan of Ouseley and Deffaudis for a naval expedition into the Paraná River did not receive Aberdeen's blessing. Both banks of the Paraná were Argentine territory, he observed. Then he enquired of Ouseley: 'Is this quite consistent with your instructions? It is not easy to see in what this proceeding differs from actual war.'[35] But however premature or aggressive such an expedition might appear from London, Aberdeen knew that it was impossible to stop it. The expedition entered the Paraná on 8 November – weeks before the dispatches which first referred to it even reached Europe. For the time being events were beyond the control of the British and French governments.

6· An Expedition into the Paraná, 1845–6

The Paraná was the greatest of the Plate's tributaries. It ran up between the states of Buenos Aires and Entre Rios, Santa Fé and Corrientes, and then continued, as the River Paraguay, way beyond the limits of the Argentine Confederation. For hundreds of miles it was navigable by foreign warships and farther still for merchant craft. Freeing the river to foreign navigation was not a priority, but it had been one of the general goals set out for Ouseley's guidance.

It was well known in Montevideo that merchant vessels, many with British cargoes bound for that port, had been stranded in the Paraná since the outbreak of hostilities associated with the Anglo-French intervention. Merchantmen had entered the river in the months after August 1844 when Rosas had reopened the Paraná to trade and thereby effectively acknowledged that his economic blockade of the littoral states was damaging the customs revenues at Buenos Aires.[1] Rescuing these ships now, and allowing others waiting in the Plate the chance to move up river, gave a naval expedition the cloak of commercial benefit regardless of any link it might have with other operations. In drawing up terms of reference for the naval commanders on 9 October 1845, Ouseley and Deffaudis therefore stressed that the expedition into the Paraná 'is exclusively commercial, and it is of importance that under no circumstances is it to take a political character.'[2]

Even if sincere, this was a forlorn hope – as Ouseley conceded shortly after. Since there was no real confidence that the blockade of Buenos Aires could force the Argentine troops out of Uruguay, diversionary tactics were required. If the navy alone had any chance of achieving the desired withdrawal, this 'can only be effected by an expedition up the Paraná'.[3] The squadrons would find much needed supplies and provisions and, more important from the viewpoint of worrying Rosas, communication could be established with his enemies in Paraguay and with the rebellious government in Corrientes. By the end of October all was ready. The men from the 45th regiment now defending Montevideo freed the necessary ships and sailors to enable an impressive force of five British and four French warships with two armed tenders to be assembled. The man chosen by the admirals to take overall command was the most flamboyant of the captains in either squadron – Charles Hotham. The French ships were under the orders of Captain François-Thomas Tréhouart.

Entrusted with the most important action of the intervention, Hotham's preparations were thorough. It was known that the Paraná had been recently fortified by Argentine batteries and that many troops were stationed along its banks. By entering the Paraná the British and French squadrons were bound to meet serious resistance and become involved in fighting which would require the disembarkation of seamen and marines. In the first untroubled week in the river much time was spent rehearsing military manoeuvres: every evening dummy landings from small boats were intended to prepare the sailors for what lay ahead. Writing home, Hotham referred to his new role 'acting as General Officer of infantry teaching my men how to withstand a charge of cavalry'.[4] This lasted until 18 November 1845. On that afternoon, and by now about 100 miles up river, the flotilla saw for the first time the Argentine flag flying over four batteries which commanded the Paraná from cliff tops above the promontory at Vuelta del Obligado.

These batteries had to be destroyed; if they were not, every man-of-war subsequently passing this point would have to fight a separate and hazardous action. Yet this was no easy matter. The Argentine defences contained 22 guns and were constructed with the two outermost batteries 60 feet above the water and the inner two sheltered in a valley. In support were about 3000 Argentine troops which, in the opinion of nearly all Hotham's commanders, made an assault by way of a landing impossible. The other great problem was that the ships could not sail past the batteries' guns returning fire as they did so. The river was blocked by 24 hulks chained together across it and these were defended from the far bank by the Argentine warship *Republicano*. On top of this, the strong current flowing back down the Paraná made it difficult for sailing ships to manoeuvre. Hotham insisted that there would have to be a landing to capture and spike the enemy guns. Before men went ashore, however, a sustained bombardment would be required. When the fire from the batteries had been sufficiently diminished, a passage could be cut through the three chains which linked the hulks and some of the warships could then slip through and begin firing at the batteries on another flank. Much would depend, inevitably, on the accuracy of each side's gunnery.

The action at Obligado took place throughout the day on 20 November 1845. Hotham and Tréhouart divided their eight sailing ships into two divisions. One was to form a line about 700 yards down river from the batteries while the other stationed itself opposite the Argentine guns at the far bank. The three steamers in the squadron were held back out of range, since they were too valuable to risk in an early exchange of fire. The battle started at 9.40 a.m., when the batteries opened up and throughout the morning dominated the engagement. By noon, Hotham's only noticeable success was that *Republicano* had been hit and was deserted and on fire. Two of his ships had lost much of their sails and rigging and had been raked across their decks by grapeshot several times. Another was so 'very much cut up' that she had to be brought out of the action altogether.[5] But the firepower of the warships, and the batteries' shortage of ammunition, finally told. *Republicano* blew up and two of the batteries ceased firing within the space of half an hour.[6] Hotham thus decided that it was time to send out boats to cut the chains between the hulks which straddled the river.

Once a gap had been created between the hulks wide enough for the three steamers to pass through, the fate of the batteries was sealed. Flanked by continuous fire from all sides, the Argentine gunnery became occasional and uncertain, although it could not be silenced completely for another three hours. Hotham's gamble on a landing could not therefore begin until early evening. Over 300 British seamen and marines were met with 'a brisk fire of musketry' as they came ashore,[7] to be followed by about 400 French sailors who joined the engagement. The battle was decided when the English charged up from the beach towards the enemy, who fired a few shots and then, to Hotham's immense relief, broke and fled. 'Half the courage displayed in the afternoon that they had shewn in the morning and very few of us would have returned,' he later confessed to Inglefield.[8] The day had cost 29 dead and 84 wounded from the combined squadron. In the days which followed, the Argentine guns were removed as trophies or sunk in the river and the battery positions were dismantled.

Victory at Obligado accomplished, Hotham progressed to the next stage of his mission which was to establish contacts with the governments of Paraguay and Corrientes. Leaving the squadron, Hotham and Tréhouart set out for the Paraguayan town of Assumption.

Hotham's instructions from Ouseley were to discuss, albeit unofficially, religious toleration, freedom of commerce, the need for low duties on foreign trade entering Paraguay and, of course, the general political and military situation within the Argentine Confederation. The Governor, or President, of Paraguay was General Carlos López who, having recently declared war against Rosas on 4 December 1845, knew precisely what the British and French wanted. Although Hotham had no authority to make any political treaty or alliance, he obviously had come to reassure the Paraguayans, and the governors of the states which bordered the Paraná, that Anglo-French incursions into Argentine territory were directed solely against Buenos Aires and posed no threat to those who likewise opposed the regime of General Rosas. Hotham, of course, also came to investigate the military strength of these states with a view to their likely effectiveness against Rosas' forces, and, as Ouseley had wished, to encourage them in their struggle. López, Ouseley knew, wanted international recognition for Paraguay as a sovereign nation and access to the Plate by free navigation on the Paraná. Both these ambitions were denied by the pretensions of Rosas, who still cherished the notion that Paraguay should be an Argentine state whose foreign relations, therefore, might be determined by the government of Buenos Aires.[9]

After a few interviews with López, Hotham was confirmed in his view of the value of political contact. 'The moment is remarkably opportune,' he concluded, 'the *de facto* independence of Paraguay is menaced. Now she will gladly seek those European alliances to which a year ago she was indifferent.'[10] In the longer term, of course, Britain's gain lay in opening these inland regions of South America to foreign trade by treaties of commerce and friendship and Hotham saw unlimited opportunities for the future. As for López's military strength, Hotham estimated that the former could put 60,000 fighting men in the field. Corrientes could produce a more modest 8000, but since the two states had formed a military and political alliance their combined strength would be impressive. In January 1846 General Paz commanded a combined force of 9000 men assembled in Corrientes with the express intention of invading the neighbouring state of Entre Rios. Such an invasion would, of course, prevent any troops from Entre Rios being sent to assist Oribe's army outside Montevideo. Hotham and Tréhouart sought a meeting with Paz at once. 'We were desirous that no misconception as to the presence of the allied squadrons in the Paraná should arise,' Hotham reported to Inglefield. 'We plainly stated that the object of our visit was commercial and had no reference to the political condition of Corrientes.'[11] Hotham returned to the squadron in the Paraná well pleased with his political foray. His reception by both López and Paz had been encouraging. More to the point, the latter's incursion into Entre Rios had gone ahead and there was every confidence of success.

The first news from the Paraná of the victory of Obligado reached Montevideo in mid-December 1845. Ouseley and Deffaudis naturally were delighted. Meanwhile naval operations along the coastline of Uruguay had continued and, at Ouseley's prompting, the navy supplied a further 940 pounds of gunpowder to the garrison at Montevideo. Far more impressively, he was able to put ashore a further 652 officers and men for the defence of the town from another troop transport ship which had been diverted from Rio de Janeiro. These were soldiers of the 73rd regiment. By late January, 1846 a total of over 1400 British soldiers and marines were stationed on the inner lines, raising morale in the city considerably and freeing yet more Montevidean soldiers for action elsewhere. To support the Uruguayan garrison at Colonia, in January 1846 an Anglo-French column of 160 men attacked and captured one of the outposts of Oribe's army just outside the town and drove off the anticipated counter-attack.[12] Encouraged by the way his campaign was progressing, Ouseley again urged Aberdeen to issue a formal declaration of war in order to give greater confidence to Rosas' enemies in the region. Quite unreservedly he asserted that 'we should try to help General Paz and Paraguay overthrow Rosas,' and that with a few more steamers and 2000 extra troops from Europe this might still readily be achieved. 'It is at Buenos Aires that the battle must be fought,' Ouseley exclaimed. 'The blow that upsets Rosas gives this country [Uruguay] peace and destroys Oribe.'[13]

*   *   *

At the end of January 1846 Aberdeen's correspondence dating from early December reached Montevideo. It was obvious that the governments in London and Paris were worried about the course which the intervention was taking, but Ouseley chose to interpret this not as a caution or reproach but as an indication that politicians in Europe did not understand the scale and importance of the operations under way. War, and the ultimate replacement of Rosas by Paz, was the only real security for the independence of Uruguay, Ouseley replied; if Oribe were allowed to return to power the republic would become a client state of Buenos Aires and European trade would gradually be excluded from La Plata. Ouseley reserved the most strident defence of his actions for his response to Aberdeen's request to reembark the 45th regiment from Montevideo. The decision to deploy the men had been taken only after serious discussions with Deffaudis and the two admirals and was a decision 'forced upon me by circumstances such as Her Majesty's Government cannot have foreseen when preparing the instructions which I have had the honour to receive.' 'I could not, consistent with my duty, allow the troops now here to depart,' he wrote formally to Aberdeen on 31 January.[14] Ouseley was convinced that once the governments in Europe were given the correct perspective in which to judge the actions of their envoys, the intervention would be allowed to proceed along the lines that he recommended.

In London there was no chance that Aberdeen would prove open to persuasion. For one thing, the War Office was not pleased that the 45th regiment had been detained in Montevideo. The men were not equipped for action, the Foreign Office was informed on 14 January, and should be sent on to South Africa immediately. In addition to grumbles from the War Office, the Foreign Office continued to receive representations from commercial houses and public criticism, most of which simply wanted an end to the armed intervention by Britain and France. A deputation of merchants who traded in the River Plate complained at length about the collapse of British exports there – down from values of £289,362 in 1842–3, £233,736 in 1843–4 and £199,990 in 1844–5 to a paltry £19,304 in 1845–6. The value of the Buenos Aires paper dollar had fallen from its value of 4d when Ouseley had arrived in La Plata to only 2d by the beginning of 1846.[15] This halved the worth of British property and outstanding debts in the city which previously had been calculated at about £700,000. Blockade and warfare only damaged British economic interests, they continued: 'our worst enemy could not desire to inflict greater injuries upon us.'[16] Aberdeen was urged to compel Ouseley to act in accordance with his own government's wishes. The remedy demanded by the merchant body for present evils was to call off the intervention and to allow Oribe to return to the Uruguayan presidency before requiring fresh elections to be held.

That was going too far for Aberdeen, who approved the fact that Ouseley had spurned Rosas' peace offering at the end of October 1845. On that occasion Rosas had done no more than to restate arguments put forward before diplomatic relations had been broken. The merchants wanted peace at any price, whereas Aberdeen had the standing of the government to consider, both at home and abroad. A complete climb down was out of the question. Britain and France were openly committed to the independence of the Banda Oriental and Oribe could not therefore be allowed to take office at the head of a foreign army without any expression of the will of the people. Aberdeen clung to the solution which he had suggested at the beginning of December 1845: a convention with Rosas, and if necessary Oribe, which provided for an Argentine withdrawal. 'It is the retreat of these troops which will be the means of giving a fair character to a transaction which in other respects might not be quite so creditable to the efforts of two great nations,' he pronounced. 'If this were done other difficulties could be solved easily,' he continued, including the difficulty of what to do about Oribe.[17] 'Although we may not now call him the legal President of the Uruguay, I should be most happy to see him installed as such.' What was needed was a form of words to get the British government out of what Aberdeen saw only as a 'most embarrassing position'.[18]

On top of these considerations came reports of the Paraná expedition which reached his desk towards the end of January 1846. There was no denying the skill and courage of the British and French forces or the admirable way in which they had worked together at Obligado, he assured Ouseley. However, success did not justify the venture, which remained 'an act of aggression upon the territory of the Argentine Confederation' and made a diplomatic convention such as he desired even more difficult to achieve.[19]

To complete Aberdeen's discomfort, Guizot, under pressure in the Chamber of Deputies, had been obliged to release the text of his instructions to Deffaudis, and the British government now had to lay similar papers before Parliament. 'The publication of these instructions will unfortunately render it manifest to everyone that our proceedings in the river Plate are at variance with their letter and spirit,' Aberdeen lamented. 'They place Rosas in the eyes of the public as a person who has been treated with violence and injustice.' As for Hotham's political contacts in Paraguay and Corrientes: 'he does not seem to have the least notion of what he is going about, and I am sure that I am quite unable to explain it.' Even if the regime in Buenos Aires was as evil as Ouseley described it, still the British government was not justified in siding with Rosas' enemies within the Argentine

Confederation. In short, Ouseley had violated his instructions: 'You are proceeding in an erroneous direction. You are engaged in active hostilities instead of keeping peace constantly in view.'[20] Well before Ouseley's letter of 31 January had reached the Foreign Office, therefore, Aberdeen had decided to withdraw from a conflict which he had become convinced served no useful purpose.

The expedition into the Paraná divided not only Aberdeen and Ouseley. It also led to the first difference of opinion in the affairs of La Plata between the British and French governments. Despite his distaste for this incursion into Argentine territory, Aberdeen did not feel able to withdraw unilaterally. To his dismay, however, Guizot seemed well satisfied with what Deffaudis and Ouseley had accomplished and had no intention of sending out instructions recalling the French squadron from the Paraná. Guizot's government was not so popular or secure in Paris that it could afford to disapprove a triumph of French arms, and particularly not at English instigation; only an appeal to the gravity of what might lie ahead stood any chance of persuading Guizot to do so. Cowley, in Paris, was therefore to emphasize to Guizot that the Paraná expedition 'involves too great a departure from the principles which were from the first laid down by England and France to be justifiable' and that it 'might, not improbably, involve us ultimately in a war with the Argentine Republic of which all the responsibility would fall upon ourselves'.[21]

At an interview on 1 February 1846, Guizot replied to Cowley that he had heard nothing from Deffaudis. He spent much time extolling the splendid spirit of cooperation between Deffaudis and Ouseley and between the naval forces which surely, he added, was important in improving the good feeling between the British and French governments such as both desired. Guizot conceded, in private, that he shared Aberdeen's disapproval of too vigorous a strategy within Argentine territory, but when he later learned that Aberdeen had written to Ouseley on 4 March 1846, effectively requiring that the Royal Navy be withdrawn from the Paraná, he was not slow to reprimand Cowley that this step had been taken without reference to the French government. After a few days of calm reflection, however, Guizot recognized that Aberdeen had presented him with a *fait accompli*. Guizot also appreciated the pressures under which his counterpart laboured in London when the French embassy there assured him that Aberdeen was more preoccupied with events in South America than with the Spanish marriages. He told Cowley that he would compromise by giving Deffaudis discretionary powers to withdraw warships from the Paraná at a suitable moment. That was good enough for Aberdeen. Profuse in his tactful apologies for having instructed Ouseley prematurely, he believed that at least the first hurdle had been cleared in reining in the two diplomats in Montevideo.

The British government's vulnerability was exposed in Parliamentary debates in February and March 1846. In the House of Lords Aberdeen was condemned for his 'impolitic course'. Britain was not the guarantor of Uruguay, Lords Beaumont and Colchester reminded him: her mediating role in 1828 did not commit the government to war in Uruguay's defence. Britain had neither rights nor obligations in La Plata. The intervention with France had no basis in legality nor had it any practical value. If the objective of policy was to safeguard trade then demonstrably the destruction of British commerce in the region was a damning verdict on Aberdeen's judgment: 'Had we not produced a much greater interruption to our commerce by our own blockade of the port of Buenos Aires?'[22] In the Commons Peel had to face Palmerston's invective. The nation had the right to know 'whether we are now at war with Buenos Aires or not'. 'Transactions have taken place there of a very warlike description,' Palmerston pointed out. 'The language of the government, when asked upon this matter in Parliament, has been the language of peace; but the acts of our authorities there have certainly been acts of war.' Did the Prime Minister believe that peace was compatible with blockade, the capture of towns, the seizure of Argentine shipping and territory and a naval expedition deep into the interior? Peel replied that there were precedents for naval action without war being declared. He also took this opportunity to deny that the engagements in the Paraná river had been foreseen. But his defence was not convincing. At the end of the exchange a Member rose to impress upon the House that 'he was at a loss to know what was war, if this was not.'[23]

Much of the disquiet voiced in open debate was shared by Aberdeen's colleagues in Cabinet. For that reason, too, he could never be persuaded by Ouseley's representations from Montevideo. The Lord Privy Seal, Lord Haddington, remarked dryly that Inglefield's dispatches to the Admiralty showed 'a very *fishy* state of affairs in the Plate.'[24] The old Duke of Wellington, as Commander-in-Chief of the army and Minister without Portfolio in Peel's government, continued to moan that British troops had been diverted to the River Plate without any authorization from London. Wellington described Ouseley,

Deffaudis and the admirals in the Plate as nothing less than 'pirates'. William Gladstone, the Secretary of State for War and Colonies, informed the Admiralty that Wellington in future 'wishes to have the troops about to sail from this country for India secured from kidnapping at Rio or La Plata'.[25] Wellington was furious that the 45th and 73rd regiments had been landed to assist in the defence of Montevideo. There they had been placed 'under the command of a revolutionary General,' he fumed, 'and engaged as parties in a civil contest.' 'I know nothing of any of these operations in La Plata,' Wellington insisted, 'excepting that there is a congress sitting either at Buenos Aires or Montevideo consisting of Her Majesty's plenipotentiary, a plenipotentiary from the King of the French, a French and an English admiral in a sort of conference and carrying on war.'[26] On whose orders or authority these diplomats and admirals acted, Wellington was at a loss to understand.

Lord Ellenborough, as First Lord of the Admiralty, was no less disturbed by developments in the River Plate or by the naval build up there. He certainly could offer Wellington no reassurance as to the purpose for which the two regiments had been diverted nor any expectation of their early departure from Montevideo. 'It is clear that our troops alone keep the enemy out of the town,' he replied gloomily. 'Within all is anarchy, with some bloodshed, and no public force – the few armed men remaining being Foreigners or Blacks. Such is the state of things we are protecting.' Of more pressing concern for the Admiralty was the state of the ships on active service and a growing uncertainty as to the task which they were expected to perform. Inglefield's dispatches did not make good reading. In the Paraná, vessels were shot at from points which they could barely reach with their return of fire. Men were being lost and ships damaged in conditions quite unsuitable for naval combat, Ellenborough recorded. The fleet in the River Plate could not secure fresh provisions and the crews were consequently weakened by scurvey. Too many officers and seamen had been sent ashore and stores of ammunition were running low. 'I never read a more deplorable report of the state of a squadron,' he informed Wellington on 11 June 1846. By this time the Admiralty was aware that Aberdeen was making diplomatic efforts to extricate the British government from the armed intervention in La Plata – and not a moment before time, Ellenborough concluded. 'It is evident that we have undertaken what it is impossible to accomplish,' he confided to Wellington, 'and that all that remains to us is to back out with as little disgrace as we can.'[27]

Ellenborough, like others in the government, questioned the wisdom of maintaining a sizeable naval presence in a region of such little importance to Britain's economic or imperial power. In February 1846, during the first of the Sikh wars in India, he expostulated with the Prime Minister on the folly of keeping forces in La Plata when requirements elsewhere were so great. 'Depend upon it, all minor considerations must be thrown over,' he implored Peel, 'and our whole energy directed to the saving of an empire which has been placed in extreme peril by defective dispositions of force.'[28] Nor was saving India his only worry. The Oregon boundary dispute made war in North America once again a real possibility in the early months of 1846; Ellenborough feared that France would quickly join the conflict on the side of the United States. The navy was also required to keep ships in the Pacific following the annexation of New Zealand in 1840, he continued; the proposed acquisition of Labuan would increase the navy's commitments even further – as indeed did the need to protect James Brooke in Sarawak after 1841 and British traders in Borneo. 'Nothing can be so inconvenient as the dispersion of our force,' Ellenborough reflected in May 1846;[29] on 17 June he wrote to Aberdeen asking precisely the size of squadron required in La Plata and why it was already so large when the demands from elsewhere were so great. Finally, there was Ireland, from where the Admiralty proposed to withdraw a battalion of marines in order to cover its shortages elsewhere. Because the 45th and 73rd regiments were stranded in Montevideo, the garrison in Ireland was deficient by several hundreds of men, the army remonstrated in May 1846, 'and for this interruption to our arrangements we are indebted to Mr. Ouseley and Admiral Inglefield.'[30] Faced with this variety of complaints both from political opponents and from within the government as to the worth of his policy and the commitment of scarce resources in the River Plate, Aberdeen had little alternative but to disown the intervention.

*   *   *

The large overlap in communications meant that even by the end of March 1846 Ouseley had received nothing from London dated later than the beginning of February. Although he knew of the government's uneasiness about the Paraná expedition, he certainly did not know of Aberdeen's instructions of 4 March to recall it. He had received, however, clear word to embark the 45th regiment and to send it away from La Plata and he now had to decide how to proceed. Knowing that his appeal to Aberdeen of 31 January could only just have reached the Foreign Office, Ouseley remained quite confident that all could still be satisfactorily explained. What was needed, he appealed again to Aberdeen, were more troops from Europe and not the withdrawal of the few already in Montevideo. Having begun the intervention, prestige required that Britain and France saw it through; if they did not, then their standing and influence in South America would be irrevocably weakened and Britain would have deserted a people to whose support she was bound by international commitments.

Convinced that in the end his arguments must prevail, Ouseley wrote another clear statement of the case for war as the only realistic hope of succeeding against Rosas. The navy had done well, he emphasized, with the blockade of Buenos Aires efficient, the Paraná expedition a spectacular triumph and Oribe's supply lines by sea greatly impeded. But on its own the navy could not do the job. Oribe's army beat the Anglo-French blockade of his supply ports by means of overland routes and provisions from Brazil. Ouseley was also aware that the city of Buenos Aires avoided any serious discomfort from the blockade by drawing on the resources of its hinterland. To break this deadlock, Ouseley argued, the intervention required five or six thousand men who could drive the Argentine army out of Uruguay and even proceed to capture Buenos Aires itself. Ouseley seemed convinced that Rosas could never raise a force capable of defending the city against a determined landing; the *porteños*, he assured Aberdeen, would willingly join with anyone who could free them from bondage. As for negotiating with the government in Buenos Aires, that was a trap to be avoided, Ouseley concluded, since Rosas would merely drag out any talks and try to play off Britain and France one against the other.

Ouseley's obstinacy in maintaining British troops at Montevideo reflected also the pressures on both him and Deffaudis as a consequence of their increasing, and by 1846 obvious, involvement in Uruguayan politics. By retiring to Montevideo in August 1845 after the collapse of their negotiations at Buenos Aires, the two diplomats could not, of course, avoid giving the appearance of having sided with the government in Uruguay. Furthermore, the importance which both men attached to preventing the fall of Montevideo subsequently and inevitably drew them into the daily problems of the city's defence. They had also engaged in joint actions with the Uruguayan army at Colonia, Maldonado and in the Uruguay River. Less conspicuously, British and French warships acted as escorts and suppliers for the Uruguayan army and its flotilla of armed vessels. During September and October 1846, carpenters and armourers from the British squadron were ashore at Martín García fitting Uruguayan gunboats for active service. The cost of equipping the ten vessels which made up the Uruguayan navy was borne by Ouseley and Deffaudis, who each drew credit on his government to the value of £1000.

Equally important was the involvement of the two Ministers with the revenues of the Uruguayan government. As commerce and shipping dwindled at the port, and as Oribe's army had effectively cut all ties with the interior, so the government had become dependent on loans raised within Montevideo which could only be secured against the precarious receipts of the Customs House. As early as August 1845 the authorities had turned to Ouseley and Deffaudis to help raise money, either by means of official British and French guarantees of repayment for the benefit of potential investors or else some milder statement that Britain and France would at least use their diplomatic influence in the future to ensure that contracts were honoured. The first was out of the question. Aberdeen reluctantly approved the second option while making it clear that diplomatic support for the creditors of the Uruguayan government did not imply a financial commitment on the part of Britain. In November 1845 the government in Montevideo raised 300,000 dollars (£60,000) secured on the mortgage of a 25 per cent share of the Customs House receipts due for the year 1848. This loan was to be paid to the government in six monthly instalments. The anticipated value of the quarter share of the 1848 customs revenues was as high as 600,000 dollars. To ease this deal, Ouseley and Deffaudis agreed that the loan might be made under the 'general diplomatic guarantee' of the British and French legations.[31]

Such involvement in the military survival and financial solvency of Uruguay could not but lead the two Ministers also into trying to secure political stability in the capital. This was never going to be easy. The defenders of Montevideo, though they feared Oribe, had little else in common. Factional rivalry and personal ambition marked the ebb and flow of political fortunes even as the enemy was at the gates. Native *caudillos*, the foreign legions and the political refugees from Buenos Aires seldom agreed on a common polity. Central to much of the intrigue was General Rivera, much weakened as a national figure after India Muerta but still with a loyal and disruptive following on the streets of the capital. Having fled to Brazil, he announced his intention to return to Uruguay a few months later in what British and French officials saw as a most unwelcome development. In August 1845 Turner instructed Inglefield to ensure that Rivera got no passage on a British warship; he also contacted the Montevidean government and Brazilian and Sardinian diplomats in the city 'with a view to avert, if possible, his arrival'.[32] Ouseley went so far as to persuade the government in Montevideo to prevent even Rivera's secretary from landing.

By November 1845, then, it was clear that Ouseley and Deffaudis wielded considerable influence in local politics. At a time of disagreement among the anti-Rivera factions, Turner assured Aberdeen that stabililty continued nonetheless: 'the state of parties in Montevideo is not, in some respects, a matter of great importance at present, as the plenipotentiaries of Great Britain and France are now enabled, from the influence which the intervention necessarily gives them, to dictate in a great degree to the Montevidean government the measures to be adopted in the present contest.'[33] Turner's point was not lost on Montevideo's politicians. Francisco Magariños, then Uruguay's Minister to Brazil, complained to Rivera on 10 December that Ouseley and Deffaudis treated the government like boys who had not reached the age of majority.[34]

To the evident distress of Ouseley and Deffaudis, Rivera arrived in the harbour at Montevideo on board a Spanish merchant craft in March 1846. The two envoys tried to arrange with the Montevidean government that he be dispatched immediately on a diplomatic mission to Spain on the pretext of ratifying a recent treaty. It was too late, however, to prevent rioting and political demonstrations on the streets in his support. On 29 March martial law was declared in the city amid a revolt in the army and the collapse of public order. For their personal safety, Suárez and government ministers took refuge in Ouseley's house during six days of turmoil in which the city became virtually undefended. A strong detachment of British soldiers was moved up to the advanced posts on the outer lines on 1 April in case of a sudden assault, while others remained at the Customs House, the barracks and the diplomatic residences. In desperation, the authorities asked Ouseley to use the 45th and 73rd regiments to pacify the town by firing on rebellious units of the Uruguayan army, but Ouseley refused to do this. On 6 April, after Ouseley, Deffaudis and the British and French admirals had all participated in mediating between the factions fighting inside Montevideo, Rivera was allowed to land in the hope that tranquillity could thereby be restored.[35] The crisis eventually passed when Rivera agreed to accept a post as Commander-in-Chief within the existing government, but not before it was discovered that one of the government ministers, Francisco Muñoz, had been intriguing with insurgents in the city. Turner reported this to Aberdeen on 18 April and informed him of the outcome: 'in this critical state of affairs, at Mr. Ouseley's request, I joined him in recommending to the President and to M. Vázquez that M. Muñoz should be removed from the government, and he was accordingly dismissed from his office.'[36] Given his prominent role in preserving the vestiges of administration in Montevideo, it was not surprising that Ouseley should still implore his chief to allow him to retain the regiments at his disposal.

From April 1846 onwards Ouseley and Aberdeen were locked in a correspondence in which there existed almost no common ground. As far as Aberdeen was concerned the whole intervention to restore peace between the warring states in La Plata had gone alarmingly wrong and he had now succeeded in convincing Guizot of that. The only action by Ouseley which he approved was the latter's refusal to allow British soldiers to be used to crush the uprising in Montevideo. Aberdeen read Ouseley's dispatches with utter incredulity. 'It is marvellous that you should still continue to talk of the necessity of declaring war against Rosas, and to repeat that you must have troops of some kind or other. Now I have explicitly declared that we have no intention, nor ever had any intention of declaring war against Rosas,' he rebuked Ouseley, 'and, further, if I had 20,000 troops to spare I would not sent one of them.' 'Without any declaration of war you are making war in a manner the most discreditable and disadvantageous to us,' he continued. Aberdeen refused to countenance any meddling in the political struggles within the Argentine Confederation, to which Ouseley, Deffaudis and Hotham attached such importance, and he did not accept Ouseley's absurd distinction between a war declared against Rosas as separate from one against the Argentine states.

Aberdeen, in fact, appeared to be convinced by the arguments of many British merchant houses whose appeals for an end to the intervention continued. In particular, he rejected Ouseley's portrait of

Rosas as uniquely antipathetic to European values and to British commerce. Much was wrong with Rosas' regime, Aberdeen conceded, 'but I assure you that the most respectable merchants in this country bear testimony to his good conduct towards us, and while they admit his moral defects and vicious character of his domestic policy, they are unanimous in declaring that in our commercial dealings with him we have no cause of complaint.'[37] The merchants' stance was this: Montevideo was defended only by its foreign population of French, Basques, Italians and by the British soldiers ashore there. The natives of the city, and of the Banda Oriental as a whole, were not nearly so hostile to Oribe as Ouseley and Deffaudis claimed; they were, in any case, so heartily sick of war that they would readily accept Oribe's return. Peace would follow, the merchants concluded, when Oribe was restored to power and Argentine ambitions in Uruguay were thereby satisfied. Logic and favourable circumstances for foreign trade both demanded, therefore, that Rosas and Oribe should be supported.

On 19 June 1846 the Admiralty was told of the widespread misunderstanding which existed as to the navy's role in defending Montevideo and opposing Oribe. All that the ships at anchor there were expected to do was to keep a few marines at the Customs House and to provide at that point a temporary place of safety to which British citizens could flee in the event of a collapse of the town's defences. The Admiralty was reminded that Britain was not a party in the struggle between Oribe and the Uruguayan government. Five days later, orders went out to Inglefield informing him that he would soon be moved to another command and requiring the relocation of the ships on his station.

Until the end of his tenure at the Foreign Office, Aberdeen continued to reproach Ouseley for the way in which he had become a pawn in the politics of Montevideo and had busied himself in matters of warfare and internal intrigues in the Platine states which had compromised the reputation of his government. He had also involved his government in expenses for the provisioning of British troops on land, for supporting the forces of the Montevidean government and for rescuing that government's financial credit in a time of crisis. Merely by supporting the Montevidean war effort, Aberdeen observed, Ouseley had already run up bills of over £20,000 which were both unauthorized and objectionable. 'It was not by prolonging the existence of any of the ephemeral governments of the Oriental state, nor by ministering to their extremities, that any object of your mission could be served.'[38] His final private letter on 2 July 1846 marked the breach between them: 'It is useless to discuss further at present the affairs of the river Plate. We look at them from a point of view essentially different.'[39] Aberdeen's frustration, however, was not to be prolonged. Racked by the problems of Ireland and the importation of foreign grain, the Tory party had disintegrated and Peel resigned. The Whigs were back and Palmerston returned to the Foreign Office.

Before he lost office, however, Aberdeen had realized that events could not be left to drift with Ouseley and Deffaudis, as was clearly shown by his approach to Guizot for a common change of policy and his letter to the Admiralty on 19 June. Since the beginning of April 1846, in fact, Aberdeen had wished to send a fresh mission to Buenos Aires to negotiate with Rosas but had been obliged to wait until the French government sanctioned the idea. Ouseley's relations with Rosas and Oribe clearly precluded him from making any such approach. With Guizot's concurrence, Aberdeen therefore appointed Thomas Samuel Hood, formerly Consul-General at Montevideo between 1823 and 1843, as a special envoy charged by both the British and French governments to reopen communication at Buenos Aires and to submit proposals there which Aberdeen believed were 'well calculated to bring all hostilities in the river Plate to a speedy termination'.[40] It was intended that Ouseley and Deffaudis should assist Hood in every way. On 19 May Aberdeen made it perfectly plain to Ouseley that a new phase of the intervention was under way. When peace was restored Ouseley would be replaced; furthermore, his suitability for another posting would depend upon his efforts now to get a settlement. His conduct was thus disowned by deed as well as word and, most galling perhaps, he was expected to help undo the wrongs of which he stood accused.

Ouseley never accepted Aberdeen's opinion and he made no effort to conceal that fact even after the latter's firm instructions of January and February had arrived in April 1846. He rejected any suggestion that a political deal to restore Oribe to power in Montevideo could be other than detrimental to Uruguayan independence. Ouseley's obsessive view of Rosas as the source of all disorder in the area, and as the eternal enemy of British economic enterprise, was encouraged by the British merchant houses in Montevideo who petitioned in support of the forceful measures which he and Deffaudis had for months directed. However, Ouseley was resigned to withdrawing the two regiments ashore, as Aberdeen had emphatically requested, despite his conviction that this would spell the end for Montevideo. Justifying all that he had done to defend the town, and the initiatives elsewhere that he had taken, he reminded Aberdeen of his great distance from London and how so often instructions drawn up there were either inapplicable or else impossible of fulfilment on arrival. The Paraná expedition and the accompanying attempts to encourage separatism within the Argentine Confederation remained, for Ouseley, the only way of forcing Rosas' troops out of the Banda Oriental and he professed continued dismay at Aberdeen's unyielding disapproval. Thus the auguries were not favourable for a meeting of minds when Hood arrived in La Plata on his special mission at the beginning of July 1846.

During the time that Ouseley and Aberdeen had conducted their disparate correspondence, the British and French naval squadrons had remained in the Paraná. Having returned from Paraguay and Corrientes, Hotham and Tréhouart now had to devote their energies to the third purpose of the expedition, which was to shepherd merchant ships safely out of the river. By May 1846, 110 vessels had been collected into a large convoy to be escorted down to Montevideo. Before then, however, it had become obvious that the Anglo-French squadron would have to fight its way out of the Paraná. Undeterred by the defeat at Obligado, the Argentine army had constructed another two cliff-top batteries at a position known as San Lorenzo.

At this point the Paraná was almost a mile wide and commanded by about 20 guns which had been cleverly concealed behind woodland. This would make accurate fire from the warships extremely difficult. The river was not blocked, as it had been at Obligado, but the prospect of shielding a large merchant convoy while under fire posed particular problems. Some of the warships had already tangled with the batteries at San Lorenzo and received a mauling from sustained grapeshot fire.[41] Amid the chaos of escorting merchantmen, Hotham dreaded the possibility of his ships running aground under the enemy's guns. Surveying the cliff tops, he therefore decided to place his faith in a small island in the river which alone gave a clear sight of the Argentine batteries.

The key to passing San Lorenzo was to be a battery of Congreve rockets which two young officers established on the island at the beginning of June 1846. Hotham's tactic was to set up distracting fire from this unexpected quarter and hope that its accuracy would be sufficient to disrupt the Argentine gunnery. The steamships in the river would keep up a bombardment of their own and under this cover, and with the current, the other warships would marshal the merchantmen past as quickly as possible. On the morning of 4 June the five steamers of the Anglo-French squadron took up position and opened the attack on the Argentine forts while the rocket brigade began its fusillade from the island. The Argentine batteries responded immediately. 'The enemy brought into play from 16 to 20 guns,' Hotham recorded. 'During five months they had prepared heated shot and studied every strategem to secure themselves and punish us.'[42] Nonetheless, while the enemy batteries were fully engaged, the sailing ships slipped by with the convoy. Many of the merchant craft were hit several times but in the three and half hours of battle the squadron amazingly incurred no casualties. Hotham's plan had succeeded beyond all expectation. 'This was a pretty affair,' he wrote home, 'and pleased me better than Obligado.'[43] When the Paraná expedition with its merchantmen reached Montevideo later in June 1846, Hotham was greeted by the population almost as a national saviour. The cargoes on the overladen convoy ships were valued at about £500,000. Ouseley believed himself vindicated; he had never lost faith in the expedition nor accepted any of the rebukes which had arrived from London. But the news he had for Hotham would not be welcome. In the latter's absence, and while performing his heroic feats of arms, the British government had abandoned the idea of an armed intervention and was now effectively to leave Montevideo to its fate. Hotham himself was to leave within weeks for a command on the West Africa station.

7· Hood's Mission to La Plata, 1846

'Your long experience and accurate knowledge of the affairs of the river Plate point you out as one who may be eminently useful in contributing to the pacification of those countries.'[1] With this lofty compliment Aberdeen introduced the dispatch of 19 May 1846 which set out his instructions to T.S. Hood. Hood was expected to profit in his dealings with Rosas from his friendship with Manuel Oribe – a friendship which had developed during the latter's presidency of Uruguay. After presenting the new British and French proposals at Buenos Aires and obtaining Rosas' agreement, Hood would travel to the Cerrito and secure agreement from Oribe. Only then was he to introduce himself to Ouseley and Deffaudis and put into their hands the instructions which he carried from the British and French governments requiring the two diplomats to gain the consent of the government in Montevideo to all that Hood had previously agreed with its enemies. It was a measure of Aberdeen's anxiety to disengage from hostilities that the propositions which Hood carried were openly acknowledged as but modifications of terms which Rosas had put forward on 26 October 1845 and which, at that time, had been dismissed out of hand by Britain and France.

In the weeks after Hood left England, however, the state of affairs in Uruguay changed. General Rivera raised a small army of 700 men at Colonia in May 1846 and sailed into the River Uruguay, capturing the town of Las Vacas from Oribe's forces. Advancing farther, he surprised the encampment of one of Oribe's commanders, capturing essential supplies, ammunition and, most prized of all, about 2000 horses. Encouraged by these triumphs, Rivera attacked and took the town of Mercedes on 14 June with similar rewards of stores, cattle and horses and a great quantity of hides and merchantable produce which was sent back to Montevideo. By July Oribe no longer appeared impregnable. His army was suffering desertions on a growing scale; meanwhile, Rivera's forces had grown to 2000 men as he liberated tracts of the country. To Ouseley, of course, all this was evidence of how Oribe's cause was beginning to crumble. Ouseley conceded that there was still about 7000 soldiers at the Cerrito, of whom about 4000 were the Argentine army, but by mid-1846 Oribe had been obliged to pull back his forces from the district of Maldonado and concentrate all his efforts on the campaign at Montevideo. Ouseley lost no time in forwarding to London reports which he had received of how, as they withdrew, Oribe's soldiers burnt the land, poisoned the wells and herded hapless civilians before them.

Beyond these setbacks in the war in Uruguay, by the middle of 1846 Rosas had to balance a variety of other considerations in conducting his diplomacy. Although he derived a wry comfort from the protests of the foreign merchant houses at Buenos Aires against the effects of the Anglo-French blockade, he also knew that it was damaging his own revenues at the port. Since about 90 per cent of the income for the state of Buenos Aires came from port and customs dues, this was a serious matter. Those duties had raised nearly 33 million dollars in 1843, over 29 million dollars in 1844 and almost 28 million dollars in 1845. The total for 1846 was to be 6 million dollars.[2]

Rosas also had to accept that it was futile to expect foreign assistance. He was still keen to play the American card and to present his cause as that of a weak but proudly independent New World republic standing up to aggression and injustice from natural enemies in Europe. In doing so, indeed, there had been initial grounds for optimism. Since the allied intervention had begun in 1845 the Press in Brazil, in much of Spanish America, in Spain and in the United States had evinced sympathy for the Argentine resistance and had roundly condemned the colonial aspirations and bullying tactics of the British and French governments. Alvear had done much in Washington to publish news from La Plata – and to some effect, he assured Tomás Guido on 31 December 1845. 'There is a universal agitation here,' Alvear reported. 'Public opinion here is favourable to us, as is that of the government.'[3]

Secretary of State Buchanan was admittedly unstinting in expressing admiration for the spirited defence of its territory by a sister republic. Both he and President Polk applauded the 'heroic struggle' which Rosas was conducting. Britain and France had violated the principles of international law, Buchanan informed Brent: 'We cordially wish the Argentine Republic success in its struggle against foreign interference.' But the crucial part of Buchanan's message stood out even amid his florid prose: 'existing circumstances render it impossible for the United States to take a part in the present war.'[4] For one thing, the Oregon boundary settlement in the spring of 1846 had improved relations with the British. For another, Polk remained a realist. His ambitions, therefore, were limited to the essential interests of his nation over Texas and the Californias.

Yet these matters for reflection and doubt in Rosas' mind were, to some extent, offset by encouraging signs elsewhere. The resistance shown to the allied squadron in the Paraná was not, of course, the Argentine triumph which the propaganda outlets in Buenos Aires portrayed, but it had focused national consciousness on an external threat and in that way had bolstered Rosas' standing as defender of the Confederation. As Guido astutely observed from Rio de Janeiro, the Argentines did not need to win – they just needed to keep fighting. 'Time is our powerful ally,' he concluded on reading the accounts from Obligado.[5] Another source of inspiration for Rosas was the information coming out of London that Ouseley had fallen foul of his own government. Rosas was assured, correctly, that Aberdeen had disapproved the diversion of the 45th and 73rd regiments into Montevideo and that neither the British nor French government would ever sanction land troops for action in La Plata.[6] Although Rosas had failed with his diplomacy to drive a wedge between Ouseley and Deffaudis, he had good reason to believe that he had succeeded in straining the resolve of the British government.

For Rosas, however, the intervention was not simply an international dispute from which he could extricate himself by means of a negotiated compromise with Britain and France. As both Ouseley and Deffaudis had, of course, immediately recognized, the struggle of the government at Buenos Aires to resist the foreigner was bound up with Rosas' broader struggle to preserve the Confederation of the Argentine states and his own authority within it. The two diplomats were right to see the divisions among the governors of the littoral states and the growing resentment at Rosas' centralized authority as the Achilles' heel of his regime. The expedition into the Paraná and the encouragement which it was intended should be given to Paraguay and to the proponents of independence in Corrientes and in Entre Rios had a sound strategic logic. There was much talk in the 1840s at Montevideo, and within the riparian states of the Paraná and Uruguay, of new structures in the region; some dreamt of a new nation to be created from the territories of Entre Rios, Corrientes, Uruguay, the Rio Grande and perhaps even Paraguay.[7] Such schemes remained in the world of political speculation, but for Rosas they provided an additional threat to the Argentine Confederation beyond the normal aspirations of provincial autonomy.

To succeed in their plan, though, Ouseley and Deffaudis needed support from the man who emerged in 1845 as the new political force in the Argentine – Justo José de Urquiza, Governor of Entre Rios since 1841, and whose loyalty to Rosas since 1843 had been essential to Oribe's campaign in the Banda Oriental.[8] That loyalty was greatly strained by the end of 1845. Many looked to him as a truer federalist than, and a natural successor to, Rosas. Urquiza certainly did little to discourage such notions. Beyond that, he now realized that campaigning with Oribe in Uruguay between 1843 and 1845 had weakened his standing at home. The absence of his Entre Rean army had permitted insurrection once again in nearby Corrientes, where in 1843 the federalist regime was supplanted by Governor Joaquín de Madariaga.

Madariaga had consolidated his hold in Corrientes by handing over command of the army to the talents of General Paz in January 1845. Faced by this threat to his north, and now menaced by the Anglo-French fleet in the Paraná, Urquiza took his leave of Oribe on 10 November 1845 and returned to Entre Rios in the following month. Early in 1846 he again established his power base, having secured his reelection to the governorship on 15 December. He then gained some minor advantages against the invading armies of Corrientes and Paraguay during which he fortuitously captured Madariaga's brother and through whom he sent out feelers for peace. Paz could not be beaten in the field but, equally, the army of Corrientes could never prevail after disputes arose with the allied Paraguayan commanders and, more damaging still, between Paz and Madariaga. Madariaga was tempted by Urquiza's hints at a settlement and in March 1846 Paz's army was effectively taken from him and Paz himself forced into exile.[9] But, to Rosas' disgust, Urquiza was not inclined to press home this military good fortune. Instead, Urquiza seemed content to offer the Argentine states a different vision of federation from that propagated by the regime in Buenos Aires. Urquiza appeared willing to disregard Rosas' wishes and to conduct his own diplomacy with the secessionists in Corrientes.

Ouseley was encouraged by this and, even more so, by the rift which was clearly developing between the two *caudillos*. Ouseley now regarded Urquiza, with his standing army of about 6000 men, as the key to the struggle in La Plata. While the naval expedition was in the

Paraná, Ouseley knew that Urquiza would distance himself as far as he dare from Rosas. Once the Anglo-French squadron returned to the Plate, however, Urquiza's inclinations would be less predictable. It was with particular relief therefore that Ouseley and Deffaudis received political agents from Entre Rios in June 1846 since their presence in Montevideo was taken as a sign of Urquiza's continuing neutrality. Ouseley stressed publicly his inability to concern himself with the internal affairs of Entre Rios or with the political ambitions of its ruler, and declined to enter into direct negotiations with Urquiza. But he assured the latter's representatives that Britain and France sought only peace and commerce with Entre Rios and were in dispute only with the government at Buenos Aires. 'At the same time I did not discourage the idea of a final separation from the Argentine Confederation,' Ouseley confessed.[10] By threat or by persuasion, Urquiza had to be kept west of the Uruguay River, thereby depriving Oribe of this potentially decisive ally.

This had an added urgency now that the British regiments were to be withdrawn from the lines at Montevideo. Unable to postpone their departures any longer, Ouseley finally made arrangements for the 45th regiment to sail on 4 July. The 73rd regiment sailed a fortnight later. All in Montevideo lamented the departure. To take their places and to keep up morale among the citizens, 339 sailors and 311 marines from the British ships were put ashore and Inglefield himself set up a headquarters in the town. Lainé landed 252 French sailors, thus providing a joint force of 902 fighting men from the squadrons. In the meantime British and French warships assisted Rivera's campaign in the countryside as best they could by ferrying his soldiers and supplementing his often meagre military provisions.

Hood had no knowledge of these events, nor did he consider that any developments in the war were pertinent to his mission. He sailed directly to Buenos Aires, arriving off the city on 2 July, and found himself well received by Rosas and Arana. From there, he wrote to Ouseley requesting that arrangements should be made for warships to carry him wherever he wished to go and to provide safe and unhindered passage; in the meantime, he insisted, the two admirals 'must take for granted what I am not now at liberty to explain'.[11] Ouseley knew little of Hood's mission. Not until 15 July did Aberdeen's dispatch of 19 May reach him, which only stated that Hood came to La Plata with the full authority of the British and French governments to put proposals to the government at Buenos Aires and that, after securing agreement, Hood would deliver these terms to the two Ministers for presentation to the government in Montevideo. This manner of proceeding was hardly calculated to flatter Ouseley's sense of dignity, although the tone of Aberdeen's correspondence in recent months should have prepared Ouseley for that. As wounding to Ouseley's pride was Aberdeen's assumption that Ouseley was now required to present what was in effect an ultimatum to the Uruguayan government. Whatever terms Hood agreed with Rosas were not afterwards negotiable. If the Uruguayans accepted them, then peace was restored on conditions imposed by others. If they rejected them, then Ouseley and Deffaudis were at once to declare that the intervention by Britain and France was at an end and that its failure was the fault of the Uruguayan authorities who alone would be responsible for the consequences.

The propositions which Hood handed to Arana on 6 July 1846 were intended to bring an immediate end to hostilities at Montevideo and to establish a timetable for the withdrawal of all foreign participation in Uruguayan affairs. An armistice was to be declared and, once enforced, Britain and France would request the disarming of all the foreign legions in Montevideo. Simultaneous with this disarming of all foreigners inside the city, Rosas would withdraw his troops back into Argentine territory. Immediately after this the British and French navies would raise the blockade of Buenos Aires, evacuate Martín García and repair and return all captured Argentine warships while saluting the flag of the republic in the process. Britain and France would concede that the Paraná was an inland waterway subject only to Argentine laws and regulations. They would concede also Argentine rights of belligerency as a sovereign power, thereby acknowledging the shaky base under the laws of nations for the allied intervention. In return, Rosas and Oribe were to declare that they would abide by the results of a free election to the presidency to be held in Uruguay as soon as the armed foreign presence in the country had ended. Finally, a general and complete amnesty in Uruguay would be proclaimed under which the lives and property of natives and foreigners alike were to be respected and all lawful claims upheld regardless of past political loyalties.

Arana could give no reply to all this. Two weeks later, indeed, Hood was still waiting in Buenos Aires for a response, but in his meetings with the Foreign Minister he found the Argentine position encouraging and conciliatory. Arana told him on 17 July that some British and

French merchant vessels still stranded in the Paraná would be allowed to pass unmolested down river and that even warships in the river would no longer be fired upon by Argentine batteries unless in self-defence. With such peaceful sentiments expressed, Hood wrote to Ouseley, the time had surely come to reciprocate by ordering all warships to keep out of the Paraná. Two more weeks passed, however, before Hood received the news for which he had been waiting: the Argentine Confederation officially accepted the British and French propositions. Hood at once boarded his warship waiting off Buenos Aires and sailed for Montevideo. The original plan to go directly to Oribe's camp at the Cerrito had to be abandoned as a safe route was not obvious. Ouseley, Deffaudis, the two admirals and the government in Montevideo all agreed that Hood should be put ashore at Buceo, where he would not be in danger from the fighting around the capital. Hood reached the Cerrito on 2 August. He remained there for two further weeks during which time Oribe's acceptance of the Anglo-French propositions was also received. 'The principal object of my mission has been fully and I hope satisfactorily accomplished,' he wrote to Aberdeen on 13 August.[12] Now he would go back to Montevideo and present the two diplomats with their instructions on how to complete the task.

Hood was not so naive as to believe that success could be quite this simple. In fact neither he nor Aberdeen had anticipated any great difficulties with Rosas and Oribe. The real problem was how his mission would be received at Montevideo. Inside the city news of Hood's visit to Buenos Aires gave rise to the gravest alarm. Hood's affinity with Oribe was public knowledge and he therefore lacked any credibility as an impartial negotiator. The Consul-General advised Aberdeen on 13 July that regardless of the terms arranged, the foreigners in the city would never allow Oribe to enter peacefully; their land, possessions and their lives would not be safe if he returned to power. Two thousand Spanish Basques in Montevideo had begun arming themselves. They would join the other foreign legions, now estimated at 4000-strong, and deserters from Oribe's army who had taken refuge in the city. Rumours of what Hood might have proposed to the Argentine government made matters even worse. It was believed that the British and French governments were about to recognize Oribe as legal President without any election and that he would be allowed to enter Montevideo at the head of his Argentine army, who would then begin a search for all Rosas' political opponents in exile. Commercial life in the city was paralysed by this latest collapse of morale and the merchant community were again enquiring how best they could leave or at least protect their property. Deffaudis observed that before Hood's arrival Montevideo had been well on the road to economic recovery. In streets damaged by fighting, buildings were being repaired and the arrival of so many cargoes from the Paraná had brought work again for the labouring classes in the port and warehouses.[13] The confidence born of this, and of the belief that the tide of war had turned against Oribe, was now shattered by Hood's mission and the betrayal of the Uruguayan cause by Britain and France which it seemed to represent. Ouseley and Deffaudis could scarcely fail to be moved by the plight of the beleaguered population all around them. But beyond that, as Hood was well aware, the two Ministers had their own reasons for resenting his arrival. Although they could not overtly oppose his mission, nonetheless they would do their best to undermine it.

Ouseley publicly declared his willingness to cooperate with Hood. To Inglefield he wrote that it was their duty to assist Hood to carry out the wishes of their government. But his indignation that a man previously of only consular rank should be Aberdeen's medium for public disavowal and that he, as an accredited Minister Plenipotentiary, should be kept in ignorance of Hood's proceedings could not be disguised. In subsequent communications with Hood his tone became distant. To Aberdeen he wrote privately about Hood's movements in La Plata and pointedly apologized for troubling the Foreign Secretary 'upon a subject that it is evident you did not intend to mention to me'.[14] Deffaudis was equally frank. Guizot had not favoured him with any warning of Hood's arrival nor one word as to the object of the mission; he had been left like an augur of ancient Rome, he complained, to divine the intentions of his government in Paris.

It was Hood's letter recommending the removal of all warships from the Paraná which first provoked the two diplomats into a display of defiance. Deffaudis told Ouseley that he did not consider that Hood had the authority to advise on such a matter. Ouseley was more than happy to notify Hood that he had no option but to act fully in conformity with his French colleague. Hood wrote at once to London of his 'apprehensions of opposition from Mr. Ouseley and the Baron Deffaudis'.[15] As yet there had been little opportunity for opposition, since Hood had not presented the two Ministers with their instructions from Europe and they still knew nothing of his negotiations. But they were further incensed when Hood hoisted the Union Jack over the building in which he stayed at the Cerrito, which not only gave Oribe an implicit political recognition but also meant, according to Ouseley, that the Montevideans risked firing on the British flag in the course of the continuing fighting.

Of course, Ouseley and Deffaudis were right to be suspicious of Hood. He was not in La Plata on a fact-finding mission but had been sent, in the light of his former intimacy with Oribe, to rescue the British government from an international embarrassment. Hood arrived with fixed ideas about the factions in Uruguay: his first report on the condition of Montevideo was written three weeks before he even set foot there. The city, he judged from accounts, was 'a perfect Pandemonium'; party strife and personal rivalry were all-consuming in its politics.[16] Fixed in Hood's mind, too, were the notions that Deffaudis and French interests were the true obstacle to peace in the region, that the French would never make a settlement with Rosas on any terms and that Ouseley would consistently support French intrigues on the pretext of acting in concert with his French colleague. Hood's task, of course, was to make terms only with one side in the conflict: he was not charged to find common ground or a compromise acceptable to all parties. It was his firm opinion that the ordinary citizens of Montevideo wanted peace on any terms and were frustrated in this end only by the venal regime which governed them – a regime fully supported, indeed kept in power, by the British and French intervention. 'I am disgusted and sick of everything connected with our intervention and the way it is conducted,' he informed Aberdeen late in August 1846. In Montevideo 'there is really no other government here than Mr. Ouseley and the Baron Deffaudis; everything is done by their consent.'[17] Hood and the two diplomats approached the war in La Plata from irreconcilable perspectives from the outset. Once Hood presented himself and his peace terms at Montevideo on 15 August, however, the gap between them was no longer one simply of initial standpoints but now enlarged by the result of his weeks of secret negotiation.

On examining the outcome of Hood's meetings with Rosas and Oribe, Ouseley and Deffaudis were at once confirmed in their suspicion that the terms agreed were quite unacceptable. They declared that Hood had exceeded the limits of the concessions which the propositions of the British and French governments had authorized. First, he had not gained Oribe's own signature to the agreement but merely that of one of his political supporters acting in the guise of a Minister of Foreign Affairs, as if in a recognized government. This not only pandered to Oribe's pretensions as legal President but made commitments undertaken on his part less binding, and therefore even less reassuring to the population inside Montevideo for whose benefit they were intended. More significantly, though, Hood had agreed to lift the blockade of Buenos Aires simultaneously with the declaration of an armistice. No wonder, Deffaudis and Ouseley exclaimed, he had encountered no Argentine resistance. Proposition number four clearly stated that 'immediately after the foreign legion and other foreigners in Montevideo shall have been disarmed, and the Argentine troops withdrawn from the Oriental Republic, the blockade of Buenos Aires shall be raised.'[18] If the blockade was now to be lifted before Rosas withdrew his troops, then all remaining leverage on him to honour the peace agreement had been given away. Hood claimed that he had authorization to make this change. The two Ministers merely informed him that they did not recognize his mission as completed since he had failed to gain Argentine agreement to the original proposals – which was the sole purpose of his coming to La Plata. Ouseley wrote to Hood on 22 August stating that the Ministers hoped Hood would return to Buenos Aires and this time make it plain to Rosas that modifications to the propositions were not on offer and that the Argentine government and Oribe must accept them as they originally stood. Hood agreed to go back, but it was obvious even to him that his mission was by now in serious trouble.

* * *

In London, Palmerston knew nothing of Hood's progress. On returning to the Foreign Office on 6 July 1846 he approved Hood's mission and, like Aberdeen, hoped for a rapid withdrawal from the intervention. He did not wish to contradict anything that Aberdeen had written Ouseley in the weeks before July; on the contrary, a firmer hand was needed to bring both Ouseley and the navy under control. The same pressures which had convinced his predecessor that the policy in La Plata had proved an error found Palmerston equally amenable to persuasion. The association of merchants trading in the region warned Palmerston that the intervention was bound to end in failure and, of course, with further and immense damage to trade. All this was considered to be obvious at the Foreign Office by July 1846.

However, since Hood was already at Buenos Aires, Palmerston needed to take no fresh initiative but just to wait for what he hoped would be good news. Of more concern to him was the way in which British naval officers were acting, both in their support for the Montevidean authorities and in their conduct of the blockade of Buenos Aires. The navy had been sent to the River Plate to provide leverage for stopping the war – not to engage in operations which extended it further. Even among the naval commanders there were serious doubts. One of them wrote home after the battle at Obligado: 'I am sure the affair here must please at the Admiralty. How the policy will be relished at the Foreign Office I do not venture to surmise.'[19]

Palmerston's return to the Foreign Office in fact coincided with news of a number of naval indiscretions. First, at Buenos Aires where neutral merchant shipping was being captured without any adjudication as lawful prizes by a properly constituted Court of Admiralty. Secondly, at the nearby port of Ensenada where, on 21 April 1846, British and French boats had destroyed five Argentine merchant ships at their moorings. Inglefield and Lainé knew that their blockade orders of October 1845 did not permit such an operation and attributed it to an 'excess of zeal' by one of the British commanders.[20] Palmerston, unfortunately, was in no mood to turn a blind eye. The action at Ensenada was, he told the Admiralty, 'wholly unjustifiable, entirely illegal, and for which a serious responsibility will attach'.[21] Not only that, but the whole blockade of the Buenos Aires coastline was of questionable legality, Palmerston continued. Britain and France were not at war with the Argentine Confederation, nor had they sustained injuries at the hands of the government at Buenos Aires which would justify interference with neutral shipping. Orders were later sent to the commander on the Brazil station making perfectly clear that, in future, he should abstain from any aggressive operations against Argentine territory and that he should confine his actions to what was strictly necessary for the protection of British subjects, their property and commerce.

While Palmerston took matters in hand in London, Hood continued his efforts to gain acceptance for his propositions. By August 1846 he was resigned to the fact that Ouseley and Deffaudis between them might well succeed in wrecking his peace mission. His relations with them became accordingly ever more strained. 'I never can get Mr. Ouseley to listen to anything about my mission,' Hood wrote to Aberdeen.[22] Ouseley's stock response to all Hood's remonstrances was that the Foreign Secretary could not possibly know what measures were required in La Plata and that the instructions which Hood had been given were based therefore on a misunderstanding of the true situation. Deffaudis and Ouseley took a quite different view of the propositions from that which their governments had intended, Hood continued: 'They see difficulties, or create them, at every step.'[23] Not only did they insist on Oribe's own signature and on the strict order of disengagement whereby the Argentine troops should leave Uruguay before the blockade on Buenos Aires was lifted, but the two Ministers also specified that any convention must include the government of Montevideo as a party and could not simply be an arrangement between Rosas, Oribe and the European powers. Everyone knew, of course, that neither Rosas nor Oribe would ever give such recognition as a legally constituted government to the defenders of Montevideo.

The return to Buenos Aires proved, as Hood had predicted, a disaster. At his first meeting with Arana, Hood was made to feel the absurdity of his position – withdrawing a modification to the original propositions to which he had previously agreed. Hood tried to justify the need for this by explaining the breakdown of communication between Deffaudis and his government in Paris. But Arana would have none of it; he would consent to a simultaneous lifting of the blockade with the declaration of an armistice but to nothing more. Back in Montevideo on 8 September, Hood received a note from Ouseley informing him that since the Argentine government had refused to accept the Anglo-French propositions as originally submitted, the two Ministers now regarded his mission as ended. Deffaudis made it known that he would in future decline any communication with Hood, and Ouseley, to keep faith with his instructions to work at all times with the French envoy, therefore told Hood that he too must terminate all correspondence in the matter of the intervention. The Argentine rejection, he concluded, precluded all hope of settling present difficulties and was greatly to be contrasted with the willingness shown by the authorities in Montevideo to accept in their entirety the propositions in the original form on 27 August. Hood's two months of negotiations had come to nothing. His efforts thwarted, and his government's desire for peace frustrated, Hood wrote to Palmerston on 13 September expressing the hope that he would not be blamed. He had acted according to the powers vested in him 'and as far as the Earl of Aberdeen intended I should act'.[24] This said, and with no object in remaining, he sailed for England and looked forward to the chance to explain in person the reasons for his failure.

As Hood blamed his lack of success on the behaviour of Ouseley and Deffaudis, so Ouseley had no hesitation in recounting Hood's inadequacies for the task entrusted to him. First, he impugned Hood's standing as a disinterested public servant. Hood had ties with four commercial houses in Montevideo, and perhaps two more at Buenos Aires, all of which derived their profits from trade conducted under favours bestowed by the regime of Rosas. Second, Hood had gone directly to Buenos Aires ignorant of the true state of affairs in the Banda Oriental. For this reason, too, he was prejudiced in favour of Oribe. Hood had believed that the majority of the Uruguayan population were sympathetic to Oribe. He had also accepted that British commercial houses were being damaged by the blockade at Buenos Aires. Both these assumptions were fundamentally wrong, Ouseley reported. The gaucho population of the interior, and most of Montevideo, were fiercely resistant to Oribe's return. As for British traders in La Plata, the warehouses in Montevideo were piled high with merchandise awaiting shipment to Europe. Ships bringing British exports to the region could easily transfer cargoes to coastal vessels for conveyance to markets on the Paraná River and to the smaller ports and inlets along the Uruguayan coastline. The fallacies upon which Hood based his judgments thus made it impossible to have confidence in him.

A week later Ouseley wrote to Palmerston in a somewhat harsher tone: 'It is my duty earnestly to caution Your Lordship against the exaggerated and *ex parte* statements of Mr. Hood; doubtless deceived by his own warm predilections, unaware of the great changes that a few years have effected in these states, and purposely misled by false statements of Generals Rosas and Oribe, his reports must be received with great caution.'[25] The solution was, of course: 'Your Lordship must therefore be informed faithfully of all by me.'[26] Hood's verbal assertions as to the present views of the British and French governments differed so greatly from those contained in the written instructions sent to the two Ministers that Ouseley and Deffaudis could do nothing but refer all points of issue back to Europe. But it was not simply Hood's opinions and his bias which had rendered him unfit for his duties. His behaviour, as Ouseley frequently commented, was also such as to antagonize all those with whom he most needed to work. The style of his correspondence was dictatorial; his manner in conversation was too often insulting. Captain Hotham had witnessed Hood's conduct too, and in the rift with Ouseley he clearly took the latter's side. 'Should the negotiation fail I am sure the blame will not be with Mr. Ouseley,' he confided to a friend at the Admiralty. Both Ouseley and Deffaudis had 'borne with treatment from Mr. Hood which, to say the least, has been anything but courteous. I understand that Hood complains of incivility from the French: he cannot say so of the English.'[27]

A further charge against Hood was that he made no effort to disguise his partisan feelings. At the Cerrito he had acknowledged Oribe as President of Uruguay and had promised him an entry into Montevideo without the need for fresh elections. In his communications with Oribe from on board a British warship Hood had used small Argentine vessels to penetrate the blockade of Oribe's supply ports – a needless and provocative measure which Ouseley deplored since Hood knew perfectly well that a flag of truce was available to him at all times under which his mission could be safely conducted. On one occasion at Ouseley's house in Montevideo this had led to a sharp exchange between Hood and some British and French naval officers. Furthermore, during his time at Montevideo Hood made no effort to make any contact with officials of the government, refusing thereby to acknowledge its legitimacy despite the fact that British diplomatic and consular staff were properly accredited to it. Arrogance and presumption as to his powers of discretion had coloured all that he had done – not only in all these respects, Ouseley regretted, but even more significantly in the way in which he had behaved towards, and indeed grossly offended, French allies.

Hood was blatantly distrustful of the French, and of Deffaudis in particular. Ouseley in fact complained to Palmerston about Hood's 'violent anti-Gallican prejudices'. Inglefield remonstrated with Hood to curb unguarded and intemperate expressions: with a large and volatile French community in Montevideo, and French warships in the vicinity, this was not the time for sowing discord and poisoning relations. But Hood replied, according to Ouseley, that the sooner the French knew that Britain must one day be at war with them, the better. At Buenos Aires, and with Oribe, Hood's hostility to French interests had been freely expressed and his indiscreet language had quickly reached the ears of French diplomats. On 12 September, as Hood was departing for England, Ouseley reflected on the damage done to Anglo-French relations by Hood's presence at Montevideo: 'If we are not to quarrel with the French, Mr. Hood must not return under authority to La Plata.'[28]

Most biting of all Ouseley's indictments of Hood, though, was that of sheer incompetence as a negotiator. Hood might conceivably have gained acceptance of the British and French propositions in their original and intended form, Ouseley considered, had he not crassly made it known to Rosas at the outset that he would accept a modification in respect of lifting the blockade before an Argentine troop withdrawal. This done, Rosas and Oribe simply insisted that lifting the blockade on the declaration of an armistice was *sine qua non* for any agreement. Hood claimed that he carried secret instructions from Aberdeen but, Ouseley never tired of remarking, since these were not shown to the two Ministers they had no way of knowing whether Hood was authorized to make modifications to the propositions and had no option but to assume that he was not. 'The line that I have endeavoured to follow is that expressly pointed out in repeated written communications,' Ouseley reassured the Foreign Secretary.[29] Nothing had arrived from London or Paris to indicate that anything else was required.

Poor as Hood's negotiating strategy may have been, there was no real chance of persuading Rosas to accept the propositions in their unmodified state. Rosas could not, and would not, withdraw his troops before Oribe was back in the presidency; at the same time, until the last Argentine soldiers had crossed the River Uruguay it was absurd to expect the garrison in Montevideo and the foreign legions there to lay down their arms. Inglefield was pessimistic even before the terms of Hood's proposals were announced. Hotham likewise saw no diplomatic solution to the conflict: 'Simple as Mr. Hood's mission might appear we on the spot perceive difficulties almost insuperable,' he confided.[30] Neither side in the war was ever likely to reject the propositions outright. As Hotham well understood, 'it was the interest of both parties to place themselves well with the European governments and to throw upon its rival the obloquy of the failure.'[31] Simple military facts weighed against successful implementation of the terms on offer. How could Oribe ever agree to the withdrawal of his Argentine supporters and to a general disarming of all foreigners in the Banda Oriental? He did not have even 1500 authentic Uruguayan soldiers in his army, Hotham estimated, and would not outnumber the native troops defending Montevideo. The original proposals offered Rosas little more than the opportunity to admit defeat; Hood, by modifying them, gave Rosas the chance of victory but in the process wrecked the mission by evoking the implacable hostility of Ouseley and Deffaudis. In truth, neither Rosas nor the two diplomats yet felt that they were beaten.

The events of mid-1846 had done nothing to alter the views of Inglefield either, who remained a firm supporter of the position taken by Ouseley and Deffaudis and who rejected Aberdeen's reproach that his squadron had become too involved with the Montevidean cause. It was not possible, he wrote to the Admiralty, to defend British life and property in the city without defending much of the city itself. Furthermore, none of the early actions by the navy had been disavowed in London. 'Her Majesty's Government had approved of powder being supplied to the Montevideans from the squadron without which supply the town must have fallen; the same approval had also been extended to the detention of the Buenos Airean squadron,' he reminded the Admiralty, 'and to the *forcible* transfer of Colonia and Martín García to the Montevidean government. Blockades were established and likewise approved of.'[32] It was his duty to see this policy through to its end. His government having declared in favour of Uruguayan independence, it was his obligation as a naval commander to ensure that Britain's national honour was upheld and that the foreign army on Uruguayan soil was not triumphant. Since May 1845 Inglefield's willingness to interpret all instructions in the loosest sense possible had been crucial to Ouseley's ability to follow the line of policy which he and his French colleague had taken. It was, of course, precisely this scope for individuals misconstruing the wishes of the government which Palmerston was determined to bring to an end.

But if Inglefield was unshaken in his convictions by Hood's mission, Ouseley was even less moved by the experience of the past two months. Up to the moment that he heard of the change of government in London he maintained in his correspondence with Aberdeen that he had done nothing outside the latitude of his instructions. With feigned indignation, Ouseley deeply regretted Aberdeen's suggestion that he had persevered in disregarding clear instructions or had misinterpreted, wilfully or otherwise, the objects of the Anglo-French mediation. He and Deffaudis had never lost sight of the great end for which they laboured, which was peace, not war. But both believed, with the advantage of local knowledge, that the only way to peace was through a vigorous campaign against Rosas and his whole regime. Their contacts with the opponents of Rosas in the interior were not, as Aberdeen had reproached him, meddling in another nation's internal affairs. The Argentine Confederation, he rejoined, was but a loose assemblage of separate states in which no one held sovereignty over any other: there was no federal authority acknowledged in a settled constitution and only Rosas pretended otherwise in claiming for himself dictatorial powers. As for Aberdeen's abhorrence of a war with Buenos Aires, the cost of such would amply be repaid by the opportunities for commerce which would be opened up throughout the region by Rosas' political demise. Territories alongside the tributaries of the Plate would gain access to European trade to the betterment and prosperity of all concerned. 'I hope to be pardoned for stating my conviction, confirmed by the events of the last few months,' Ouseley defiantly proclaimed, 'that had the recommendations which Baron Deffaudis and myself conscientiously made to our governments been promptly acted upon the object of the allied powers as relates to the expulsion of the Argentine troops and the independence of the Banda Oriental would have been attained.'[33] September 6 brought fresh hope for Ouseley. News of a new chief at the Foreign Office meant an unexpected second opportunity to convince his government that he had been right all along.

8· Ouseley Continues the War, 1846–7

By the end of 1846 the weight of opinion reaching the Foreign Office from chambers of commerce, manufacturers and merchant houses undoubtedly condemned the armed intervention and the concomitant disruption of economic activity throughout La Plata. But commercial opinion was not unanimous. Ouseley had supporters, especially among the 32 British trading firms established at Montevideo. Of these, most could also boast interests at Buenos Aires; when they clamoured for a vigorous defence of Uruguayan independence against the Argentine invasion they claimed, therefore, a neutral stance and an interest in the economic potential of the region as a whole. In reality, of course, most of the merchant houses in Montevideo were compromised by their involvement with the authorities there, and in particular by their contributions to government loans in previous years.

Faced with the cost of war in 1842, the Uruguayan government had raised the standard import duty and also introduced a special levy of 8 per cent as a war tax charged essentially upon the foreign trading houses. The government applied pressure on the merchant community again in 1843 in order to gain some further advances. These measures, however, proved insufficient to meet the government's mounting expenditure. In 1843 the government therefore obtained the assent of the legislative assembly to raise a loan of 500,000 dollars (£100,000) secured by the sale of a portion of the customs receipts for the following year.[1] Still more was needed. Ouseley and Deffaudis thus actually encouraged the merchants to take up the new 300,000 dollar loan of 1845 by promising that diplomatic efforts would be made to ensure repayment. As substantial creditors of the regime, the merchants inevitably saw their only hope of debt recovery in a successful conclusion to the war brought about by Anglo-French participation. In May 1846 the British merchants and residents in Montevideo therefore petitioned Ouseley in favour of continuing the intervention and in particular begged the British and French envoys to provide the garrison in the city with more essential supplies.

Ouseley's arguments towards the end of 1846 for sticking to the intervention policy were inevitably a mixture of what he really believed and what he thought might now most influence Palmerston. First of all, there was no alternative if Uruguay was to be safeguarded and Rosas' expansionary schemes thwarted. Great damage would be done to Britain's political standing in the Americas, he warned, if the principle of Uruguayan independence was abandoned. Secondly, there was the issue of relations with France: not only would his own position with Deffaudis be awkward if Britain withdrew unilaterally from combined operations, but the government in Paris would also rightly consider itself deserted by such an act of bad faith. More than that, what would French policy in La Plata be if France were left alone? A withdrawal by Britain from the intervention, Ouseley pointed out, in no way meant the end of France's involvement. The French government would not be able to abandon the thousands of French citizens both in Montevideo and settled in its hinterland. Ouseley raised the spectre of a ministry in Paris led by politicians who might be determined to court popularity by a blatant anti-English stance, and to pander to the worst expressions of nationalist sentiment by advocating a strong assertion of French rights and interests without any heed as to the consequences. French troops and warships would then be free to conduct war against Buenos Aires, in the course of which British commerce would be all but eradicated. With Montevideo occupied by regular French forces and with the influence of the volunteer French legion stronger than ever, the government in Montevideo would be reduced to the status of a puppet, unable to end the war by negotiation even if it wished to do so. The Banda Oriental, for the independence of which the intervention had been devised, might in the end become a victim of French colonial ambitions.

Unfortunately for Ouseley, his ability to control events on the spot steadily diminished towards the end of 1846 and early in 1847. One factor in this was the latest instructions which the Admiralty had sent to Inglefield, which were followed by the decision to replace him, as of 9 November, with a new commander on the Brazil station. To the end of his service in South America Inglefield supported, and was guided by, Ouseley. His successor, Captain Sir Thomas Herbert,[2] proved far less pliable and indeed brought more specific orders from London which, as Ouseley declared on reading them, left absolutely no doubt that 'it is clearly the wish and intention of Her Majesty's Government to withdraw from the joint intervention at the earliest possible moment.'³ 'He tells me that he is *not* to act in concert with the French, nor to take directions from me,' Ouseley observed. 'I am thus relieved from any responsibility arising out of the movements of the squadron.'⁴

A further problem for Ouseley was the change in the consulate at Montevideo. Until mid-1846, first Dale and then Turner had been strong advocates of the intervention and much in favour of naval operations. At the end of June 1846 Martin Hood was appointed as acting Consul-General. Martin Hood was the son of T.S. Hood, whose peace mission to La Plata Ouseley had done so much to discredit. The two men were soon at loggerheads as Hood resurrected past complaints against the Montevidean government to which Ouseley and Deffaudis had always turned a blind eye. One issue was the way in which General Rivera had pressed British residents at Las Vacas into military service for the town's defence, while his own Uruguayan soldiers went off into the interior in search of supplies and cattle. Sensing the futility of protesting to Ouseley, these British subjects had in the past accepted their fate with resignation. To a new and sympathetic consul, however, they remonstrated loudly and young Hood assured them, in reply, that they could not be compelled to bear arms in a foreign war. Ouseley reproached Hood for taking up the cases. Foreign residents commonly performed 'urban service' on the streets of the capital and Ouseley saw no irregularity at Las Vacas nor any reason to raise the matter with the Uruguayan government.⁵ But Hood refused to leave it there. This was military service and not street patrol duty, the consul insisted. Since Las Vacas had been abandoned by Rivera's forces, by what right could foreigners be obliged to defend it against attack? Writing to the Foreign Office in December 1846, Hood pointed out that such practices were not confined to Las Vacas. 'There is not one town on the whole coast of the Uruguay which is at present garrisoned by troops belonging to General Rivera: he has removed from them every disposable force and then he has compelled the foreigners to take up arms and defend the towns, making them mount guard on the fortifications.'⁶ Hood dismissed Ouseley's excuses on behalf of the Uruguayan government. By condoning such flagrant breaches of the rights of foreign subjects, Ouseley placed British lives in great peril. Men could not claim to be neutrals in a war when they fought on one side; if Oribe's army captured towns which had, in effect, been defended by Englishmen then the latter could expect little mercy as vanquished belligerents.

Martin Hood similarly exposed Ouseley's improper silence about the way in which British and French marines and sailors were being used on the lines at Montevideo. They were not simply protecting those quarters of the city in which the large foreign community lived and conducted their businesses, as Ouseley and Inglefield had so often argued. Between June and November 1846 Rivera had weakened the garrison by 1000 men in order to continue his operations inland; this was hard to justify on any military grounds save that it drew the British and French servicemen ashore into assuming a greater responsibility for holding the town. A strong sense of duty required that all this be reported, Hood wrote to Palmerston. Whether duty or family vendetta, the effect was that by early 1847 Ouseley's credibility was irrevocably damaged.

A third consideration which greatly weakened Ouseley's ability to control events was the progress of the war itself. Before July 1846 the Montevidean cause had been reviving. Minor military successes had both boosted confidence in the city and enabled the Uruguayan forces to regain the initiative. By the new year, however, the tide of the war had turned once more. Ouseley was adamant that T.S. Hood's negotiations had given Oribe time to resupply his forces and to prepare an expedition from the Cerrito to find and destroy Rivera's army in the interior. Rivera, meanwhile, having left Las Vacas, moved farther up river to the town of Paysandu, and on 26 December commenced an action from which there were to be serious repercussions. After a five-hour bombardment from two French warships in the River Uruguay, Rivera's soldiers and a column of French sailors attacked the town and forced a surrender. Once inside, the victors ran amok, killing, looting and, in the process, murdering a large number of prisoners taken. After two days of bloodshed, the Montevidean forces abandoned the ruins of Paysandu when reports arrived that a large part of Oribe's army was nearby. The reports were accurate. The remains of Rivera's ill-disciplined army were finally caught at el Cerro de las Animas, Where Rivera himself was fortunate to escape with his life. Now in all Uruguay, only Colonia and Maldonado, with their British and French garrisons, were still under the control of the beleaguered government in Montevideo.

For Ouseley the rout in the upper Uruguay was a crushing setback. As Martin Hood observed at the end of January 1847, Rivera's cause 'is lost forever, and that cannot but be confessed by Ouseley and Deffaudis.'[7] But the manner of Rivera's passing was also important.

The rampage by his followers at Paysandu was a propaganda disaster which could never be explained away, and which Hood and Herbert described fully in their dispatches to London as indicating the unworthiness of the Montevidean regime to receive any further British support. Worse still, it appeared to have moved General Urquiza in Entre Rios to renounce his neutrality and reenter the war on the side of Rosas and Oribe – something, of course, which since the end of 1845 Ouseley and Deffaudis had tried to avoid. Urquiza's breach with Rosas had naturally been a source of great encouragement for the Uruguayan government. In August the rift had seemed complete when, quite contrary to Arana's directives, Urquiza signed the treaty of Alcaraz with the Madariaga government in Corrientes which, in effect, exempted the state of Corrientes from its obligations under the federal pact of 1831. Towards the end of 1846 Urquiza had taken a further step of defiance: he offered his mediation to the warring parties in Uruguay, thereby distancing himself from Oribe, recognizing *de facto* the regime in Montevideo, and usurping Rosas' authority to conduct foreign relations on behalf of all the states of the Confederation. After the sack of Paysandu by a largely foreign army supported by foreign warships, Urquiza withdrew this mediation offer and thus left the Montevideans once again facing a united Argentine challenge.

With these different and apparently insuperable obstacles to the defence of the Uruguayan republic, by early 1847 Ouseley's only hope of continuing an effective intervention with the French lay with a change of heart in London in response to his impassioned appeals. That, however, was not realistic. The pressures which had worked on Aberdeen to end military involvement and to send T.S. Hood to find a settlement had intensified in the months since Palmerston's return to office. Merchant houses continued to complain of the damage which the blockade at Buenos Aires inflicted on their business and British manufacturers were still denied access to their markets. Hides and other produce from the Pampas were still in storage on the quayside and diminishing every day in value. An annual trade worth about £2 million was thereby stopped, Palmerston was reminded by a petition from London merchants. The commercial lobby had placed its faith in T.S. Hood's trip to Buenos Aires as an earnest of the resolve of the British government to end such a deplorable state of affairs. Now that Hood had failed, Palmerston was left in no doubt that a new initiative was expected.

One hundred merchants, bankers and manufacturers from Glasgow urged the Foreign Office to heed a letter to *The Times* on 30 December 1846 calling for an end to the intervention. Fifty Manchester merchants demanded a return to unrestricted commerce in La Plata. Forty Midlands manufacturers from Nottingham, Derby, Belper and other industrial centres likewise urged an end to the blockade and to the damage it was doing to their communities. From Liverpool, whose traders had led the campaign against government policy since the autumn of 1845, came fresh intelligence about the seizure of cargoes, almost at random, both by British warships acting on behalf of the Uruguayan authorities and by armed vessels of the Montevidean flotilla. These acts were little less than piracy. Such seizures were often for the personal gain of Montevidean commanders; they were, however, invariably acquiesced in by Ouseley and Deffaudis as a desperate means of financing and supplying the war effort. 'If these or other vessels carrying on the trade are molested who have we to complain of but the late Government?', the Liverpool house of Nicholson, Green & Company enquired of Palmerston. The British government had 'interfered in the domestic quarrels of these countries which but for intervention would long since have settled their own differences and we should have been at peace ere this, whereas now we see no end to our troubles and losses.'[8] On top of this came further representations from the Admiralty, which by the winter of 1846-7 wanted a quick end to operations in the south Atlantic.

From among Ouseley's arguments to justify the intervention only one touched Palmerston – the problem with the French. The rest, Palmerston had either heard before or dismissed as the ramblings of a wayward envoy. A unilateral withdrawal from the intervention which left the French free to act alone as belligerents might indeed have serious consequences; Palmerston thus acknowledged that an intervention jointly entered into must be jointly ended. The Earl of Auckland, First Lord of the Admiralty in November 1846, confided to his friend Hotham just how serious this worry about French intentions was now within the government: 'If it were not for this consideration there could be little doubt of our at once withdrawing our force.'[9] Palmerston became still more wary as doubts grew about Guizot's honesty at the time of Hood's peace mission. In November 1846 it transpired that Guizot might not have sent the instructions to Deffaudis, which he had assured Aberdeen would be sent, authorizing the acceptance of Hood's modified propositions. When asked frankly by Lord

Normanby, the new British ambassador in Paris, if this was so, Guizot was evasive and replied only that he could not remember but would institute enquiries in his office. Two months later Normanby confirmed that Deffaudis did not receive any instructions to accept Hood's terms until after the mission had already failed – as a result largely, of course, of Deffaudis' own opposition to it. Palmerston left no doubt as to his view: 'I am not without suspicion that some of the people in and about the French government who are strong for Deffaudis and Montevideo would wish to shape our proceedings and to make them fail.' 'We must have our eyes open to this,' he cautioned Normanby. 'We have a strong commercial interest in getting rid of the blockade; the French have no great interest about it one way or another.'[10]

Although he needed an agreement with Guizot which would end British and French intervention simultaneously, Palmerston's willingness to work with France was at best grudging. Throughout the years of Tory government since 1841, he had sniped at Aberdeen's policy of cooperation with Guizot both in his parliamentary speeches and in his loyal mouthpiece among the Press, the *Morning Chronicle*. It was inconceivable, therefore, that he would do anything after 1846 to revitalize Aberdeen's concept of *entente*. In fact, Palmerston did not even inherit a functioning relationship with the French. During the last year of Peel's administration Aberdeen had been isolated in believing that cooperation with Guizot was either possible or beneficial – so much so that he had offered to resign in September 1845, only to be told by Peel that the government was too weak to carry on without him. For the first half of 1846 Aberdeen and Guizot had merely kept up the pretence of a diplomatic understanding; neither had wished publicly to admit that their collaboration went no further than private correspondence.

In Paris, Guizot too had found himself increasingly alone in expressing any willingness for an Anglo-French accommodation. For much of 1846 he battled with a hostile Chamber where any mention of *entente* at once reduced his government's majority to a negligible margin. Moreover, the reappointment of Palmerston to the Foreign Office soon removed all restraints on the expression of Anglophobe emotions. Guizot's estrangement from London was highlighted by Normanby's arrival as ambassador in August 1846. Normanby was a prominent Whig aristocrat and a friend of the new Prime Minister, Lord John Russell. He knew little of French politics, had no previous diplomatic experience and behaved from the beginning with an exaggerated assessment of his own dignity and importance which rapidly incurred Guizot's displeasure and led to a personal and lasting dislike. Under Normanby, the workings of the Paris embassy devolved heavily on the First Secretary, Lord William Hervey, who was a staunch supporter of Palmerston and his antipathy towards France and who also personally detested Guizot. After only a few days in Paris, Normanby detected a distinct chill in the diplomatic climate. 'I find the prejudice against Palmerston so much stronger than I could have expected and existing with such inveteracy in such high quarters,' he advised Russell. 'It will require your constant vigilance to soften down the tone of communications.'[11]

Guizot's reaction to the new government in Britain was to stage a diplomatic *coup* of his own. On 27 August, in Madrid, it was announced that the Queen of Spain and her sister would marry simultaneously and that the Infanta Louisa would marry Louis-Philippe's son, the Duke of Montpensier. This news was received in London with indignant fury. Guizot had promised Aberdeen that this would never happen. Henceforth Palmerston faced the problem that if Isabella died childless then the throne of Spain would pass to her sister and thereafter to her children by a French prince, who would effectively unite the crowns of Spain and France. Any hope which Guizot held, though, that his bold stroke might weaken Palmerston's standing in Cabinet was sadly disappointed. Palmerston rallied his colleagues and his foes alike, to the cry that Guizot had acted beyond the pale of political behaviour and had proved conclusively that the word of a Frenchman was worth nothing. Aberdeen, in opposition, acknowledged that 'the cordial understanding which formerly existed, is necessarily at an end; and it will require much caution, prudence and temper to prevent that coolness which is now inevitable, from degenerating into actual hostility.'[12] Russell wrote to the French chargé d'affaires in London in October reminding him that, 'I came into office convinced that a cordial understanding with France was beneficial to both nations.' After the French government's deceit over Spain, however, 'I can no longer believe that M. Guizot attaches any value to that friendship.'[13]

Guizot tried to play down the affair and hence to minimize the rift with England. His rash diplomacy had backfired and Thiers levelled the accusation that, by wrecking any chance of reasonable relations with the Whig government in London, Guizot had left France more isolated and vulnerable in Europe than ever before. So exposed was Guizot to attack that by October 1846 Normanby was in no doubt that Louis-Philippe was already looking around for a way to dismiss him. Seeing Guizot in such political distress, and hoping to augment it, Palmerston would not hear of any reconciliation. He thus declined Guizot's invitation for a joint protest to Austria against the suppression of the free state of Cracow in October 1846. With regard to Spain, Palmerston told the French government in December that the only acceptable solution was that the children of the Infanta and the Duke of Montpensier should be barred by Spanish law from succession to the throne. In such uncompromising mood, therefore, it was infuriating for Palmerston to find himself dependent on Guizot in La Plata.

On 20 November 1846 Normanby was asked to sound out Guizot on the possibility of raising the blockade at the same time as an armistice was declared at Montevideo. Palmerston stressed the urgency of the matter, but throughout December 1846 and January 1847 Guizot made it obvious that he would not be pushed into any agreement. To make matters worse, by February 1847 contacts between Normanby and Guizot had virtually ceased and the two men were openly insulting each other in Parisian society. Guizot had publicly accused the ambassador of conspiring with his opponents to bring down the ministry. Normanby demanded an apology and Palmerston, again not slow to grasp his opportunity, insisted that ambassadors should be withdrawn if none was forthcoming. The personal dispute between Normanby and Guizot was superficially settled with a pre-arranged handshake at the Austrian embassy in March, though this did little to remove the bitterness created by their professional differences. Normanby afterwards informed Palmerston that he still intended to keep his contacts with Guizot to a minimum. Amid such scenes, agreeing a strategy for terminating their involvement in South America was nigh impossible.

Furthermore, Guizot was being widely criticized for a failure to assert French interests and to support the pro-French regime in Montevideo. He could not, therefore, consider ending the intervention on terms other than could be presented to the Chamber as a vindication of his policy. In these unhappy circumstances Palmerston was resigned to the need for another diplomatic mission to try to bring the factions in La Plata together. It was suggested that Lord Howden, before assuming his duties as Minister to Brazil, should call at Buenos Aires and try to succeed where Thomas Hood had failed a year before.

Guizot accepted the idea of a new diplomatic initiative. He approved of Howden, with whom he spoke in Paris early in February 1847 and in whom he found at least a patient listener for his plea for an improvement in Anglo-French understanding. Guizot was not enthusiastic, however, about the British government's plan of procedure. Palmerston wanted the mission to end with a convention to be signed by all parties to the war and by the two great powers. This would provide for a cessation of hostilities, a lifting of the blockade, the withdrawal of Argentine troops from Uruguay, disarming of all the foreigners in Montevideo, the return of all captured ships and territory and a free election for the Uruguayan presidency. All signatories would therein acknowledge the independence of the republic. Guizot favoured greater flexibility, although he gave no convincing reason why. He also decided to send his own special envoy, Comte Colonna Walewski, with identical instructions to those of Howden and with a specific request to act as one with Howden in using their discretionary powers. In March 1847 the naval commanders in the Plate were sent orders to carry out the wishes of Howden and Walewski in supervising and enforcing the terms of any settlement achieved – though Palmerston pointed out to the Admiralty that enforcement was not to be by violent means but rather by the moral influence of a firm and united Anglo-French position. Before he left Europe in March 1847, Howden received one other important communication. Enclosed in a despatch from Palmerston was a letter addressed to Felipe Arana, formally announcing the recall of Ouseley from his post.

9. The Diplomacy of Howden and Walewski, 1847

Howden had been a soldier and a politician before settling for the diplomatic life. He was aide-de-camp to the Duke of Wellington in 1817–18 and had been present at the sea battle of Navarino in 1827. Before he succeeded to the peerage, he sat in the Commons in 1829–30. He had undertaken special diplomatic missions to Greece and Egypt in 1827 and to Belgium in 1832, before being sent to Madrid in 1834 where his fluency in Spanish could be put to service. Howden's current instructions, issued by Palmerston on 22 March 1847, contained a draft convention which it was hoped would be acceptable at Buenos Aires. In so far as it conceded all that Rosas had asked of T.S. Hood in 1846, there was indeed some chance of success.

Under the terms of this draft, Rosas and Oribe would agree to order the Argentine troops out of Uruguay and to an election for the presidency. In return, Britain and France would, on signature, lift their blockade of Buenos Aires and arrange the disarming of the foreign garrison in Montevideo. The captured warships, cannon, flags and Martín García would all be returned to the Argentine Confederation, whose full right of belligerency was to be acknowledged. The rivers Paraná and Uruguay were to be designated interior waters subject to the territorial rights of the countries through which they flowed. All parties to the war would declare hostilities ended and grant a general amnesty to past opponents. All would affirm, too, the independence of the republic of Uruguay. How such a convention could be arranged was for Howden and Walewski to decide. If Rosas objected to signing an agreement which implicitly recognized the regime in Montevideo, then a convention *à trois* between Britain, France and the Argentine Confederation would suffice: Rosas would sign for Oribe while the two European powers would pledge fulfilment by the Montevideans. If Oribe signed any document, his style should be no more than that of a military commander claiming to be the legal President of Uruguay but in no way acknowledged as such. If, however, negotiations could not be concluded satisfactorily at Buenos Aires, then Howden and Walewski were to cross the Plate and try to arrange an armistice between besiegers and besieged at Montevideo such as would allow a free election to the presidency to be conducted.

By the time Howden reached Buenos Aires on 10 May, he faced the familiar problem of how to follow instructions conceived months beforehand. Since Rivera's defeat in January 1847 the weakness of the Montevideans had been increasingly revealed. The garrison needed further supplies of gunpowder, which Ouseley and Deffaudis arranged should be provided by the naval squadrons. But the pressing difficulty lay in defending the towns of Colonia and Maldonado, which precariously held out against attacks by Oribe. Ouseley knew from British residents at Colonia how weak the defences there were; it was really held by a small body of British and French sailors which Herbert reinforced with a further 20 marines at the end of 1846. The Uruguayan army virtually abandoned the town in January 1847, leaving the naval commanders to protect the local British and French nationals and to hold it as the essential *point d'appui* for the ships blockading Buenos Aires. Maldonado was no better placed. Since February 1847 British and French warships had been ferrying Uruguayan soldiers and their supplies from Montevideo to this last redoubt in the east of the country, and the ships had used their guns on several occasions to disperse Oribe's soldiers who were advancing to the outskirts of the town. Rosas appeared to be closing in for the kill in Uruguay.

Within the Argentine Confederation Rosas had also strengthened his hand in recent months. The threat from Urquiza had receded as he had chosen to display loyalty by sending soldiers to assist Oribe and by pressing Madariaga in Corrientes to renegotiate the treaty of Alcaraz. Urquiza sensed that Rosas had skilfully used the cry of the nation in danger to gain support. A military challenge to Rosas would have meant an alliance with the European powers in their effort to break down Argentine resolve to defend the nation's integrity, and Urquiza recoiled from this dangerous step.[1] On 30 March 1847 he increased the pressure on Madariaga to agree to new treaty terms, thereby leaving the secessionist movement in Corrientes isolated and vulnerable. With the war in Uruguay and resistance to the Europeans going well, and with Urquiza's ambitions in check, Rosas had actually turned the Anglo-French intervention to his own advantage and now had no apparent interest in a rapid end to the struggle. Terms which he would have agreed with Thomas Hood in 1846 might well seem less tempting when coming from Howden a year later.[2]

In the meantime Ouseley kept up an active support for the Montevidean government as best he could. On 6 April 1847 he wrote to Herbert expressing his opinion that recent orders from the Admiralty to reembark marines and sailors from the city need not be followed. Such orders were, like so many others forwarded to 'this distant station', Ouseley emphasized, 'conceived under erroneous impressions as to the real nature of our position here.'[3] Herbert retorted that it was not for him to question the assumptions upon which his orders were based but rather to do his duty and obey them. He did, nonetheless, agree not to remove any men from the lines of Montevideo until Howden reached Buenos Aires, and even after that time to embark his sailors only gradually so as to prevent panic in the town. That the defences of the city were in such a parlous state was in any case the responsibility of none but the Montevidean authorities themselves, Herbert continued. They had depleted the garrison to no avail and, though warned that the withdrawal of British marines was nigh, they had done nothing by way of preparation.

Ouseley also, on occasion, impressed upon less senior commanders the need to do their duty by the Uruguayan cause. He did not believe that Herbert was capable of acting impartially and he feared that Herbert's sympathy for Rosas and Oribe would spread throughout the squadron. By the spring of 1847 relations between Ouseley and Herbert were certainly at a low ebb. Herbert was jealous of any meddling in the operations of the ships on his station. In particular he took great exception to a letter interfering with naval orders which Ouseley had written on 3 February to one of his captains. Herbert condemned this as a 'very extraordinary letter for a diplomat of your experience to write to a junior officer under my command.'[4] In reality there was little that Ouseley could now do for the Montevidean government, given the nature of his instructions from London and an unsympathetic commander exercising a tight control of the squadron. It was a marked change from the authority which he had wielded in 1845 and early 1846, when he had effectively taken control of the war and had seemed likely to determine its outcome.

Howden was quick to appreciate the state of affairs in Uruguay. Oribe was well placed for victory while Rivera had been disowned and deserted by virtually all his former supporters. Montevideo was in a hopeless state. Its government was weak and bankrupt and at the mercy both of foreign legionnaires and of the merchants and speculators who provided what little remained of the sinews of war.

Moreover, the effort to weaken Rosas by the blockade at Buenos Aires had proved almost ludicrously ineffective, Howden reported to Palmerston: 'the regular English and French square-sailed trader is kept out, while the native coaster and smuggler, in a shallow, difficult navigation, does just what he likes.'[5] Howden was also convinced of another factor which must affect the course of his diplomacy – that the French would do very little to assist the object of his mission and that his colleague, Walewski, with whom he was supposed to maintain the closest harmony, was not a man to be trusted. Howden had heard of Walewski's remarks before leaving Paris to the effect that he would not hesitate to foment disputes between Entre Rios, Corrientes and Buenos Aires if he thought that some leverage on Rosas might thereby be gained. *En route* for La Plata, Howden and Walewski had met in Brazil, where Howden professed astonishment at the latter's casual suggestion that they should get the signature of the government in Montevideo for their convention before going on to Buenos Aires. Such a procedure would at once have destroyed any chance of success, since Rosas would never even consider a peace proposal which had been offered first to a regime which he did not recognize and which his army had spent nearly five years trying to overthrow. Walewski also expressed the view that as the diplomatic representatives of great powers they should not meet directly with Oribe but instead should deal with him through attachés. Again Howden saw the danger of a slight to Latin pride. Of these proposals by his French colleague, Howden wrote to Palmerston: 'it is evident that they were only *feelers*, but I trust they are not forerunners of the animus that I am to find in my companion.'[6]

For all these forebodings, the initial meeting with Rosas was cordial and free from expressions of entrenched opinon. As an extraordinary gesture of conciliation, Rosas refused to accept the notice of Ouseley's recall in any public manner. However much an impediment to peace Ouseley had been, and grateful as he now was that the British government had recalled him, Rosas declared that he bore no enmity towards Ouseley and did not wish to appear in any way to triumph over him. Howden was deeply impressed. On 14 May he and Walewski presented their draft convention to Arana and made it clear that, while negotiations were in train, the British and French warships conducting the blockade would do nothing beyond what was technically required to maintain it.

A week passed before any reply came from the Argentine government: it was a request from Rosas for Howden to call on him privately at midnight on 22 May. In a two-hour 'soliloquy', Rosas extolled the virtues of the English and of the lasting debt of gratitude felt by every Argentine for Britain's early recognition of their nation's independence. Conversely, the French were widely distrusted in La Plata and their interests were directly opposed to those of Britain and the Argentine republic. French plans to establish a dependency at Montevideo would, Rosas explained, 'steep the Uruguay in blood', imperil Britain's treaties with the Argentine Confederation and threaten to drive everything English out of the entire region. Howden confessed to Palmerston that it was hard to follow the meaning of much of what Rosas had to say, but that the tactic employed was the obvious and usual one of sowing as much discord as possible between British and French opinion.

Eventually Rosas got to the point. He no longer needed to sign any agreement to which the soi-disant government in Montevideo was a party. Oribe now controlled the Banda Oriental. Things were much changed, therefore, since he had given his consent to the modified propositions of Thomas Hood in July 1846. There was no arguing with the logic of what Rosas was saying, nor did Howden make any effort to do so. He stressed the need only for a practical and businesslike end to the war in which there would be no reason to consider national pride. Rosas interrupted him to raise the question of Oribe's style of address. Legal President he was, and as President he must be referred to in any convention which the Argentine Confederation signed. Argentine flags would need to be saluted, too, as was consistent with the nation's honour; Rosas complained that he could find no mention of this in the Anglo-French draft. On this last point, Howden assured him that his flag would be saluted as often and in any way that he liked. But as for Oribe, Howden explained, 'I never could or would call him legal President,' and, he continued, 'I should never be pardoned by my government if I yielded.'[7] Howden suggested that they might construct a range of titles for Oribe so long as that particular formulation was avoided. For once Rosas was silent and gave no indication of his feelings. The day after the interview Howden wrote to Palmerston that he remained optimistic of reaching an acceptable agreement despite Rosas' clear refusal to treat with the government in Montevideo. Much would depend on the content of the counterproject still awaited from Arana.

Such optimism as Howden had, however, was never shared by

Walewski, who appeared to have decided before he even reached the River Plate that his instructions were incapable of implementation. Walewski's main concern by the end of May 1847 was apparently just to disengage from all negotiations in such a way as to leave with Rosas the odium of failure. For that reason he reverted to his earlier suggestion that the two diplomats should try to find agreement with the other parties in the war, Oribe and the Montevidean government, before allowing themselves to be kept waiting at Buenos Aires until Arana deigned to send a reply to their draft convention. Howden still would not consider this. Unsatisfactory as Rosas' methods of negotiation were, he was nonetheless the principal figure in the war without whose consent any terms agreed with the others would be of little value. Walewski also pressed the idea that Argentine troops might be brought home from Uruguay in British and French warships. This, Howden replied, might well serve to speed up their departure when the time came, but the suggestion was hardly likely to appeal to Rosas, who would interpret the plan as an attempt to make his army appear as prisoners of war returning home on foreign vessels. Sufficient tensions soon existed for Howden to confide to Palmerston that 'Mr. Hood had incomparable advantages in treating alone.'[8] But Walewski too had his suspicions – in particular of Howden's impartiality as a diplomat, since the latter seemed increasingly to favour the views and opinions of the Argentine authorities.

It would have been difficult for Howden not to be impressed with his favoured status in Buenos Aires and perhaps to feel, therefore, that he was uniquely placed to succeed. His arrival in the city had been a spectacular affair, with the streets lined by crowds cheering as his carriage passed. Such spontaneous enthusiasm as he saw that day clearly reflected both the anxiety of the ordinary citizens of Buenos Aires for an end to years of warfare and blockade and their confidence that he, as a British diplomat, was the man who could fulfil their hopes. His warm reception by Rosas, the latter's personal charisma and his expressions of such high esteem for all things British had a marked effect on Howden. So too did his infatuation with Manuelita Rosas, with whom he spent much of his time in May 1847 riding out across the Buenos Aires countryside and on whose account, understandably, he felt far less concerned than Walewski at the slow progress of negotiations. In the circumstances, Walewski might have excused himself for thinking that in his hands alone lay the fate of the doomed garrison and inhabitants of Montevideo.

Diverted as he was, Howden did gain one important advantage while at Buenos Aires: Herbert managed to arrange an armistice in the fighting in Uruguay. Rosas was ill-pleased when he heard of this. Oribe had apparently succumbed to the persuasion of the British naval commander without checking first with his ally. The price for a ceasefire was to have been a simultaneous lifting of the blockade. Oribe had stupidly thrown that away and had handed to the British and French a valuable counter. A ceasefire, therefore, was one thing less that Rosas could now offer when drawing up a response to Howden and Walewski's draft convention. Arana finally presented the Argentine reply on 30 May, but, on inspection, Howden found the terms offered to be so objectionable that he did not even bother to consult Walewski before conveying his unease. Relying once more on Herbert's tactful ways and popularity, he sent the latter to speak with Arana and to observe how certain stipulations from the draft appeared to have been omitted. Herbert's excellent relations with Arana, as indeed with Oribe in gaining the armistice, enabled some things to be said by him which could not, without a diplomatic row, be said by others. The essential point conveyed, however, was that nowhere in the Argentine response was there recognition of, and support for, Uruguay's independence and that without this as a preamble the convention was dead and the negotiations over. Again Herbert gained his point; Arana assured him that some suitable mention of Uruguay's status would be inserted. Predictably, however, the next step was a summons for Howden to see Rosas once more alone.

In this interview, at the beginning of June 1847, Rosas failed again to detach Howden from his French colleague, despite a lengthy tirade against French ambitions and intrigues in South America, with much of which Howden secretly agreed. On 3 June Howden and Walewski returned their official answer to Arana's version of a draft convention. Cautious to the point of obscurity, they stumbled towards an explanation of what was wrong with the Argentine proposals. There was, as Herbert had unofficially informed Arana, no mention of guaranteeing Uruguay's independence. Furthermore, Arana made the execution of such a convention conditional on its ratification by Oribe, even though Oribe himself would not, in Arana's draft, be a signatory of the agreement. In these circumstances, Howden and Walewski observed, it was Britain and France who were making all the concessions: raising the blockade, returning captured vessels of war, handing back Martín García and engaging to do all they could to disarm the foreigners in Montevideo. Arana committed the Argentine government to nothing – not even to a withdrawal of troops across the River Uruguay since this technically could be vetoed by Oribe. What was needed, they continued, was a separate convention between Britain, France and Oribe. After the conclusion of this, the two great powers could then treat with the Argentine Confederation on such matters as touched upon its interests alone. All were agreed that the Hood proposals of 1846, as modified by Rosas, would form the basis of agreement. What was sought, the two envoys optimistically concluded, was merely a practical form of giving them both expression and execution.

Howden knew that he would never get an agreement from Rosas which specifically guaranteed the sovereignty of Uruguay. Enemies of Rosas would always cite this refusal as evidence of his territorial ambitions, but Howden assured Palmerston that there was a less sinister explanation. Rosas saw the affairs of La Plata in terms of his *sistema Americano* and was determined not to admit the right of any European power to intervene in South American politics. To sign a convention with Britain and France which dealt with the question of the independence of any South American state was, therefore, ideologically unacceptable as well as an international humiliation. This did not mean that a form of words suitable to all parties could not be found. On 5 June Rosas sent a member of the Buenos Aires Hall of Representatives to sound out Howden on a compromise. The contracting parties might recognize that none of them had selfish or separate objects in view and that they all desired nothing more than to uphold the peace and independence of the states of La Plata, as already recognized by existing treaties. The sovereignty of Uruguay was, of course, enshrined in the treaty between Brazil and the Argentine Confederation of 1828. 'I thought it was better to accept this proposition, than to run the risk of a rupture on this point,' Howden informed the Foreign Office.[9] He undertook to recommend this neutral statement to Walewski since it gave the two European powers sufficient to justify their intervention. Again Arana had been given an indication, unofficially, of how best to phrase his next proposal. Thus the only serious problem after the first week of June appeared to be that relating to the status of Manuel Oribe.

Arana did not reply until 13 June. In his response even the points of known agreement were dealt with amid excessive elaboration. Howden and Walewski were wrong to assert that as things stood it was Britain and France who were making all the concessions in an effort to reach agreement. Arana reminded them that Buenos Aires had agreed to a suspension of hostilities and that it waived its undeniably just claims to compensation for injuries committed against Argentine territory. His honour satisfied by this declaration of Argentine magnanimity, Arana next spelt out the form of words needed to satisfy all parties as to the integrity of Uruguay – secure in the knowledge that such a formula was already unofficially agreed. There were still differences on two points, however. The first was Arana's persistent, but to Howden flippant, claim that the River Uruguay should be recognized as a waterway subject to the laws and regulations of the Argentine Confederation. Howden decided to say nothing on this issue. By ignoring the Argentine assertion and by abiding by the British draft, which stated more vaguely that the river was an interior waterway subject to the rights conferred by international law, Howden calculated that Arana ultimately would have to drop his wording.

The second difference concerned Oribe, and here Arana offered no reason to anticipate any surrender. Howden knew that Rosas could not make any concession in respect of his ally. Having fought for years to assert Oribe's right as legal President of Uruguay and consistently recognized him as such, Rosas could hardly be expected, when undefeated in the field, to change the designation accorded to the General – and even less so when to all the world it would appear that Rosas had bowed to foreign pressure. Likewise, of course, Britain and France could not suddenly acknowledge Oribe to be President, having resisted his cause for so long and within weeks, indeed, of Ouseley having officially taken his leave of the authorities in Montevideo as the recognized government of Uruguay. 'Only one means of getting out of this difficulty occurred to me,' Howden reflected.[10] The separate texts of the convention would refer to the General differently, with the British and French envoys declaring what they neither recognized Oribe as President nor were their governments influenced in their relations with the republic of Uruguay by the fact that he was thus described in the Argentine copy. Walewski and Arana seemed to agree to the principle. It was not a very satisfactory form of agreement, as Howden was well aware, but by now the only alternative was a breakdown in negotiations altogether. Even after accepting Howden's idea of varying texts, Arana once more withdrew into dignified silence. Towards the end of June the British Minister resolved to see Arana alone in a final effort to agree a draft convention which might solve outstanding problems by the time-honoured practice of avoiding them.

A private interview with Arana was bound to bring matters to a head, since Arana had told Herbert several times that the French were the obstacle to an agreement. By coming alone, and by offering the opportunity for a confidential conversation, Howden called the Argentine bluff. If Rosas wanted peace in La Plata, as he claimed he did, then let the parties sign a simple document in which the Argentine government agreed to withdraw its troops from Uruguay and in which Britain and France specified the concessions that they would make in return. Oribe would not be mentioned. But Arana clearly could not or dared not accept. Howden suggested that the Argentine government might write in advance to Oribe inviting him to dismiss his auxiliary Argentine troops. If Oribe agreed to do so, then the simplified convention could be signed at Buenos Aires and Rosas could show to the world that his ally had not been abandoned but had been amply consulted beforehand. Arana did not reply to this; later, however, Howden heard that Rosas would not consent. His final initiative to break the deadlock having failed, Howden was left to wonder whether he had not perhaps been impulsive in acting alone.

Howden, though, could not have allowed the negotiations at Buenos Aires to drag on any longer. By late June 1847 he was all too conscious of the interminable delays in correspondence with Arana and frustrated by the latter's utter inability to negotiate on any point without constant reference to Rosas. Now, more than ever, Rosas had every reason to drag out the negotiations. In fact, with Oribe so well positioned in Uruguay and with the British manifestly anxious to extricate themselves from the intervention, there was really very little need for Rosas to conclude an agreement at all. Howden and Walewski had simply come to look foolish, waiting week after week at Buenos Aires for a convention which, quite possibly, Rosas had no intention of signing.

There was another pressing reason for bringing the negotiations to an end, with or without success. Howden felt unable to sustain the blockade of Buenos Aires any longer. It had long been a sham, he reminded Palmerston: 'This blockade fails so utterly in all the contemplated purposes of such a measure, that the sooner it is got rid of the better.'[11] Ouseley and Deffaudis had manipulated shipping in the Plate by giving merchantmen clearance to enter Buenos Aires provided that they called first at Montevideo and paid port duties there. In this way the blockade had been used as little more than an income-generating device for the Montevidean authorities. The consuls of the

United States, Sardinia, Denmark, Portugal and Hamburg at Buenos Aires were protesting at these abuses and at the capricious manner in which British and French naval officers seemed to put the blockade into practice. Howden confessed that he had no answer to give to the consular community which could justify the way in which the blockade had operated. In any case, they were not demanding a justification for the past but an immediate lifting of the blockade so that normal trade could be resumed.

Until now, Howden had drawn some comfort from the easy relationship which he had established with William Harris of the United States legation, who had tacitly supported the Anglo-French intervention and had used his influence with Rosas in favour of the peace proposals. As soon as Howden reached the Plate, Harris had announced his willingness to cooperate with him and indeed leaned further towards the European powers than his government's policy of neutrality strictly permitted. Harris, in fact, was largely untroubled by directions from Washington, where Buchanan and Polk remained indifferent to contacts with the Argentine Confederation. Buchanan did not even bother to enquire as to the British and French governments' intentions in La Plata with respect to the joint mission of Howden and Walewski, despite Harris' advice and request that he should do so. For his part, Rosas had grown distrustful of the United States government because of what he regarded as the war of conquest it had launched against Mexico in 1846. Nonetheless, Harris felt that he should not acquiese any longer in an improper and damaging blockade and at the end of June 1847 told Howden that he could assist the latter's diplomacy no longer. Deprived of the good offices of the eminently obliging and reasonable Harris, Howden reported to Palmerston, there was less chance than ever of Rosas being persuaded to sign a satisfactory convention and no reason therefore for not yielding to the wishes of the consular community in Buenos Aires.

Howden and Walewski officially broke off their negotiations with the Argentine Confederation on 29 June. Rather unexpectedly, it was on the question of navigation rights on the River Uruguay that a final meeting with Arana foundered. Arana would accept nothing less than a specific reference to Argentine jurisdiction – a point which Walewski was not even prepared to discuss. Relaying the bad news to Palmerston, Howden stressed that every effort had been made to find agreement with the Argentine government but, consistent with the triumph of its forces during the past year, that government's bargaining position was unassailable. Having failed at Buenos Aires, the two diplomats prepared to depart for Montevideo, where they hoped to be able to put the armistice between Oribe and the Montevidean authorities onto a more dependable basis than merely that of a temporary ceasefire. On this Howden and Walewski could easily agree, but on other matters planned by Howden there was bound to be trouble. Howden wished to reach agreement with Oribe on how to hold elections for a new President in Uruguay and bring him to a political accommodation in the meantime with the present government. He also wished to begin withdrawing British sailors from Montevideo. But the real issue of contention with the French, as he knew, would be the blockade, which he assured Palmerston on 30 June he would lift at the first opportunity. At Buenos Aires Howden and Walewski had shared a common purpose. On crossing the River Plate their disparate interests would soon surface again.

* * *

Initial impressions of Uruguay confirmed Howden's worst fears of a regime at Montevideo which survived only by virtue of foreign assistance. His arrival coincided with the fall of Maldonado to Oribe. The same fate would soon befall Colonia, he surmised, since most of its defenders were unfit for military service and its garrison was provided for only by the British and French navies. Looking at the defences of Montevideo itself, Howden estimated a force of about 2400 French, Basques and Italians supplemented by a small contingent of 300 Uruguayans and a legion formed by 300 liberated slaves. Against these, he calculated, was ranged Oribe's army of 10,700 men. Howden saw but one end to this state of affairs: he thus resolved to persuade the Montevideans to surrender to Oribe on terms which he and Walewski could guarantee. Knowing the effect which this idea would produce in Walewski's mind, Howden wrote to his French colleague on 5 July explaining his thinking 'in the most unreserved manner'. By all means the two envoys could try to persuade Oribe to end the war with an armistice and a political compromise with the authorities in Montevideo. But realistically this was highly unlikely, given Oribe's military position. "It is my opinion (and it is my duty, after the most mature and anxious deliberation, to communicate it to you),' Howden insisted, 'that we should propose to the government of Montevideo to capitulate on the most favourable terms with General

Oribe.'[12] If the Montevidean government agreed, then Britain and France would lift the blockade of Buenos Aires, retaining only Martín García and the captured Argentine vessels until further instructions came from Europe. If the government in Montevideo, or the foreigners who commanded its forces, refused, then the two Ministers would declare their mission ended and that no further support from the allied squadrons could be expected. Walewski was taken aback. Under no circumstances, he replied on 7 July, did instructions from Guizot or Palmerston authorize them to enter into any initiative to bring about the surrender of Montevideo. If Oribe would not accept a lasting armistice then their mission would indeed be at an end, but this did not mean that Montevideo was to be told to capitulate. Clearly the only chance for their joint mission ending in harmony lay in the remote hope that they might somehow convince Oribe that he should abandon the war.

After informing Suárez of their plans, Howden and Walewski rode out to the Cerrito on 8 July 1847. Oribe seemed agreeable enough and was willing to accept an armistice for six months, during which time the contending forces would retain their current positions and provisions would be allowed into Montevideo from the Uruguayan interior. Howden and Walewski undertook to lift the blockades on both sides of the River Plate. On their return to Montevideo, Walewski declared that he would only be a party to such an armistice if the Montevidean government first approved its terms. Howden replied that he did not think this to be necessary, but he had no means of overruling his colleague. Oribe meanwhile told Walewski's aide that he would sign nothing which did not acknowledge him as President. This could well bring all efforts to extend the ceasefire to an end, Howden realized. He confirmed in a letter to Walewski on 13 July that 'I entirely agree with you that it is not possible for us to affix our names to a document thus headed.'[13]

In the end it was not Oribe who wrecked the negotiations but rather the government in Montevideo. On 15 July it simply announced that the terms of the armistice were refused. Howden, of course, saw the hand of French diplomacy at work here: this was why Walewski had insisted that the Montevidean authorities should have a power of veto. Up to the last minute Walewski urged on Howden the limits of his duty in so far as the termination of their mission meant that the *status quo* remained. Howden, however, had made up his mind. On the same day as the Montevidean government rejected the terms of armistice, he wrote to Herbert requesting the latter to raise his blockades both of Buenos Aires and of Oribe's supply ports on the Uruguayan coast and to cease all other naval measures. The years of naval cooperation with the French were over. In explaining what he had done to Palmerston, Howden craved indulgence 'for the grave responsibility I have incurred in alone raising the blockade.'[14]

Howden sailed for Rio de Janeiro on 25 July 1847, disillusioned and even bitter at having reached agreement neither at Buenos Aires nor in Uruguay. Looking back over his ten weeks in La Plata he reflected on the complex reasons for these failures. First of all, he wrote to Palmerston, his mission with Walewski had been conceived on the dubious assumption that in 1846 T.S. Hood had come close to producing a diplomatic *tour de force*. Manifestly he had not, and in his correspondence Hood had portrayed both Rosas and Oribe as more conciliatory and eager for a settlement than was the case in reality. Hood had concealed crucial difficulties respecting Oribe's ambitions, Howden concluded, 'merely to make people suppose that he had arranged in six weeks the whole question of the Plate.'[15] That being so, Howden had naturally encountered problems which could not have been anticipated in London or Paris.

A second crucial factor in his failure was the burden of cooperating with the French who, Howden believed, were widely disliked throughout the region. Howden was convinced that on his own he could have settled a convention with Rosas. In Uruguay, he found that the same distrust of French intrigue 'pursued me into the camp of the Cerrito' and made Oribe more wary of reaching an agreement than he otherwise would have been.[16] Despite his earlier suspicions of Walewski, Howden conceded that when all was over his French colleague had not personally undermined the mission. The real problem lay with Walewski's compatriots in Montevideo and the extent to which the charade of an indigenous government there was so utterly in the hands of unscrupulous foreigners.

Howden provided evidence to show that by 1847 Montevideo was not under the control of Uruguayan nationals. Ouseley and Deffaudis had, since the armed intervention began, been the dominant force in the city; the armed legions of French, Basques and Italians under colonels Jean Thiébaut and Garibaldi had also acted much as they pleased and with scant regard for local sensibilities.[17] They controlled the streets and, since Frenchmen were predominant among them, the atmosphere was inevitably that of a city under occupation. Likewise, the French controlled the city's Press. They were instrumental, too, in presenting the Uruguayans to the world at large as a weak but freedom-loving people locked in a life or death struggle with a murderous tyrant from across the water. This was a romantic, but somewhat selective, portrayal of the war. The true nature of the contest, Howden wrote to Palmerston in disgust, is that ' between a small number of foreign shopkeepers, artisans, and labourers (whose defences are manned by French and English sailors) and a larger number of Orientals.'[18] Furthermore, behind these foreign elements in the city hid, in the shadows of political intrigue, the moneylenders and mortgagees of the Customs House revenues. Such men as these, Howden reported, comprised 'that abominable species of British subject that you meet with abroad' who 'are always setting England against the government of the country they live in'.[19]

Howden, in fact, warned Walewski while they were at Montevideo of the machinations afoot to make them abandon the legitimate goals of their mission. On 14 July, with hope still alive that an armistice with Oribe might be reached, Howden wrote that 'I am aware that the whole foreign population of Montevideo and the Buenos Airean emigrants in that town are using every morning and evening their ceaseless endeavours to persuade you to change your first opinions and to recede from your first intentions respecting the consummation of this armistice.'[20] But there was no saving Walewski. On 20 July Howden informed Palmerston that the pressures from French nationals and from the new French admiral, Joseph Le Predour, had quickly gained the upper hand and that Walewski's thinking had 'changed by being exposed, through his residence in the town, to every sort of argument, entreaty and attempt at intimidation'.[21] Howden himself had avoided such exposure. He had stayed on board a British man-of-war at anchor off the city as much as possible, and on the occasions when he had gone ashore he had been studious to avoid all contact with the British merchant body, for whom he displayed nothing but aristocratic contempt. 'You cannot imagine such a sink of iniquity as is this Montevideo,' he assured Palmerston.[22] In circumstances like these it was not to be wondered that his meticulous attempts to find peace in La Plata had been frustrated.

Howden was particularly scathing of Ouseley's behaviour over the years – not just in the way in which he had allowed the blockade to be conducted but by the way in which he had identified with the British merchants and loan jobbers in Montevideo. With regard to them,

Howden explained to Palmerston, 'Mr. Ouseley was in the habit of writing addresses to be presented to himself by them on all occasions when he wanted a little confirmation of his intentions, and they are extremely angry at not having been able to give me some political lessons.' As for Ouseley's pathetic pandering to French ambitions: 'It is humiliating to see the way in which we have been playing the exclusive game of France, and recklessly ruining immense commercial interests for nothing by a senseless blockade.'[23] Once Ouseley had gone, of course, it was also possible to discover from the legation archive the extent of his dubious activities in support of the regime in Montevideo. Ouseley left no proper accounts of his disbursements to the authorities in the city. When he transferred his authority to draw sums on the British government to Martin Hood on 7 June 1847, Ouseley was vague about the amounts involved or the purpose for which past payments had been used. 'A general account has been kept against the Oriental government including all expenses incurred in securing their independence,' Ouseley minuted, 'and the amount to be regarded as a subsidy.'[24] When the consul turned to Howden for advice, he was told at once that Ouseley's practice of assigning subsidies to the Uruguayan government was 'perfectly ludicrous'. 'I feel sure,' Howden urged, 'that you will not for a moment adopt that foundation for burdening Her Majesty's Treasury.' Ouseley's general account, in fact, ran to over £70,000 – more than £50,000 of which had gone in aid, disbursements, rents and other expenses. In Howden's opinion it was 'wholly extraneous to any legitimate purpose,' and lavish to an extent which 'quite astounded me'.[25]

Howden could prove to his perfect satisfaction, then, why his armistice had been rejected by the Uruguayan government. Dependence on French ships, French sailors ashore and the French legion left the government no scope for independent policy. It had become, Howden believed, but a tool of French expansionist ambitions in South America – to serve which end the war would need to be continued. He was well aware that in sections of the Press in Europe he would be much criticized for his failure to keep faith with the population of Montevideo and with a cause so often represented as the embodiment of nationalist ideas and a symbol of liberty in the New World. Nonetheless he had felt it right to break with the French and to end the joint naval intervention; it had been done 'for the commercial and political interests of England.'[26]

Howden need not have worried how his news would be received at the Foreign Office. Palmerston was relieved. 'The combined operation of our two naval forces, which has been miscalled a blockade, has for a long time past been something very like a system of piracy,' he replied to Howden on 2 October 1847, 'and I am very glad that you have at last got us out of it.'[27] Of course, the problem of La Plata remained much as before, and Palmerston lost no time in raising it once more in Paris. There was still a need to stop the war in Uruguay and a need now to persuade the French government to follow Howden's example and to instruct their naval commander in the Plate to lift his blockade also. Guizot was not receptive to this suggestion. There had been no thawing in relations between Paris and London in the course of 1847. Furthermore, the news from France seemed to indicate that Guizot's ministry was in terminal trouble. Normanby and Hervey wrote of dissent within the government as well as pressure from opponents over foreign affairs. Guizot was thus in no position to make concessions to Palmerston about French interests in Uruguay when Normanby called on him on 18 September.

Guizot listened patiently while the ambassador went on to express Palmerston's wish that France would end her blockade. Then Guizot asked whether or not Normanby was aware of how the intervention in La Plata had started. It was Aberdeen and not he, Guizot pointed out, who had suggested the idea and it was the British government which had taken all initiatives. France had cooperated fully as an ally, only to find now that the British had abruptly terminated the policy unilaterally when it had become unpleasant for them. Normanby said meekly that he could not recollect exactly how the whole affair had begun, but that the real problem in any case was how best to end it. Guizot concluded this uncomfortable interview with the remark that he did not question the propriety of Walewski's actions. Two days later he summoned the ambassador back to the Foreign Ministry and this time drew Normanby's attention to glaring inconsistencies in the British position. According to Palmerston, the government had approved of Howden lifting the blockade. But according to Russell, to whom the French ambassador had spoken in Downing Street, this was not the case: the matter was still under consideration and indeed the blockade might yet be reinstated. Perhaps Howden had mistaken his instructions? Guizot concluded. Normanby was happy to pass the whole matter back to the Foreign Office without comment and to await fresh advice from London.

Although he could not say so to Guizot, Normanby too had reservations about the manner in which Howden had broken with Walewski and lifted the British blockade. 'I cannot but feel,' he confided to Russell, 'that by Howden's own account there was in the last stage of the business rather a *"manque de procédé"* towards his colleague which under all the circumstances of the moment is much to be regretted.'[28] Nor was Normanby the only one to express such doubts. The Chancellor of the Exchequer, Sir Charles Wood, after seeing the diplomatic papers was moved to write to the Prime Minister that, although he was no supporter of the naval intervention, nonetheless Howden's tone towards Walewski had been neither conciliatory nor likely to produce a cordial cooperation.[29] Palmerston, though, was untroubled by these diplomatic niceties; nor had he any difficulty in answering Guizot's query. Anything which the Prime Minister had said was based on incomplete information: only the Foreign Office was fully aware of what had taken place in La Plata. Howden had done right to lift the blockade and it was unfortunate that Walewski had not seen fit to follow. Normanby was told to remind Guizot of the spirit of the instructions issued to Howden and Walewski, which was that since the two powers had undertaken the entire intervention in order to protect the republic of Uruguay, once the two powers had negotiated peace terms sufficient for that end it was quite unreasonable for the Uruguayan government to reject them and still expect material assistance in the war. Howden had merely applied the overriding principle of his instructions to circumstances as they had developed. There was no possibility of the Royal Navy resuming the blockade. There were only two questions to be debated, Palmerston informed Normanby on 8 October. First, would the French squadron persist alone in the discredited blockade, which might lead it eventually into serious difficulties with other powers? Second, what diplomatic measures should Britain and France take 'to disencumber themselves finally, but with honour, of the very embarrassing and unsatisfactory interference which they have now so long been carrying on in the river Plate?'[30]

Even Normanby had a moment of sympathy for Guizot, whom he knew had effectively been discarded by the British and could not survive in power for long. It was not surprising that Guizot took the news of Howden's actions in La Plata and of Palmerston's endorsement of them very badly. The intervention policy was all that survived from his friendship with Aberdeen and from the days, therefore, when he could defend his ministry with the argument that France had renewed her stature in international affairs by virtue of collaboration with, and at least some concessions from, Britain. 'In this case it was obvious that *here* there must be some rankling soreness felt that the last remaining link of the *entente cordiale* should have been so abruptly snapped,' Normanby advised Russell.[31] But like it or not, Guizot saw the overwhelming logic of the position which Palmerston had taken. In a long dispatch of 12 October 1847 to the French ambassador in London, he spelt out the dilemma for his government. Ignoring the issues of who had initiated the intervention in 1844 and the perfidiousness of the British in now jettisoning it, the French were faced with three options: reopening negotiations with Rosas while keeping up whatever pressure could be applied by a blockade; sending a military expedition to drive Oribe out of Uruguay; or, finally, dropping the mediation, as the British had done, seeking in so doing only an armistice between the warring parties on such terms as gave assurances about Uruguayan sovereignty. Realistically, a new approach to Rosas in his moment of diplomatic triumph was a waste of time. As to sending out an expedition of several thousand soldiers, the two governments had firmly resolved at the outset that they would never commit troops to fight on land. An army of occupation in the Banda Oriental, even if militarily successful against Oribe and the Argentines, was a commitment of indeterminable duration and might lead to difficulties out of all proportion to the importance of the original purpose. Only the third option, to follow the British, seemed practicable. This would mean a further attempt to bring Rosas, Oribe and the defenders of Montevideo together in some peaceful formula. Guizot would therefore wait to hear from Palmerston what the British proposed to do next.

10· Palmerston's Search for a Peace Settlement, 1848

The months which followed Howden's departure from Montevideo witnessed political convulsions there which were linked to the gradual tightening of French control. Divisions had emerged among government ministers between those in favour of continuing the war at any cost and those who favoured negotiations with Oribe. On 12 August 1847 Martin Hood wrote to Palmerston that this had come to a head with the resignation of two of the senior men from Suárez's government. A petition of over 220 respectable signatories had been collected and presented to the President which urged an accommodation with Oribe, but this had been rejected outright by Suárez after visits from the French consul and the landing of an additional 100 French seamen. 'It has the appearance certainly of intimidation having been resorted to,' Hood complained, 'for the purpose of driving the government and the people to comply with the wishes of the French authorities.'[1] Other manifestations of French control in Montevideo were, as Howden had suggested earlier, to be found in the Press. Those who opposed the war policy of Ouseley and Deffaudis had often cited the subservience of the city's main newspapers to the two envoys. In the years since 1839 the *Nacional*, the *Courrier de la Plata* and the *Conservador* had been controlled and edited by political exiles from Buenos Aires, all of whom were implacable enemies of Rosas and had used their papers to inflame the passion for armed combat.[2] The *Courrier de la Plata* was notoriously the propaganda agent of French interests in Uruguay. Deffaudis had supported its foundation in 1846 and had, it was no secret, exercised considerable editorial control over it. The French envoy had paid the paper a monthly subsidy of 200 dollars to keep it going, which was subsequently extended by Walewski. All the while that British diplomats had worked to foster the spirit of the *entente cordiale* in La Plata, Hood wrote bitterly, their French counterparts had been at work behind the scenes to portray the British and their diplomatic overtures for peace in the most unfavourable light.

At the time of Walewski's sojourn in Montevideo the French certainly did not anticipate an imminent military collapse. In August and September 1847 the new French Consul-General, Devoize, still assured Guizot that, even if the French navy ended its blockade at Buenos Aires and its support for the Montevidean authorities, the defenders would fight on rather than throw themselves upon Oribe's mercy.[3] As 1847 ended, though, two important developments undermined Montevideo's capacity to continue its defiance. One was the government's dwindling resources, particularly the rapid decline in the Customs House receipts now that the British had lifted their blockade at Buenos Aires. Once again there was no money to pay the soldiers and the government's only resort was to raise subscriptions and emergency levies from among the already impoverished inhabitants. The second development was the loss of Joaquín Madariaga in Corrientes, whose revolt against Rosas had made him, in effect, an ally. Throughout the year Madariaga's independent stance had grown less secure as Urquiza in Entre Rios had backed away from his own challenge to the authority of Buenos Aires and had shown himself inclined to side with Rosas in restoring unity within the Argentine Confederation. On 13 September 1847 Urquiza presented an ultimatum to Madariaga requiring him to acknowledge the status of Corrientes as demanded by Rosas. When this proved insufficient, Arana insisted on a military invasion of Corrientes in order to restore a federalist government there.[4] Urquiza did not feel strong enough to refuse this and a few days later he mobilised his army of 7000 men. On 27 November Urquiza routed Madariaga's smaller force at the battle of Vences and installed a new Governor in Corrientes. Any challenge to Rosas from within the Argentine was thus ended for the time being.

The increasing French control of Montevideo made Palmerston ever more aware of the need for a peace convention in La Plata such as would allow for a total withdrawal from the joint intervention. For this, of course, he still needed to work with the French government. But if cooperation with Guizot had been a bitter pill for him to swallow in 1846, it seemed an even less palatable proposition by the autumn of 1847. Palmerston had spent a good deal of energy in 1847 trying to convince the Cabinet of the need for greater public expenditure on sea defences, and in particular of the merits of his scheme for raising and funding a militia force in England which could defend the country in the event of a French invasion. Anglo-French diplomacy remained poisoned by Guizot's handling of the Spanish marriages. In fact friction between the two governments increased in the summer of

1847 as Queen Isabella, still childless, began to lose political credibility in Spain and to mutter threats of abdication. A further dispute had arisen between Palmerston and Guizot concerning the prospect of civil war in Switzerland. Guizot wanted to arrange a five-power declaration which would uphold the cantonal sovereignty enshrined in the treaty of Vienna. Palmerston, in July 1847, refused to give Guizot the satisfaction of a diplomatic success and declined to participate. This, as so often, left Guizot vulnerable to attack in Paris over the ineffectiveness of French foreign policy. Palmerston's intention was to prevent any international intervention in Swiss affairs and in this he scored a notable triumph.

Political unrest in Italy was another contentious issue where Palmerston appeared to care as much about isolating and discrediting Guizot as about the problem at hand. The Prime Minister favoured a softening of attitude towards the French government and a cooperation in Italian affairs where common objectives could be found. But Palmerston rejected any approach to Guizot. Only civil war in Portugal and Britain's treaty commitments to protect the Portuguese crown could induce Palmerston to tolerate any agreement with France. In June and July 1847, intervention by Britain, Spain and France proved necessary to preserve the authority of the Portuguese monarchy. It was, therefore, a measure of his resolve to escape from the entanglement in South America that he agreed with Guizot to send there yet a further joint diplomatic mission. This time the task was to be undertaken by one of Palmerston's friends, Captain Robert Gore R.N., who had been a loyal Whig Member of Parliament between 1841 and 1847 and upon whom Palmerston now conferred the title of Commissioner Extraordinary. This commission was to be the first of Gore's assignments. After what they hoped would be a successful conclusion, he was to present fresh credentials at Montevideo which would mark his appointment as Britain's new chargé d'affaires and Consul-General to the Uruguayan republic. At the Foreign Office the practice of drafting instructions to new emissaries *en route* for La Plata must have seemed, by the end of 1847, depressingly familiar. Since February 1845, Ouseley, T.S. Hood and Howden had all set forth equipped with copious guidance.

As French Commissioner Extraordinary, with whom Gore was to act closely in all matters, Guizot appointed Baron Jean Battiste Louis Gros, who had formerly served as France's chargé d'affaires in Colombia. Common instructions were to be sent, although by now such expressions as full and frank cooperation and preserving a good understanding between British and French agents surely sounded a little hollow. Nonetheless, because Gore's mission was less ambitious than previous ones, optimism prevailed. This was not to be an Anglo-French approach to Buenos Aires to construct a broad settlement of Argentine and Uruguayan claims. Gore and Gros were sent solely to Montevideo 'to re-establish order and peace on the left bank of the river Plate'.[5] What was sought was an armistice, not a treaty. This time the parties to be squared were Oribe and his enemies inside the capital – not General Rosas.

On arrival off Montevideo, Gore and Gros were to make a declaration that their joint proceedings were aimed only at bringing peace to the region. This declaration was to be sent to Oribe, to the government in Montevideo and to the authorities in Buenos Aires. Thereafter, with all suspicions formally allayed and diplomatic sensitivities duly addressed, the serious object of the mission was to begin. First, the two commissioners would invite Oribe to confirm once more that should he enter Montevideo, under whatever circumstances, he would grant amnesty to the native inhabitants and provide for the safety of both the persons and property of its foreign residents. Second, they would approach the Uruguayan government with this fresh assurance and invite it to negotiate formally, helped by the good offices of Gore and Gros, with Oribe. It was unlikely, Palmerston hazarded, that either side would refuse to comply with the commissioners' request. If all reason failed, Gore was to remind Oribe gently that a British squadron still lay at anchor in the river and would, if necessary, again unite with the French to sever his supply lines. As for the Uruguayan government, should they refuse the opportunity to treat with Oribe under British and French auspices, then Gore and Gros should say at once that the French navy would cease all its remaining interference with Oribe's lines of communication and that their two governments would consider all attempts to mediate in the war on behalf of the Uruguayan nation to be peremptorily brought to an end. Assuming that both parties wished to talk, especially when faced with the alternatives, Gore and Gros were to propose to both sides the following arrangements.

Agreement would be required on only four points. First, that Oribe should dismiss the Argentine troops serving under his command. Second, that the various foreign legions inside Montevideo be disarmed and disbanded. Third, that these two operations should take place simultaneously. Fourth, that both operations should be supervised and assisted by the British and French naval commanders. Either party rejecting these terms was to be deemed unwilling to enter negotiations and should be treated accordingly. When agreement on all four points was achieved, the two commissioners were to make two concluding declarations to the Argentine government to which no response would be expected or required. First, that since the Argentines had consistently claimed that they acted only as auxiliaries of Oribe, the British and French governments had felt it sufficient to deal only with him. Second, that Britain and France considered the government at Buenos Aires bound by existing treaties to respect Uruguay's sovereignty. Local circumstances, Palmerston conceded to Gore, might require some slight modification in procedure but in essence the points to be proposed bore of no compromise.

A further cause for optimism in London at the end of 1847 was that there no longer seemed any reason to doubt Guizot's sincerity in wishing to conclude matters. As if to acknowledge that one of Walewski's insuperable difficulties earlier in the year had been the conduct of French officials in Montevideo, Guizot wrote to Devoize in December, at the same time as Gore and Gros received their instructions. Success for the two commissioners would depend very much upon the influence of the French consulate with both the native government and the foreign legions within the city: the duty of the consul was to give the commissioners whatever help was needed. Guizot even indicated a major change in French policy. Whereas Walewski had not been empowered to recognise Oribe as legal President of Uruguay, Devoize might, 'en dernière analyse', counsel the Montevidean authorities to accept him as such and also use his best efforts to gain such recognition for Oribe from the chiefs of the legions.[6] The British government could scarcely ask for more.

Gore and Gros were greeted in the Plate by a raging south Atlantic storm in the middle of March 1848. It was several days before they could send out their initial communications to the conflicting parties and to the government in Buenos Aires. Oribe replied immediately that he would accept the assistance of the commissioners in reaching a peace with the defenders of Montevideo. On 2 April the government inside the city gave a similar response, despite rumours that the foreign legions would stage a *coup* if it showed any willingness to negotiate. As a precaution Le Predour landed an additional 120 sailors from his squadron as a show of support for the Montevidean authorities. Gros at once invited the British to do the same. But Gore would not be drawn into having marines in the town again. Herbert put a force of 200 men on board a steamer at anchor inside the harbour, from where they could be rushed ashore if need be. That was a sufficient safeguard for the lives of British subjects, Gore insisted; that was the limit of his responsibility. On 7 April the commissioners visited Suárez and called upon the Uruguayan Foreign Minister. The following day they rode out to the Cerrito to talk with Oribe. Pleasantries were exchanged all round and the point was clearly made that Gore and Gros came not as negotiators but merely as intermediaries.

In presenting their peace proposals Gore and Gros made one important addition. Using the discretion which their instructions allowed them, they asked of both parties that as part of a peace convention, and in deference to Oribe's insistence, the latter should be declared President. At the Cerrito there was naturally profuse praise for this statesmanlike suggestion. In Montevideo, the Foreign Minister, Manuel Herrera y Obes, was devastated. When the two commissioners called to receive the reply of the Uruguayan government on 12 April, Herrera launched into an emotive appeal to the time when Britain and France had supported his nation in its hour of need. Gore and Gros made no direct response save to observe 'that the two governments have now changed their opinions and are most desirous to see peace.' Nonetheless, Herrera exclaimed theatrically: 'death before dishonour.' He would never have any part in recognizing Oribe as something which plainly he was not. 'We advised him to weigh calmly and consider well before he came to any determination,' Gore later informed Palmerston.[7] Gore had formed the impression that there was no means of securing peace other than by declaring Oribe President and only then carrying out the four main propositions contained in their instructions.

Although Gros had gone along with this, he now expressed his misgivings. On 29 April he informed Gore that he was not happy with the procedure and he suggested that the inclusion of Oribe's presidential status in the propositions made to both parties exceeded the limits of their authority. The instructions were, Gros reminded his British colleague, that they put specific points both to Oribe and to the government which would be either accepted or refused. Technically Gros was correct; their instructions made no mention of Oribe's status. But Gore stuck to his position using the latitude which the Foreign Office had allowed him on account of local circumstances. He was gambling too, and as the weeks passed apparently justifiably, that the reality of their hopeless position would eventually persuade even the belligerent foreign legions to sue for peace and to content themselves with Oribe's oft-repeated assurances of amnesty.

Gore also knew that the Uruguayan government was bankrupt and its credit exhausted. Weeks before, on 15 March, Herrera had called Martin Hood and the other consular agents in the city to the Foreign Ministry and announced precisely that fact. He had then asked the assembled consuls to put pressure on their nationals living in Montevideo to contribute to a modest loan of £10,000 to help pay the foreign soldiers. Failure to raise such an emergency sum might result in the legionnaires ransacking the city in order to provide for themselves, Herrera intimated; even so, the consuls replied that it was not in their competence to intervene in this way. What appeared to be the final blow to morale came on 14 April 1848, when Garibaldi and a group of his remaining legionnaires sailed for Italy to join an older, and for them a still dearer, national struggle. For all these reasons, Gore reported to London in mid-May, although progress was painfully slow his negotiations were still going well. Then, just as he had convinced himself that he stood poised for triumph, all Gore's patience and achievements were reduced to nothing. A ship sailed into the harbour at Montevideo with news that Europe was in tumult: Guizot and the King had been swept away in a new French revolution and a republican movement had come into power in Paris which was dominated by Guizot's arch-rival – Thiers. Gros was arguably no longer an accredited emissary; the regime which had sent him on this joint mission to La Plata had simply disappeared.

The reaction in Montevideo was one of euphoria, especially among the French legion. It was taken for granted that a revolutionary government in Paris would take up the cause of Montevideo again and that those French nationals who had fought so valiantly within the city would now be embraced in France as brave compatriots and, more to the point, be reinforced by regular soldiers. There was no question of surrender in this, their hour of merciful providence. Gore could only curse his luck and agree with Gros that all they could do was await further news from Europe and, more specifically, fresh instructions from Paris which might either confirm or contradict Gros' original orders. Their mission was in that respect suspended, rather than abandoned. But it was questionable whether Gore was really as close to success as he had implied to Palmerston. His optimism was certainly not shared by Martin Hood, who had never regarded the French with anything other than the gravest suspicion. The intimacy between Thiébaut and Devoize augured ill for peace, Hood complained. Contrary to Guizot's instructions, Devoize used the French legion to put pressure on the Uruguayan government not to accept any deal with Oribe. By this means Devoize sought to tie Gros' hands and to annul the latter's diplomatic initiative.

Beyond this local French intrigue, though, Hood had to concede that there were those in Montevidean politics who remained unswerving opponents of Oribe and whose refusal to negotiate simply could not be surmounted. 'I have used all my influence with the hope of persuading the party in this town to accede to the proposals made by England and France,' he wrote privately to the Foreign Office, 'showing them that if they do not they are lost entirely.' 'I have shown them that they are the losing party, that they are on the point of being absolutely conquered and put down,' he continued, 'and therefore that any terms or conditions they may obtain now are so many advantages which they cannot hope for when the Intervention shall cease.'[8] Hood did all that he could to cajole the Uruguayan authorities to accept the commissioners' terms but, he reflected on 22 April 1848, it was not difficult to see why he had failed. 'Every proposition is favourable to General Oribe,' he candidly admitted. The worst that could happen for Oribe's staunchest opponents was that he would occupy the capital as legal President, and this was what Britain and France were now putting forward in the guise of compromise. Who could blame the diehards for wanting to fight on? Hood asked. 'They cannot be in a worse position and the chances are at all events in their favour – if we lose we shall be as we are now, if we gain we are better off than ever.'[9] For the war faction in Montevideo, the hope remained that although deserted by the British, and possibly by the French too, they might yet be saved at the death by Brazil. Hood thought it unlikely that Brazil would go to war with Rosas, provocative as an Argentine occupation of the Banda Oriental might be. Rumours about Brazil's intentions, however, like those of everything else, circulated freely in Montevideo.

Hood considered that there was an even more fundamental reason for Gore's failure: the factor missing from the brief of the two commissioners had been General Rosas. True, Hood's father and then Howden had both failed to solve the problem in La Plata with Rosas included in their negotiations. The corollary of that, though, was not that the problem could be solved with Rosas excluded. The Argentine

Confederation was the major power in the area and it could not simply be ignored just because it had proved uncooperative in the past. Hood warned Gore on 31 March 1848 that the official Press in Buenos Aires was full of abuse against Britain on the one subject which was always the most reliable barometer of Argentine thinking – the Falkland Islands. 'I am much afraid,' he confessed, 'that this may be the forerunner to the bad exit of the mission confided to you.'[10] Rosas would never allow Oribe to make a separate peace with Britain, France and the Uruguayan government and thereby feel humiliated by being left out.

Hopeless as his task seemed, Gore struggled on until the middle of June 1848. To make matters worse, he also became involved in a disagreement with his French colleague over the precise nature of their instructions. This was precipitated by a note dated 17 May from Oribe which informed the two commissioners that the original point accepted in April as the framework for a settlement between him and the government in Montevideo could no longer be considered as valid and that negotiations could only proceed further on the basis of T.S. Hood's amended propositions of 1846. It was obvious to all what had happened and Oribe made no effort to disguise it. Rosas had simply put his foot down and warned his ally that he was not free to make any separate deal which related solely to his own position in Uruguay.[11] Rosas would only permit a settlement which embraced Argentine interests and which brought to a satisfactory conclusion the differences between the Confederation and the British and French.

Gros wrote to Gore on the following day to say that, as far as he was concerned, this retraction by Oribe left them with no alternative but to do as their instructions required – to reform their squadrons into a blockading force and once more to sever Oribe's supply lines. But Gore rejected this interpretation. To his French colleague's dismay, he referred to the catch-all paragraph in Palmerston's instructions whereby 'if upon your arrival at the spot, any parts of the preceding plan should appear to you to require modification, you will be at liberty in that respect to employ the means at your disposal to the best of your judgment.'[12] The Hood bases of 1846, Gore stressed, did incorporate all that was currently required of the two commissioners and therefore he proposed that they should be prepared to treat accordingly. Gros retorted that this would not be a modification of the plan but rather an entirely different order of diplomacy into which they were not licensed to proceed. They had not been sent to La Plata as negotiators, he reminded Gore, but only with the task of bringing Oribe and the government in Montevideo together to make peace on prearranged terms. T.S. Hood had had full powers to treat with the Argentine authorities, whereas they had not. To adopt the Hood bases would be to enter the whole discussion of indemnity claimed by Rosas against the two powers and the status of the rivers Paraná and Uruguay. Their instructions as commissioners covered none of these points. Despite further representations to his French colleague, Gore had to back down and to recognize that his enthusiasm to free his government from its difficulty at almost any price had outstripped his diplomatic judgment. Such repentance, however, did no more than return matters to square one. It was still impossible to see how he could bring his task to any worthwhile conclusion.

Logically, having accepted Gros' interpretation of their instructions, he was obliged to accept also Gros' insistence that their next step was to reimpose a joint blockade on Oribe's supply route. On 28 May Gros asked that this should be done and Gore reluctantly agreed. 'It was quite evident to me that a great effort was making (*sic*) to get the English once more into the intervention,' Gore later reflected, 'which I was just as anxious to prevent.' In agreeing to the blockade in principle, however, Gore stated firmly that he would put on paper a formal protest since he was convinced that such an action would be illegal without first receiving confirmation from Europe. This time it was Gros who felt unsure of his position; the two men agreed to await the next ship from Europe carrying diplomatic bags. On 2 June the bags arrived, but to Gros' dismay there was nothing from Paris to give any guidance at all. Gore seized his chance to wriggle out of a fresh British naval blockade in the Plate by formally writing to Gros that, in the light of the uncertainty of events in Europe and the silence of the new regime in France, he, as British commissioner, took upon himself the responsibility of refusing to continue further with the letter of their original orders. Gore was prepared to wait but not to act. 'The chance of my colleague being left without any confirmation of his instructions by the new government of France was the only legitimate objection I could make,' he confided to Palmerston, 'and one that it was my duty to take advantage of, although at the same time, it would place me in a most disagreeable position.'[13]

On 8 June 1848 Gros conceded that the joint mission was dead. There was no recrimination. As a parting thought, however, he astonished Gore by suggesting that they should agree to pay a subsidy to the Uruguayan government of 40,000 dollars (£8000) per month to enable it to continue the defence of the capital. Gore replied that without specific authority from London he could never agree to such an expenditure. Gros did, however, finally lift the French blockade at Buenos Aires before leaving La Plata. On 12 June, Gore presented himself to the authorities in Montevideo as Britain's new diplomatic representative. Reflecting on what little could be learnt from recent events, both Gore and Martin Hood concluded that it was impossible to reach any peace in Uruguay outside Buenos Aires.

This was not lost on Palmerston, who had long since drawn a similar conclusion. Even before the news arrived that Gore had been forced to abandon his peace initiative, the British government had appointed Henry Southern as its new Minister to the Argentine Confederation. Southern had many of the qualities required for reopening diplomatic relations at Buenos Aires: he was an educated and literary man who was well versed in the culture and language of the Iberian world. Palmerston had first known him as a journalist and editor in London. Since 1833 he had served as Lord Clarendon's secretary at Madrid and had acted as chargé d'affaires there for six months in 1839. He was then first secretary at Lisbon from 1839 until 1846 and chargé d'affaires again until 1847. Southern was undoubtedly energetic and clever, but if this posting to Buenos Aires was to be a major step in his career he had to do no less than convince Rosas that all disputes between their nations since 1845 had been but misunderstandings, and that Britain harboured none but friendly sentiments towards the Argentine states. His overriding priority, however, was simply to be accepted as an accredited diplomat and thereby to restore Britain's presence in Buenos Aires. When Southern sailed, in July 1848, Parisian politics was still in turmoil and the French government would clearly take no part in the affairs of La Plata for some time to come. For better or for worse, Southern would have to deal alone with General Rosas.

11· The Resumption of Relations at Buenos Aires, 1848–9

Despite the encouragement which many in Montevideo drew from news of the revolution in Paris, in harsh military terms the war effort of the Uruguayan government had visibly disintegrated by late 1848. In July, political fissures broadened into open revolt when a military *coup* was only defeated by troops loyal to Suárez leaving the defensive lines and retaking control of the city. In August, Colonia, the last point held by the government outside the capital, fell to Oribe. The defence of Montevideo now depended upon the payment of the 40,000 dollars monthly subsidy to which Gros had committed the French government in June. 'Everything here looks as if the present state of affairs was drawing to a close,' Gore confided to Palmerston. His chief concern, as Britain's representative, was to keep clear of party feeling. 'On good terms with *all*,' he concluded, 'intimate with *none*.'[1]

Dire as the situation in Montevideo undoubtedly was, that was not Palmerston's immediate concern. What he wanted was a diplomatic settlement with Buenos Aires which merely acknowledged Uruguayan sovereignty without any regard for who or which party ruled the country. To that extent the stubborn survival of a regime locked up in the capital with which Rosas would not treat was more of a hindrance than a help to his policy. Like the merchant lobby which continued to pester him, Palmerston wanted an end to the political stalemate and a return to peace in La Plata. Thereby, he explained to the new French government in July 1848, he would be free as soon as possible from 'the fruitless embarrassments' of 'this ill-judged and unfortunate interference.'[2] To achieve this, it was essential to get Henry Southern into Buenos Aires and to reopen some form of negotiation. To lessen the chance of causing affront, Southern sailed there directly from Rio de Janeiro without calling at Montevideo or consulting with Gore or Herbert *en route*. On 5 October 1848 he ventured ashore at Buenos Aires aware, of course, of the risk of being rebuffed.

To his surprise, Southern was politely and even cordially received by political figures there and also by members of Rosas' own family.

He was invited to visit the Governor himself on 14 October, on which occasion he endured a four-hour session of diplomatic sparring. Rosas, it transpired, had much to say – at least unofficially. He had suffered the absurd lies of those who postulated that he did not want a reconciliation with London; on the contrary, what was needed was a properly signed peace treaty. Fighting between sovereign states must involve a state of war and, that being so, such a dispute could only be resolved by a formal agreement. Otherwise he would not accept a new British Minister as if nothing at all had happened since July 1845. In making this demand, Rosas had no reason to lack confidence. At home his regime seemed more secure than ever, since war with Britain and France had done much to unite the population behind him. As a public manifestation of this, in October 1848 the Hall of Representatives petitioned the Governor in glowing terms: Rosas was an example to all American states whose honour and independence might be trampled on by the injustice and force which were so much features of the foreign relations of European powers. Rosas had inspired the Argentine people's glorious defence in a time of danger.

On first encounter, Southern found Rosas excessively vain, obstinate and wild in his reasoning although, as he admitted to Palmerston, 'he has no weak point that we can touch.' Southern replied as best he could to Rosas' insistence on a proper peace settlement. He granted that 'differences of opinion and disagreeable occurrences had taken place', but this, he urged, was equally a reason for accepting him as an envoy as for rejecting him.[3] But Rosas remained impassive and, as Southern rightly realized, cared nothing for mere expressions of goodwill. Southern then asserted that Rosas was not technically justified in refusing him at Buenos Aires. Moreno had never left his post in London, nor indeed been asked to do so by the British government. Why then should Rosas deprive Britain of the same right of representation? Did Rosas realize that by denying Southern his proper status he risked Moreno's expulsion from London and hence a final diplomatic break? Again Rosas affected not to care. Clearly he neither thought the risk to be so great nor the consequences so frightening as Southern implied. As for coming to Buenos Aires without powers to negotiate and sign a formal convention, Southern had answered with feigned innocence that he could not think of any reason why such powers should have been issued. Britain asked for nothing which was not already afforded by the 1825 treaty. What need then for any fresh stipulations?

In this initial interview Rosas raised two other issues which he judged best brought into the open straight away. First, his annoyance at the way in which Gore's mission had been devised and handled. Britain and France had tried to negotiate a separate peace between Oribe and the government in Montevideo and thereby to drive a wedge between Rosas and his ally. The effect of doing so would have been to leave him in 'a ridiculous and even igniminious position,' Rosas complained; his feelings had been 'aggravated and outraged' by this clumsy diplomatic slight. As far as Rosas was concerned, he had already reached agreement in 1846 with T.S. Hood and had Howden and Walewski come out to confirm those terms then everything would have been long since settled. Once again Southern was on shaky ground in giving a reply, for it was obvious that Gore and Gros had been sent to La Plata specifically to bring about a peace which excluded Rosas. However, Southern assured his host that Gore's mission had been both 'misunderstood and misinterpreted'.[4] No disrespect had been intended in leaving the government at Buenos Aires out of the negotiations which Gore and Gros had conducted. Britain and France had simply wished to reduce the peace talks to the ostensible parties fighting the war. Rosas, after all, had always claimed that his troops acted only as auxiliaries to Oribe's army and that the Argentine Confederation itself was not at war but merely supporting its ally. Rosas said no more on this. The second issue which he raised was Britain's relations with the French and the latter's ambitions in South America.

With regard to the French, Rosas avowed that he could not comprehend Britain's motive in having cooperated with them. To him it was obvious that France intended to establish possession of Montevideo and ultimately the whole of the Banda Oriental as a colony, whereas, Rosas politely added, he had never suspected the British of territorial designs. Why had Aberdeen and Palmerston for so long allowed themselves to be used as unwitting agents of French policy? Southern rather feebly responded that the intervention with the French was now ended and that his arrival in Buenos Aires was intended to open a new phase in Anglo-Argentine relations. He acted alone as a diplomat, just as Herbert had acted independently when he had refused Le Predour's recent invitation to assign seamen to defend Montevideo. Rosas accepted these assurances. Clearly, Southern noticed, Rosas had been impressed by Herbert's strict refusal to land any of his men. These matters all discussed, Southern was left to ponder on his hours of conversation and the fact that Rosas, for all his evident civility, still refused to accept him as an appointed diplomat.

In the meantime Southern stayed on in Buenos Aires. Palmerston was assured that a variety of diplomatic and face-saving procedures would be adopted. 'This will give at least a couple of months before I can announce I intend to apply for clear instructions whether to stay or leave,' Southern judged. 'Given how slowly everything happens here this will enable me to remain in Buenos Aires "decently enough".'[5] In fact, life in Buenos Aires proved more attractive as the weeks passed than Southern had expected. He was soon prominent in local and diplomatic society and assured Palmerston on 17 December 1848 that 'I am treated with every distinction and deference this government can shew to a diplomatic agent, whether of a public or a private character.'[6] The final months of 1848 brought a more relaxed air back to the city and this was much to Southern's advantage. When the French navy had lifted its blockade in June 1848, commerce and shipping began to move again and the immigrants from Europe began to arrive. Some even came across from Montevideo and, as far as Southern could see, no questions were asked as to their role in the fighting.

Southern soon gathered information on another issue of concern to the Foreign Office in recent years – the fate of the British community which had remained in the city. The last eye-witness accounts had come from Howden while he had been negotiating with Rosas in 1847. Rosas had then boasted that all foreigners were safe under his protection: his reputation for such care was well known, he had impressed upon Howden, and was 'worth a thousand treaties.'[7] Southern found that indeed this was so. As long as the foreign community stayed indoors during the frequent military exercises and conformed to all other regulations, then their safety and property were respected. The British who had stayed on during the period of hostilities experienced nothing worse than financial misfortune caused, as so many had complained throughout, by the imprudent policy of their own government.

Between October 1848 and January 1849 Southern made only slow progress in his efforts to restore normal diplomacy. He could get no clear indication from Arana as to terms for a convention: he even came to doubt that Rosas really wanted a settlement of grievances with Britain at all. On 21 November several more hours of conversation with Rosas left Southern no nearer official recognition. Again he found the Governor 'extremely rational and moderate' but equally vague.[8] The only comfort to be drawn from this encounter was that

Rosas took the trouble to refer to the existing Anglo-Argentine treaty as binding and its provisions unaffected by recent conflict. Impatient for some greater sign of movement, however, at a further meeting with Rosas later in November Southern broached two sensitive issues by way of experiment. Knowing that Arana was drawing up a project of convention to be submitted to the British government, Southern enquired whether the same terms would be, or indeed could be, submitted to the French. The Hood bases of 1846, which when suitably modified would presumably form the basis of a comprehensive settlement, Southern ventured, had been an Anglo-French proposal. Surely, therefore, any agreement derived from them should be drawn up in terms acceptable in Paris? In reply came a gentle dismissal. 'The Argentine government looked upon France in a different light from that of Great Britain,' both Rosas and Arana insisted. This response might have appeared superficially flattering to the British but it contained no encouragement for what they really wanted – the withdrawal of both their own and French involvement from the politics of La Plata, for which purpose a broad settlement incorporating all parties was indispensable. The other issue which Southern raised was that of consular representation. Since the entire question of principle and national honour had become attached to the problem of his own official reception, why Southern asked could Martin Hood not be received as consul at Buenos Aires in order that he might perform his commercial duties? To allow this would be evidence of the conciliatory spirit of which Rosas had so often spoken in recent weeks. 'His Excellency appeared somewhat startled at my proposition, and after some hesitation said that I had broached a very delicate question,' Southern reported to London.[9] Later he heard that Arana had been told to think about this point.

While Southern struggled on at Buenos Aires, Palmerston made his position clear to the Montevidean authorities. The Uruguayan Consul-General in London, John O'Brien, provided Palmerston with the chance to do so when he begged the Foreign Office in November 1848 to rethink the way in which Britain was forsaking his country. Had Ouseley's armed intervention been continued, peace would long since have been restored to Uruguay, O'Brien insisted. Britain had shrunk from honouring its declarations of support for his people; indeed, 'it has in the last moments of their extremity abandoned them to their fate.' 'Never was there in the dealing between nations such inconsistency as that which has been pursued by Great Britain in the whole of these transactions,' he inveighed Palmerston.[10] But however impassioned O'Brien's appeal, Palmerston's ears were closed to its suggestion that Britain should again involve itself in the hostilities at Montevideo. Furthermore, he scoffed at the character of the government which O'Brien represented. The Uruguayan capital was under the military command of a handful of foreign adventurers, Palmerston replied. The authority of its nominal government appeared to be negligible and beyond the city walls it commanded not one inch of Uruguayan soil. 'It is evident, therefore, that it is the persons who exercise control in the town of Montevideo who are the causes of the continuance of the evils of which you complain.' In proposing a solution Palmerston was equally unyielding. 'Peace would be restored to the territory of the Uruguay if those persons who still hold out in the town were to make terms with General Oribe,' he sharply suggested.[11] This pressure to give up the struggle was continued in Montevideo. On 15 November Palmerston instructed Gore to raise the matter of the monthly subsidy which Gros had arranged for the French government to pay in support of the garrison. The Uruguayans would do well to consider what might be the ultimate consequence of this subsidy. Gore was told to alert the Foreign Minister that when the time arrived to repay it, the government in Montevideo might discover they could do so only at some sacrifice of national independence. Gore was to repeat Palmerston's advice that 'surely it would be far wiser for them to relieve themselves at once from this and from all other embarrassments by coming to such an agreement with Oribe as would put an end to the war.'[12] Above all, Gore should quash all rumours and destroy any pathetic hope in the city that material help would ever come from Britain which might allow its government or citizens to carry on their war.

By the middle of January 1849 still nothing had materialized to break the deadlock at either Montevideo or Buenos Aires. Arana eventually produced a draft Anglo-Argentine agreement but, on inspection, Southern found some of the terms so unrealistic that he frankly told Rosas that he could not even forward it to London. Rosas promised future discussion but evidently was in no hurry to proceed. Southern derived some comfort from the exercise in that even negotiations apparently destined to produce no reward at least justified his 'waiting decorously' in Buenos Aires.[13] Palmerston was content with this and, though he would have much preferred to see his envoy received officially, told Southern to express pleasure at the friendly manner in which these initial contacts had been conducted. There was, however, one most surprising development. Admiral Le Predour, formerly viewed by British agents as being committed to naval intervention and to the French military defence of Montevideo, sailed across the Plate and into the roadstead at Buenos Aires where, on 11 January 1849, he was granted permission to come ashore. Perhaps the French, too, were prepared to try for a political solution? Either that or, in the absence of any guidance from Paris, the navy had simply lost patience with current operations.

Very little was known of Le Predour's mission by the British diplomatic body. Gore believed that since Rosas would only treat on the basis of T.S. Hood's propositions of 1846 then logically Le Predour must be reconciled to those as a starting point. Gore also attributed this breakthrough to Southern's patient work with Rosas since October 1848, which had done much to reduce the sense of outrage and the bitterness felt at Buenos Aires against both European powers. But not all the French agents supported the Admiral's initiative. Eugène Guillemot, the chargé d'affaires at Rio de Janeiro, hastened south to Montevideo in February 1849 determined, Gore believed, to wreck any peace plan with Rosas before specific instructions came from Paris. Guillemot was a friend and long-term supporter of Louis Napoleon and his posting to Brazil reflected his particular devotion to the cause of French interests in South America and to the dream of a French colony being created in Uruguay. All this he had freely admitted to his British counterpart at Rio de Janeiro, James Hudson. Hudson was sure that Guillemot had also deliberately delayed instructions for Le Predour from Paris in the hope that this would damage the chance of a settlement with Rosas.

Southern shared Hudson's pessimism that Le Predour's best efforts for a Franco-Argentine agreement could be easily undermined. Nonetheless, he did what he could to help the process of reconciliation. 'I am doing my best because the French cause is our own,' he confided to Gore, 'and will amazingly facilitate any settlement with us *now* or *later*.'[14] He was certainly correct in believing so. On 6 March he finally received from Rosas the Argentine conditions for restoring diplomatic relations and settling the international dispute in La Plata. These terms, Southern reminisced, were the produce of 'long and laborious' meetings with the Governor; they were, he advised Palmerston, 'the only means of bringing the disastrous state of things now existing to a favourable termination.' 'The only alternative left,'

Southern concluded, 'is the adoption of this or some other arrangement which must vary but *little* from the proposed one or an open and decided rupture.'[15]

Rosas' project of convention contained the following provisions. First, the restoration of Martín García to Argentine possession, the return of all captured warships and a 21-gun salute for the Argentine flag. To this would be added the return by both parties of all captured merchantmen and their cargoes. Next, Argentine troops would withdraw from Uruguay when the French government disarmed all the foreign legions in Montevideo and concluded a treaty of peace at Buenos Aires. The British government should agree to use its good offices to persuade the French to comply. The Paraná River would be recognized as an inland waterway of the Argentine Confederation, subject to its laws and regulations alone. Britain would admit the Argentine republic's full right of belligerency comparable to that of any other sovereign state. Finally, the convention would be conditional on General Oribe's approval of it in his capacity as President of Uruguay and as an ally of the Argentine Confederation. On receiving this draft, Southern made a brief formal protest saying that he was not authorized to negotiate and that he could see no need for any convention to be signed before restoring proper diplomatic relations. He then recommended to Palmerston that the British government should accept it. To tempt the Foreign Secretary towards compliance, Southern stressed two small concessions which he had gained from Rosas after wearing down the latter's resistance. Rosas would drop the need to mention specifically T.S. Hood's proposals in this 1849 convention and he would also drop the need to secure Oribe's consent. Oribe's name would still appear in the text with the title of President, but only where he was declared to be so by the Argentine government. 'I conceive that such reference does not imply any acknowledgement of such title on behalf of the other party to the agreement,' Southern asserted.[16] Surely, at last, a mixture of words and phrases had been found whereby both nations could feel their honour saved and their interests protected.

It would be May before this news and Southern's advice reached London. Meanwhile, hopes had risen on hearing that Le Predour was also in Buenos Aires. When the ambassador of the French republic called at the Foreign Office Palmerston enquired as to Le Predour's instructions. To Palmerston's consternation the ambassador replied that as far as he knew none had been sent at all. In fact Le Predour had been left in La Plata without any credentials from the new regime in France. When instructions were drawn up they were imprecise, and then they were lost in Paris, thus ensuring further delay. Le Predour received no orders until the early weeks of 1849. To Palmerston's relief, however, the French ambassador did express 'a hope that as England and France had entered together into these affairs of the river Plate, they might also get out of them together.'[17]

More alarming, of course, was the news from Gore of Guillemot's plans to obstruct Le Predour. Palmerston urged Normanby in Paris 'to take such steps as you may think best calculated to defeat the plans of M. Guillemot,' and to remind the French government that the only object of Anglo-French intervention was to maintain the independence of Uruguay.[18] This need for concerted action with the French in settling their common differences with the Argentine Confederation was clearly spelt out by Palmerston on 21 April 1849. At the back of his mind was a suspicion of French policy in South America which the revolution in Paris and the advent of a new regime had nothing to diminish. 'It is indeed evident that if England were to make a separate arrangement, and to leave France with her differences with General Rosas unsettled,' he wrote to Southern, 'the British government would lose all right of objecting to the French occupation of Montevideo, and yet a prolongation of that occupation, ending possibly in the conversion of the country into a French colony, would be very adverse to British interests both commercial and political.'[19] He warmly approved, therefore, of Southern's assistance to bring about an agreement between Le Predour and the government at Buenos Aires.

Palmerston need not have worried. On 29 March 1849 Le Predour concluded an agreement with Rosas which he then dispatched to Paris for approval. The terms of this convention were little different from those which Southern was recommending his government to accept. Reference by name to the Hood bases of 1846 was omitted from the French convention, as it had been from the British draft. The problems of Oribe's status and of the legitimacy of the regime at Montevideo were solved by slight differences in the French and Spanish texts. Rosas had made sweeping gestures of statecraft in granting Le Predour this success. From what Gore had heard, Le Predour was treated to a lecture on why his government had no right to the same generous terms of settlement as those granted to the British. But, Rosas had magnanimously conceded, Le Predour had been so straightforward in his dealings and French politics appeared to be in such a state of turmoil that he would agree to treat with both powers in a similar way. Le Predour left Buenos Aires on 28 April to arrange an armistice at Montevideo. He would await orders from Paris, which he greatly hoped would approve of all that he had done. In the meantime he would try to bring together Oribe and the Montevidean government in some form of political compromise.

Le Predour's unexpected entry onto the diplomatic stage and his equally unexpected triumph greatly strengthened Southern's position with the Argentine authorities. So, too, did the economic boom now underway in Buenos Aires. By April 1849 cargoes of British manufactures arriving off the port could be sold on board ship as soon as anchors dropped. There was not a bale of British produce unsold in any warehouse in the city, Southern remarked, and merchants selling their goods on the vessels out from Liverpool were clearing profits of 40 per cent. In this heady climate Rosas agreed to an exchange of notes with Southern, whereby the latter would be allowed to communicate with the Foreign Ministry as a diplomat in all but name, while preserving the principle intact of no formal recognition before an agreement was signed. But Southern judged the time right to press for more than that. Rosas had unmistakably revealed his wish for a resumption of relations with the two great powers: he had even offered terms which the governments in Europe would likely find acceptable. At an interview on 12 May, therefore, Southern all but insisted on a public gesture from Rosas towards the renewal of Anglo-Argentine relations. In consequence, Martin Hood was allowed to take up his consular post at Buenos Aires and the remaining British and French warships in the Plate were allowed to communicate with the Argentine coastline.

There was, of course, one place where this news of diplomatic cordiality was received with anything but euphoria. In Montevideo, Le Predour's visit to Buenos Aires had naturally been a matter of considerable anxiety. Tension was increased by the evident expectation of French naval officers in the city that they would soon be going home. If it was really true, Gore wrote to the Foreign Office, then the defence of Montevideo was finished. The only source of income for the government, as before, was the French subsidy. The foreign legions were rebellious and quite out of control and the ministers in the government were in open dispute and disarray. Gore also reported the sad spectacle of distress within the city, with even respectable families reduced to begging in the streets. Nonetheless, the war faction, and those British traders who had long backed it, still kept a tenuous hold on power. The state of the government, Gore observed, was 'most pitiable'.[20] Of the British merchants, he advised Palmerston: they were 'a discontented set and hostile to all British agents that do not take their selfish view.'[21] These merchants blamed Rosas for all the evils in La Plata although in practice it was they who had kept the war going for so long.

Gore's frustration was eased in May 1849 when Le Predour returned from Buenos Aires. On 20 May the admiral issued an appeal to the French legion for order and cooperation with his seamen while everyone awaited news from France as to the acceptability of his convention. He announced that, for the time being, a ceasefire had been agreed with Oribe and insisted that the French legion should respect it. On 24 May the Montevidean government published its own official ceasefire pending word from France. Le Predour lifted his blockade of Oribe's supply ports and began to disperse his squadron. Within four weeks he had only five warships still in the Plate. Unshackled by any apparent communication with diplomats, or with politicians, the French admiral had stamped his authority on events in Montevideo in a manner seldom seen even in the days of Ouseley and Deffaudis – and all this without any contribution from the British.

Southern meanwhile continued with his subtleties across the Plate. He and Rosas indulged each other's nostalgia and agreed that the guns of British warships and those of the fort at Buenos Aires should resume the practice of saluting independence day and the Queen's birthday. These salutes passed off with all due attention on 24 and 25 May. In July the Argentine government began loan repayments due to British bondholders which had been suspended for some time. There was, in fact, nothing more to be done at Buenos Aires. By the summer of 1849 the initiative lay in Europe, where both the British and French governments had to decide whether to accept the conventions which Southern and Le Predour had negotiated. Palmerston did not object to the terms on offer but declined to authorize Southern to sign, on the grounds that he wanted a simultaneous agreement by the French government to Le Predour's draft, the text of which reached France in July 1849. This meant that diplomatic activity shifted to Paris, where Normanby was given the unenviable task of coaxing the authorities towards a settlement.

The overthrow of the Orleanist regime in February 1848 had done something to remove difficulties in Anglo-French relations. Clearly, with no monarchy in France, the issue of dynastic ties with Spain disappeared from the diplomatic agenda and the protracted dispute over the Spanish marriages came to an end. But a republic in Paris raised spectres from the past; it also was unlikely to be as concerned to maintain peaceful relations with Britain as Louis-Philippe and Guizot generally had been. Aside from Anglo-French relations Europe was, of course, absorbed by revolutions and their aftermath. Then, at the end of 1848, the uncertainties which followed the revolution in Paris gave way to the apprehensions which accompanied Louis Napoleon's election as President of the Second Republic. Until March 1849 there was war between Austria and the kingdom of Piedmont, while in Rome a revolutionary republic had been proclaimed in February 1849. Italy did require a measure of Anglo-French cooperation since the British were wary that any independent action by the French government might lead to too close an association between France and revolutionary movements throughout the peninsula. In April 1849 Russell felt confident enough to refer to 'our French alliance' in Italian affairs and wrote, in hope, to Palmerston that this 'cornerstone of our present policy' might be maintained.[22] There was another encouraging sign: Normanby was on good terms with Louis Napoleon, who seemed to be receptive to the ambassador's opinions and advice. But the atmosphere of cooperation was soured in June when the French government sent an army into Rome to reestablish papal rule. After September diplomatic priority had also to be given to averting conflict between the Austrian and Russian governments and Turkey over Polish and Hungarian political refugees who had found asylum on Turkish soil. As so often in the past, the need of both the British and French governments to address their difficulties in South America was eclipsed by events at home and by issues central to European diplomacy.

Normanby's immediate problem in 1849 was to find a stable point of contact with the French government as Foreign Ministers came and went. As for the affairs of La Plata, the incumbents at the Quai d'Orsay had two things in common – ignorance and preoccupied indifference. Bastide, who had occupied the post at the end of 1848, had expressed full confidence in Le Predour's judgment. But with the election of Louis Napoleon as President, the government changed. Drougn de Lhuys replaced Bastide, only to find that the latter had not been in the habit of keeping proper records. By July de Tocqueville was Foreign Minister. Normanby found him reluctant to take any decisions. Furthermore, he disliked the problems of La Plata and simply blamed them all on his predecessors. But, as the British came to realize, there was more than just administrative chaos behind this political paralysis. There was a 'strong party' in the elected Assembly who opposed any peace with Rosas on the grounds that an abandonment of Montevideo, and of the Frenchmen who manned its defences, would be dishonourable and a blow to national pride.[23] In a dispatch of 30 June 1849 Palmerston reiterated his distrust of the French. The principle of Uruguay's independence had formed the basis of the joint intervention, he reminded Normanby, and any departure from it could not fail to have a detrimental effect on relations between Britain and France. Several of de Tocqueville's friends and political associates, including Baron Gros, had been in London and had tried to persuade Palmerston to agree to an Anglo-French expedition of between six and eight thousand men to drive the Argentine army out of Uruguay. As always, Palmerston had dismissed the suggestion. His willingness to act in concert with the French went no further than signing simultaneous peace conventions in the firm belief that only by that means could he end French interference in Montevidean politics and ultimately ensure a complete French withdrawal from the region.

By August Normanby was, alas, no further on with the French. De Tocqueville made promises to settle Le Predour's convention but it was clear that there were intrigues afoot in Paris to prevent its endorsement. On 16 August de Tocqueville admitted to Normanby that he could not guarantee that the National Assembly would ratify the terms. By now neither Palmerston nor Southern felt able to wait any longer. In Buenos Aires the latter was being pressed by Arana to sign and was accused of misleading the Argentine government into believing that its proposals might be acceptable. This was a great change, of course, from late 1848 and early 1849, when it was Rosas who had spun out all the preliminary negotiations. Southern, however, thought he knew the reason why. Rosas had expanded on his schemes for developing the port at Buenos Aires, for increasing commerce and for revenue reforms. Talk of warfare was out of fashion now at Buenos Aires; Rosas even spoke of disbanding his armies, and therefore the sooner regular international relations were restored, the better for all his ambitious plans. In September 1849 Palmerston sent off full powers to sign the treaty in the form that Southern had submitted it to London. The only extra step required of Southern was to remind the Argentine authorities of the assurances, made to Howden in 1847 and to Gore in 1848, that Oribe would guarantee the lives and property of all the inhabitants of Montevideo when he entered the city. On receipt of these instructions, Southern signed at once. Peace and amity were officially restored between Britain and the Argentine Confederation on 24 November 1849.[24]

12· The Liberation of Montevideo and the End of the War

The turbulence in French politics seemed to grow worse as 1849 drew to a close. At the beginning of November de Tocqueville departed the scene along with the rest of Louis Napoleon's Cabinet. The political world in Paris talked of little else but the way in which the President's powers were expanding; most believed that Louis Napoleon had plans which would take him beyond merely serving France as the elected head of a republic. On 18 November General de la Hitte took over as Minister for Foreign Affairs. At the same time the President announced that the government would continue to recommend to the Assembly that the terms negotiated by Le Predour should be adopted. Such a recommendation, however, as Normanby knew, meant very little. De la Hitte admitted that he thought some modification to those terms would be necessary.

To Normanby's intense annoyance, his hand was further weakened by an administrative blunder in London. No one had bothered to tell him that on 3 September the dispatch had gone off to Buenos Aires which instructed Southern to sign the peace agreement on his own. For nearly three months Normanby had been telling the French government how important it was to have a simultaneous Anglo-French settlement with Rosas and how Palmerston had only delayed since July 1849 because of his belief that both powers should simultaneously extricate themselves from their difficulties in La Plata. This oversight was, as Palmerston admitted, 'a very serious omission' and one which placed Normanby 'in a very awkward situation'.[1] It was unlikely now that the French government would place any trust in Palmerston. On 23 December, with Le Predour's treaty being at last debated in the Assembly, Normanby informed Palmerston of the degree of hostility felt in Paris towards England and of the strength of the populist lobby for war in La Plata which resisted any concessions to the Argentine authorities. The debate indeed only served to confirm earlier predictions that there was no chance of ratification. There was widespread opposition to any reference to Oribe as President of Uruguay – even if only in the Spanish text. The Assembly also demanded much more from Oribe by way of assurances about life and property inside Montevideo before he could be permitted to enter the city. 'General de la Hitte begged I would impress upon Your Lordship the great difficulties under which the French government laboured in the present state of public feeling,' Normanby reported in January 1850.[2] The only good piece of news was that further negotiations with Rosas would be entrusted once again to the capable Le Predour who, having briefly returned to France, was sent straight back to his command in the Plate.

The tenor of debate in Paris throughout the latter half of 1849, and in particular the frequent abuse directed at Rosas, naturally had repercussions in Buenos Aires. Southern found the Governor once more sullen and uncooperative and still unwilling to accept him as Minister. By December even Southern's patience at this delay had become exhausted. He requested an interview and gave notice that his reception would be the subject raised. Rosas had consistently led him to believe that, once a convention was signed, normal diplomatic relations would be resumed. Now Rosas spoke of formal ratification in London providing a more suitable moment; he also mentioned the need for Britain first to fulfil an important provision of the agreement by returning his warships seized in August 1845. Southern confessed himself to be both surprised and indignant. This news would make a very bad impression in London, he replied. How could the Argentine government refuse to accept a diplomat with whom it had just signed a treaty? As for the return of the Argentine squadron, nations only signed treaties on the assumption that each party would carry out its terms: 'otherwise the whole thing was a farce,' Southern remonstrated.[3] Rosas had never seen the British envoy in such a mood before and proved quite unprepared. A week later Southern learnt that Rosas no longer demanded an immediate return of the warships but would be satisfied instead with a letter informing the Argentine authorities that the appropriate instructions had been issued to the current commander on the Brazil station, Admiral Barrington Reynolds. Southern, to his great relief, was finally received as Minister to the Argentine Confederation on 24 February 1850. He spent £200 on a public ball in celebration, which Palmerston grudgingly agreed to cover as an extraordinary disbursement.

The degree to which the British had thrown in their lot with Rosas as the best prospect for peace and political stability in the region was evident from the way in which Gore increasingly disassociated himself from the Uruguayan government and even began to conduct diplomatic business with Oribe. By the beginning of 1850 Gore was practically preparing Oribe for his return to the presidency. At the Cerrito on 17 January, Gore suggested that the General should send an agent to Rio de Janeiro. This would give Oribe a diplomatic presence in an important neighbouring state and would also help to counter the intrigues of the Montevidean envoys there who still hoped that they could persuade the Brazilian government to enter the war. Oribe, naturally, was delighted at receiving such encouragement. In February 1850 Gore visited him again. This time his suggestion was that Oribe should try to present a more democratic image to the outside world; he should call a House of Assembly, comprising delegates from all over Uruguay. Such a move would lessen the force of his critics in Paris who reviled him as a military dictator with no popular standing in his own country and who thereby prevented the French government from ratifying Le Predour's settlement with Rosas. Oribe promised Gore that he would give the matter grave consideration. Secretly, as Gore soon discovered, he had written immediately to Rosas for guidance.

Behind Gore's growing contacts with Oribe lay the assumption, of course, that resistance from within Montevideo was petering out. With its coffers empty and its former allies now concluding peace treaties with Rosas, surely, Gore reasoned, the government merely awaited the moment when the foreign legions also would at last give up the struggle. Gore dispatched to London his latest estimates of the numbers of men still under arms behind the lines. Thiébaut had about 800 men left in his French legion, while there were 300 Basques and 380 Italians. Uruguayan soldiers in the town numbered about 1400. However, Gore's assumption was disturbed in April 1850 by the unexpected arrival of French ships from Europe which brought 1500 regular soldiers to an anchorage off Montevideo. These troops proved to be an escort for Le Predour, who had arrived back in the River Plate to renegotiate his convention with Rosas. Le Predour declared that they had come to ensure that the foreign legions in Montevideo could be disarmed and disbanded and that an agreement with Rosas, which required this of him, could therefore be properly enforced. Whether this was true or not, there was no doubting the preponderant position which the French now occupied in the river. In addition to his 1500 soldiers, Le Predour had seven well-armed men-of-war, two small armed steamers and several transport and supply ships. The only other naval presence worth reporting were four Brazilian, two Sardinian and two United States vessels. The British were reduced to mere spectators. Gore could register only one modest British warship and two small steamers in the Plate.

Southern and Gore were both alarmed by the French admiral's return in force. As far as they were concerned, his chance of a successful renegotiation of the 1849 agreement was hindered, not enhanced, by so ostentatious a gesture. Neither Rosas nor Oribe accepted the pretence that the troops had come only to disband the legions in Montevideo; they believed that the troops came to intimidate the Argentine government into modifying the 1849 draft treaty. Le Predour still hoped for peace, Southern reassured Palmerston, but was also well aware that should he break off relations with Rosas, and set his 1500 men to challenge the invaders of Uruguay, he would be welcomed back to France by a large part of the elected Assembly as a national hero. It was not immediately clear what changes to the original agreement Le Predour was demanding. Normanby never discovered in Paris what the admiral's precise instructions were. Only on 1 May, nearly three weeks after Le Predour had landed at Buenos Aires, was Southern able to send to London an account of the issues under discussion. In the 1849 agreement Argentine troops were to be withdrawn from Uruguayan territory as soon as the foreign legions in Montevideo had been disarmed. Le Predour was now insistening that, before the legions were disarmed, all Argentine soldiers must have withdrawn to the east bank of the River Uruguay. They would then cross the river as soon as news arrived from Montevideo that the legions had been disbanded. This was, of course, a significant alteration. Rosas responded by claiming that in practice it annulled the French commitment to disarm the foreign legions. Once the Argentine forces were withdrawn to the River Uruguay, the French knew very well that for reasons of the men's morale and their expectation of returning home it would be impossible to take them back to rejoin Oribe's much-diminished army outside Montevideo. It was tantamount to making Oribe lift his siege without any reciprocal advantage. Le Predour also required all reference to Oribe as President of the country to be removed from the treaty in both languages. Not surprisingly, Southern reported that the talks were making no progress whatsoever. Rosas was being pressed quite publicly to make major concessions.

Palmerston's capacity to influence these negotiations in 1850 was effectively removed by a dramatic deterioration in Anglo-French relations. France recalled her ambassador from London as a protest against the British blockade and bombardment at Piraeus, while in Paris Normanby's contacts with de la Hitte became formal and infrequent. Even so, Palmerston was not deterred from urging upon the French a speedy settlement at Buenos Aires. He knew about the objections in Paris to signing any convention which would give Oribe control of Montevideo. Nonetheless he required Normanby to try to bring de la Hitte round to the British view that the return of Oribe to power in Uruguay was the only realistic solution to the conflict. But such an argument was useless in Paris. De la Hitte informed Normanby that the positions of the British and French governments were not comparable. There were thousands of French nationals in Montevideo who looked to Paris for protection. Furthermore, France had for months being paying its subsidy to the government there specifically to enable it to survive.

Despite these problems in Paris, at Buenos Aires both parties were ultimately prepared to make the concessions needed to reach a new agreement. Southern, as before, was full of praise for Le Predour's diplomatic skills. The admiral had somehow succeeded in convincing Rosas that the soldiers accompanying him were not linked to his mission. Rosas had thus felt sufficiently confident again to display generosity in agreeing to changes in the original draft. In return Le Predour had accepted the face-saving provision that Oribe's formal agreement to the Franco-Argentine convention would be sought before signature. As a further gesture, in August 1850 Le Predour reduced the subsidy paid to the Montevidean government. On 31 August, with the formality of Oribe's consent obtained, Le Predour and Arana signed a new treaty.[4] In order to disarm the foreign legions, Le Predour had landed his 1500 soldiers in Montevideo twelve days before. The city remained quiet, Gore observed in September, 'and has now quite the appearance of a French possession'.[5]

It was natural for Southern, a diplomat himself, to see the reason for Le Predour's success as finesse in negotiation and sensitivity in handling Rosas. By August 1850, however, Rosas had his own reasons for wanting finally to settle his differences with the French. Rosas' authority at home seemed a little less secure than it had been of late. Resistance to the challenge from Britain and France had reinforced his personal prestige but it had done little truly to reconcile the military governors of the other Argentine states to the excessive power wielded by Buenos Aires within the Confederation. Most dangerous among these malcontents, as usual, was Urquiza in Entre Rios. He had, of course, throughout the years of warfare in La Plata, adapted his stance towards both Rosas and the intervening European powers to suit his own military and political advantage.

Although Urquiza had backed away from an open challenge to Rosas in 1846 and 1847, Rosas had since convinced himself that he must weaken Urquiza by undermining the economy of Entre Rios and in particular the growing salt meat industry which operated so successfully through the outlet of Rosario on the Paraná River. In 1847 Rosas imposed new tariffs on goods entering Buenos Aires from the other states of the Confederation. He then prohibited the movement of metal money from Buenos Aires to the provinces, which obliged the merchants from Entre Rios to accept his devalued paper currency. Effectively Rosas decreed that Buenos Aires should be the only port available for the commerce of Entre Rios and further restrictions followed in 1849. Urquiza was aware of this scheme to isolate and to destroy the prosperity of his state, and of course his own vast estates within it, and he protested vigorously against all Rosas' measures between November 1848 and October 1849. By 1850 the Argentine was rife with rumours of rebellion. 'It is very certain,' Southern predicted, 'that General Urquiza will not long submit to the commercial thraldom in which the provinces on the Paraná are kept by the government of Buenos Aires.'[6] Nevertheless, Southern left no doubt where he thought British interests lay. Rosas, for all his faults, held the key to stability in the Argentine and thus to the long term benefit of Britain's economic contacts; he was, in short, the only force which held together the loosely linked Confederation.

*   *   *

By the latter half of 1850 the affairs of La Plata were also complicated by renewed Brazilian participation. Since her exclusion from the Anglo-French policy in 1845, Brazil had watched developments from the sidelines content, at least initially, that the European powers were prepared to take a stand against Argentine domination of the Banda Oriental. The victory at India Muerta had startled the government in Rio de Janeiro; such a display of Argentine military power had led

Brazil publicly to distance herself from the ailing regime in Montevideo. However by the end of 1846 it was apparent to the Brazilian government that the British, and probably the French too, wanted to abandon the intervention, raising the spectre of a settlement in Uruguay which favoured Rosas and Oribe. If Brazil had one overriding interest in the war it was to keep it going, Hudson informed Palmerston confidentially in September 1846. Once Rosas had restored Oribe to the presidency in Montevideo, his Argentine forces would be free to launch an expedition against Brazil and to destroy central authority in the southern provinces of the empire.

Hudson did not believe that these fears were unduly exaggerated. In a conversation with General Guido in April 1847, Hudson learnt that Rosas did intend to press Brazil for redress on a variety of Argentine grievances and contemplated the possibility of war and an incursion into Rio Grande do Sul if satisfaction was not forthcoming. Brazil's response to the faltering European presence in La Plata was to improve both diplomatic and economic ties with her neighbours – particularly with Paraguay. Some Brazilian politicians dreamt of a defensive league against Rosas which would embrace the Argentine states of Entre Rios and Corrientes, and which the government in Montevideo could also join. Certainly, Hudson concluded, Brazil would exhaust all political opportunities to contain the power of Rosas before it risked a military confrontation.

For reasons unconnected with events in La Plata, Anglo-Brazilian relations had remained at a low ebb in the late 1840s. Disputes over the commercial treaty and an anti-slave trade agreement still soured communication between the two governments. Hudson told Palmerston in January 1847, and again in February 1848, that no progress was possible with a new treaty nor with attempts to suppress the slave trade. In Brazil, he lamented, 'all parties are alike in their hatred to us.'[7] Brazil neither wanted nor indeed perceived that it needed closer ties with Britain – a dent perhaps to British pride but of limited significance for so long as Brazil was content to remain neutral in the war in La Plata. In April 1847, however, a government minister in Rio de Janeiro announced that that would no longer be possible. It was common knowledge that throughout the 1840s Brazil had, as its immediate interests dictated, opened and closed its frontiers to the soldiers of both Oribe's and Rivera's armies, and likewise its ports to the shipping of both belligerents, and that neutrality had always been difficult to maintain. Brazil was, in fact, gradually being forced into an intervention in Uruguay by the need of the imperial government to assert its authority in Rio Grande do Sul.

The frontier between Rio Grande and the Banda Oriental was loosely delineated. Several large estates in Uruguay were owned by Brazilian nationals, and cattle had always been traded freely across the border. On account of the war, Oribe had tried to stop this movement of valuable livestock out of the country much to the annoyance of the landed proprietors whose livelihoods he threatened. Foremost among these was the Brazilian Baron Jacuhy who in 1848 began to organize incursions by irregular Brazilian soldiers into Uruguay in defiance of Oribe's orders to seal the frontier. Jacuhy, whose men hailed him by his guerrilla name of Chico Pedro, conducted a series of audacious cattle raids and, inevitably, clashed with Oribe's forces in northern Uruguay. The government in Rio de Janeiro played down Jacuhy's excursions and gave little public support to his cross-border operations. But in truth it was powerless to stop him and recognized that Jacuhy had the support of the *estancieros* of Rio Grande, upon whom the writ of the imperial government in the province depended.

As the scale of Jacuhy's operations mounted, the clamour for war against Oribe grew louder in Rio Grande do Sul; so much so, Hudson wrote to Palmerston in December 1849, that if the Brazilian government did not declare war soon, then Jacuhy and his followers would declare their province a sovereign territory and join the conflict in Uruguay on their own account. Early in 1850, after an initial defeat by one of Oribe's commanders during a border raid, Jacuhy entered Uruguay with 900 horsemen and put to flight a detachment of Oribe's army. Thereafter Jacuhy joined the political struggle in the Banda Oriental by issuing a proclamation which called upon the people of the country to rise up against Oribe's tyranny and to join with the defenders of the capital. The situation on the Brazilian frontier was now so serious for Oribe that he was compelled to send troops from his army at Montevideo northwards in 1850 until, on 9 May, Jacuhy was routed in battle with the loss of over 200 of his men. Even after this, Oribe felt obliged to keep more than 3000 soldiers on the frontier to prevent any resurgence of guerrilla operations. The tide of separatism still ran strongly in Rio Grande and Jacuhy's defeat had done nothing to enhance the central government's power there. Since 1846, 9000 of the Brazilian government's 15,000 regular soldiers had been stationed in this southern province primarily for the task of averting a new outbreak of republican insurrection. By 1850 it was clear that the only way out of this dilemma for the imperial government was to yield to the call for war.

Hudson viewed Brazil's drift from neutrality with growing unease. His problem was to keep the peace between Brazil and the Argentine states, but as the months passed he became ever more pessimistic. Hudson was cynical about the Brazilian government's role in the raids across the Uruguayan frontier in 1849 and 1850. 'There is no doubt whatever that these incursions of Chico Pedro have been encouraged by the Brazilian government,' he reported to London.[8] More to the point, he continued, Rosas knew this too. At the end of August 1850, Jacuhy was warmly received by the Emperor in Rio de Janeiro despite General Guido's prior demand that the guerrilla leader should be publicly punished for his military adventures against Oribe. Jacuhy returned to Rio Grande do Sul well satisfied with his treatment and confirmed in the opinion that the central government had no option but to support his cause.

On 9 September 1850 Hudson informed Palmerston that there was no chance of preventing a break in diplomatic relations between Brazil and the government at Buenos Aires. 'I have done all I could,' he wrote apologetically, 'but in vain.'[9] Rosas had insisted that Jacuhy be punished. The Brazilian government had replied that whereas it might be required to justify irregular raids by its nationals into Uruguay to Oribe, it most certainly was not accountable to Rosas, who had no *locus standi* in Uruguayan affairs. Rosas responded that if that was the case, then his envoy would ask for his passport. The Brazilians assured him that Guido could collect his passport at any time.[10] On 2 October Guido left Rio, convinced that the Brazilian government had chosen to intervene against Oribe in the Banda Oriental and to fight a war against Buenos Aires in preference to facing a civil war in Rio Grande do Sul. An additional pressure on the Brazilian government had been the news from Buenos Aires that Rosas and Le Predour had signed a convention. The French garrison at Montevideo would be withdrawn and the foreign legions in the city disarmed, thus effectively ending all resistance to Oribe. In desperation, therefore, Brazil had to act to safeguard her influence in Uruguay and to try to confine the power of Rosas to within the limits of the Argentine Confederation.

A war between Brazil and the Argentine Confederation was potentially more disruptive to British trade than anything which had occurred in La Plata in the 1840s. Not surprisingly, Palmerston urged both

Hudson and Southern to offer their good offices to the Brazilian and Argentine governments in order to help reconcile the differences which had arisen. Both envoys were to make it plain that under the terms of the 1828 treaty between the two countries they had undertaken to give Britain, as the mediating power on that occasion, six months' notice of any recurrence of hostilities. The prospect of a major war in South America also placed Palmerston under further pressure to persuade the French to conclude their involvement in La Plata. To his frustration, Le Predour's second treaty with Rosas seemed no more guaranteed of approbation in Paris than his first, and Palmerston was now concerned that the possibility of war might become the excuse for refusing ratification. Further delay in Paris 'would shake the confidence of Her Majesty's Government in the good faith of France in regard to these affairs and would countenance the suspicion that France wished to find an excuse for continuing her military occupation of Montevideo,' he urged Normanby to inform the French authorities.[11] Britain and France had always agreed that the protection of Uruguay's independence was the basis for all that they had tried to do in the region; neither power could conceivably consent, therefore, to any part of Uruguay falling under the permanent occupation of the other. But Palmerston made no specific threat; there was, as Normanby soon discovered, no leverage available.

By the spring of 1851 it was quite obvious that the views of both the British and French governments had become largely irrelevant to what was taking place in South America. Whether or not the Assembly in Paris ratified Le Predour's treaty with Rosas was academic: its terms could no longer be executed. The time had passed when the French could bring the Montevidean government into line by threatening to abandon the town. By 1851 the departure of the French was eagerly awaited, since Le Predour appeared to have committed French troops to disbanding the foreign legions which still defended the city. The government there could also at last look with confidence to Brazil to invade and thereby save it from a surrender to Oribe. Hudson's dispatches kept the Foreign Office up to date with Brazil's preparations for war. In March 1851 he reported heavy borrowing by the government from financial sources in Rio; at the same time the government appointed Admiral John Grenfell of the Brazilian navy to command a squadron of 11 warships bound for the Plate. When Hudson asked the Foreign Minister about these moves he was told simply that Brazil could not be expected to stand idly by while Rosas made himself master of Uruguay. Hudson knew also from John Morgan, the British consul at the port of Rio Grande do Sul, of the build-up of 16,000 Brazilian soldiers on the Uruguayan frontier. In May, Hudson was curtly informed by the government at Rio that there was no obligation to give Britain six months' notice of any intended hostilities. Britain's role as mediator in 1828 had ended with the conclusion of the treaty between Brazil and the Argentine Confederation, and she no longer had any standing in relations between those two sovereign states. Unwelcome as this message was, Hudson told Palmerston plainly that Britain was powerless to prevent war once the decision at Rio had been made.

After concluding an agreement with the Brazilian government early in 1851, it was, in fact, General Urquiza who made the first move against Rosas. On 1 May he declared Entre Rios to be a sovereign nation and withdrew from the government of Buenos Aires the authority to conduct international affairs on its behalf. Later in the month a formal league was declared between Entre Rios, Brazil and the government in Uruguay. The Governor of Corrientes then joined with Urquiza and broke all links with Buenos Aires.[12] Urquiza secured another valuable political ally when the respected Uruguayan general, Eugenio Garzón, until recently a loyal supporter of Oribe, declared in his favour.[13] Urquiza and Garzón planned an invasion of Uruguay from Entre Rios, the defeat of Oribe at the Cerrito and then a triumphant entry into Montevideo. Urquiza would be hailed as liberator and Garzón acknowledged as the man uniquely qualified to rebuild national unity, and thus the obvious candidate for the presidency. On 19 May 1851 Urquiza began to move his army of 15,000 men across the River Uruguay. After nine years of siege and military stalemate, he had dramatically opened the final chapter in the war.

Within six weeks of Urquiza's invasion, the Brazilian government also made its move. Brazil gave an assurance to the government in Montevideo that its troops would enter Uruguayan territory solely to force Oribe to withdraw and that Uruguay's independence would not be in jeopardy. Faced with Urquiza from one side, the Brazilians from the other, and with defections among his own officers and men, Oribe realized his precarious position. To compound his problems the Brazilian navy cut his supply route across the Plate. Brazil also threw down a clear challenge to his Argentine ally by placing a blockading squadron at the mouth of the Paraná River, thereby cutting off Buenos Aires from the other littoral states. As a final gesture of commitment, the

THE LIBERATION OF MONTEVIDEO AND THE END OF THE WAR 183

Brazilian navy landed 800 soldiers at Montevideo – a move welcomed by the local authorities and unopposed by Le Predour's French garrison. Oribe would either have to fight or evacuate his army across the Plate to Buenos Aires. On investigation, however, the option of a retreat by sea appeared to be closed. Urquiza and the Brazilian navy were not prepared to allow Oribe's 5000 or more experienced Argentine soldiers to embark safely and sail away, later to be available to fight for Rosas when the inevitable battle took place between the contending forces within the Confederation. In desperation, Oribe turned to Gore for support. He needed assurances from the British and French naval commanders in the Plate that they would guarantee his Argentine troops a passage home, unmolested by any third party. Gore was uncertain what to do. He replied that, although the British and French navies were neutral in this conflict, their commanders might offer their moral influence to allow an evacuation on humanitarian grounds. But, as Gore wrote to Palmerston, there was no chance of weakening either Urquiza's or Brazilian resolve on this point. If Oribe would not, or could not, fight then he would have to surrender. As for Britain's best interest, he advised Palmerston on 5 September, 'I think that we had better abstain from any step that may involve us in future difficulties in these countries.'[14]

In Buenos Aires, Rosas sent for Southern to discuss the fate of his troops now acknowledged as being stranded in Uruguay. Southern was too ill to leave his house, but Rosas was soon at his bedside explaining the urgency of the problem. The conversation from Rosas was 'long and desultory', Southern later bewailed, but he did agree with the Governor that it was in the best interest of all parties that the Argentine troops be allowed to return home, since that would avert a direct military clash with the Brazilians.[15] On 30 September, therefore, Arana sent a formal request for the British Minister to press Reynolds to give a guarantee of safe passage across the Plate for Argentine soldiers. 'Our government, in its anxiety to prevent a war between two countries so important to our commercial interests, have (*sic*) made an offer to the Argentine government of its friendly offices to bring about a reconciliation between it and the Brazilian empire,' Southern wrote stiffly to Reynolds. 'I am persuaded that one of the friendliest acts of interposition which we could employ would be this one of relieving the Brazilian forces from all danger of contact with the Argentine troops.'[16] But Reynolds was not interested. His orders were to keep clear of any hostilities unless the lives of British subjects or their property were endangered and any assistance for Oribe's soldiers would constitute British naval cover for a retreating army. His last hope gone, on 8 October 1851 Oribe surrendered his army without giving battle. Urquiza had raised the nine-year siege of Montevideo.

In one of the last dispatches from Buenos Aires before he was transferred to serve as Minister at Rio de Janeiro, Southern gave his assessment of these remarkable events. He had been astonished by the success of Brazil's military and naval intervention in Uruguay. 'The standing of that country in South America is thereby doubtless elevated and her importance increased,' he advised the Foreign Office.[17] By contrast, the French position in Uruguay was eclipsed and her prospective treaty with Rosas an irrelevance. Argentine interference in the country was finished too. Southern showed shrewd judgment, for undoubtedly the balance of power among the Platine states had changed. But in looking to the future, Southern's touch was far less sure. Although he recognized that Urquiza had emerged as a formidable opponent, he did not believe that Rosas could be toppled by a military revolt. In manpower, horses and all other materials of warfare, the territory of Buenos Aires could sustain sufficient force to defeat any invader and ultimately to crush the wayward states of Entre Rios and Corrientes. Furthermore, he stressed, it suited foreign interests that Rosas should survive in power. For the European powers, Southern believed to the end that Rosas stood for an order of things which was not incompatible with economic development and in which their trade could expand and their migrants prosper.

Southern was replaced at Buenos Aires by Robert Gore, who assumed his new duties on 1 December 1851. Gore's initial advice to Palmerston on Britain's general position in the region was much the same. 'I dislike and condemn the system of Rosas, as all liberal men must do,' he considered, 'but I conceive it would be a great evil should he be vanquished, as this system gives protection to life and property – more particularly to that of foreigners, and it is based on order.'[18] Soon, however, Gore was losing confidence in Rosas' capacity for survival. By January 1852 Urquiza was reported to have taken the towns of Santa Fé and Rosario and was across the Paraná and on the southern shoreline of the Plate. Rosas had also lost the best of his commanders and would himself now have to join his army outside Buenos Aires, where his personal prestige would be necessary if his troops were to fight on.

In the event, the end for Rosas was swift and comparatively bloodless. None of the military men around him had spoken truthfully of the strength of Urquiza's army. Instead they had fed him stories of how forces loyal to the dictator were quickly closing on Urquiza's flank and rear. When Rosas rode out of Buenos Aires on 3 February 1852 to lead his men to immortality, it was in the conviction that the lines of battle would prove a mere formality. Although Gore estimated his losses by desertion at the end of January to be as high as 7000 men, Rosas still led 18,000 men onto the field. Urquiza, however, led 24,000 well trained soldiers – among them, Gore estimated, 3500 Brazilians, 1500 Uruguayans and others drawn from many of the states of the Confederation.[19] Urquiza was also an experienced battle commander, whereas Rosas most certainly was not. But vital to the outcome on the day, Gore wrote to Palmerston, was the treachery of those around Rosas who, seeing that his star had waned, had already opened channels to his enemies. Once the new recruits and conscripts of Rosas' army began to break formation, his senior commanders simply switched their service to Urquiza.

The diplomatic corps went to greet Urquiza at his camp outside Buenos Aires. After the rout of Rosas' army their main concern was to arrange for a peaceful transfer of power to the victor when he entered the city. Marines were landed from the foreign warships in the Plate to protect the diplomatic residences and the Customs House. Returning home after his meeting with Urquiza, Gore found Rosas hiding in his bed and begging his assistance to flee the country. Gore later collected Manuelita and Rosas' son and helped them to safety on board a British warship.

Rosas spent his remaining years as an exile in England, where he died in 1877. His overthrow began a new phase in Argentine history which many observers in La Plata and in Europe were quick to appreciate. Though most of them had valued the order which Rosas had imposed at Buenos Aires, and the safety in which the foreign merchant houses could therefore go about their business, the British also realized that the great wealth of the continent still eluded their reach. Within weeks of Rosas' downfall, the British government sounded out the Foreign Ministry in Paris as to a joint special diplomatic mission to the Argentine Confederation. Its particular object would be to negotiate the opening of the Paraná and other rivers of the interior to the trade and navigation of foreign nations. Liberal opinion in Buenos Aires, long suppressed under Rosas, was also in favour of greater economic contact. Urquiza proved a leader well suited to this reawakened spirit of commercial enterprise when in the summer of 1852 he asked all the governors within the Confederation to begin the collection and publication of statistical information relating to their territories. Gore, who resided at Buenos Aires until his untimely death in 1854, like others divined in these developments the end of an era in this part of South America. The introspective mentality of the gaucho was disappearing and the forces of the international economy would no longer be held back by the political sterility of a generation steeped in the traditions of the independence struggle. The isolation of the interior, and the old political divisions between federalist and unitarian, also gradually became memories from the past. The economic monopoly of the port of Buenos Aires, enforced through an invidious imposition of customs dues, gave way within two years to freedom of navigation for international trade on the great tributaries of the Plate. Waves of European migration were, in decades, to transform the character of Argentine society, while constitutional reorganization presaged the emergence of Argentina as a nation state.

For the defenders of Montevideo, of course, the war had ended in liberation several weeks before Rosas' defeat. Oribe had capitulated on terms which, in order to heal the rifts among the Uruguayan population, declared that there were neither victors nor vanquished in the struggle. Events thereafter, though, took an unexpected turn. General Garzón, who, as anticipated, had emerged as a figure of sufficient standing to unite political opinion in Uruguay, died suddenly on 1 December 1851. Nor was that the nation's only problem. On 1 January 1852 repayment was due to begin of the monthly subsidy paid by the French government since June 1848. Although the trade of Montevideo began to improve rapidly in the new year, the Uruguayan government protested that the schedule was unrealistic, requiring as it did half of the customs receipts to be set aside until the debt was cleared. A commission was established for the classification and liquidation of debt. As late as March 1853, however, only about half of the total had been properly defined. The British Consul-General, George Lennon-Hunt, estimated that the gross debt of the Uruguayan government after ten years of warfare probably exceeded £8 million. Some of that was owed to the French and Brazilian governments and to the merchant houses which had lent on the security of the customs receipts. But much of it represented a commitment to bonds and paper currency issued to employees and creditors during the war, a lot of which was redeemable at only a percentage of its nominal value.

Perhaps, therefore, the hard core of irreducible obligation could be considered as no more than £3,500,000. On top of these problems, of course, was the occupation of the country by foreign troops, albeit by those of two friendly powers – Brazil and France. Terms still had to be arranged for their withdrawal.

The 1500 French soldiers in Montevideo left on 27 February 1852. This was on orders received from Paris and apparently without condition. The Brazilians likewise had no wish to linger. In June 1852 Britain's new chargé d'affaires, Frederick Bruce, reported an amicable settlement between the Brazilian and Uruguayan governments on the recognition of existing treaties, on debt repayment and the creation of a boundary commission to settle border differences. This represented a liberal concession from Brazil. Under the terms of a treaty made in October 1851, about which the Montevideans had been in no position to argue, Brazil had originally obtained large territorial concessions as the price for her military intervention.[20] It augured well for the independence of Uruguay, Bruce reported to London. The new regime in Buenos Aires had also given a guarantee to respect the terms of this modified Brazilian-Uruguayan accord.

The future, therefore, offered encouragement. Even a debt burden of £3,500,000, Bruce considered, would offer no serious obstacle to the progress of the country if peace could be secured for a few years. Bruce rightly saw in Uruguay the enormous attraction for European settlers. 'A very few years of an industrious immigration,' he predicted, 'will swamp entirely the native race, will introduce habits of industry and order, and put an end to the domination of the gaucho.'[21] As in the Argentine, the world of the *caudillo* was giving way to a new order of trade and investment which was to tie the life of the country increasingly to the requirements of industrialized Europe. In its politics, Lennon-Hunt noted in March 1853, Uruguay displayed the trappings of a modern state. Its government pursued the path of legal and constitutional propriety and was composed almost entirely of civilians. 'The race of military chiefs that has vexed this unfortunate country for so many years is happily disappearing, and there is not at this moment a leader in the provinces with sufficient prestige to assemble 300 men.'[22] The era of savage and partisan warfare seemed finally to have passed in all the territories of La Plata.

13· Conclusion

The British drew scant comfort from their years of intervention in La Plata. At the end of 1844 they had been confident that the region's destiny lay with their ability to adjudicate its problems. In 1847, however, few disagreed with Lord Auckland that the attempt had proved a 'disastrous business'.[1] The navy had blockaded Buenos Aires, it had supported the defenders of Montevideo and it had launched an exdition into the Argentine interior. Furthermore, these naval actions, like diplomacy, had all been conducted in conjunction with the French. Yet together the greatest powers of Europe could neither stop the fighting in Uruguay nor, crucially, compel the Argentine army to leave. Britain and France had demanded that their interests and their status be respected. Rosas had defied them both.

In the light of this failure, Martin Hood confided his worst fears in June 1848. 'The course of the intervention has given to these weak states and ignorant people the idea, which has been widely propagated, that European nations have not the power to resist them,' he reflected. 'I fear very much that future years will prove that the influence and moral power which English and French agents formerly had in these countries are totally gone.'[2] Howden, likewise, was certain that Britain's reputation had been seriously damaged. Britain had sunk into 'the abominably undignified position of being exposed to the insolence of a little potentate who wraps himself up in the inviolability of his geographical position'.[3] Hood returned to this theme in January 1849. 'Rosas has unfortunately been exalted from insignificance to an idea of immense power by the very measures adopted to oblige him to listen to reason. He loses no opportunity to make us smart under the vile abuse, the insult, or the contempt which he lavishes upon us on every occasion.'[4] In 1850 he still advised Palmerston that 'we shall never have so good a footing as we had a few years ago'.[5]

Nor was it only in Buenos Aires that British representatives sustained a loss of authority. In Montevideo, resentment at the way in

CONCLUSION

which the British had backed out of the intervention after 1846, and in particular at Palmerston's abusive admonitions for the city to surrender after 1847, became more pronounced as confidence began to return in 1850. The British had soon realized that the freedom of Uruguay was worth nothing if it cost them money through interrupted commerce, Herrera observed; they soon made their peace with Rosas at almost any price to protect their stake in La Plata.[6] Uruguay's revenge came when the elected Assembly revoked the 1842 treaty with Britain as its initial ten-year period expired. This was done, as Lennon-Hunt starkly reported, on the grounds that 'sufficient support was not given by Her Majesty's Government to the government of M. Herrera prior to the termination of the late war.'[7] It was not a chance to be missed, Ellauri had counselled in July 1851: 'let us free ourselves from the ties that bind us to these perfidious governments of Europe.'[8]

This diminution of Britain's credibility on both sides of the Plate seems anomalous in an age and in a region which, it is widely held, were fashioned by her economic and political might. The middle decades of the century witnessed, it has been argued, the flow of informal empire as Britain's overwhelming dominance in trade, and a navy effectively unchallenged on the high seas, gave her government the leverage to adjust global affairs to suit her near-monopoly of industrial manufacture. Such generalizations have been proffered as a perspective for the study of nineteenth-century imperialism and, in broad debate, there is no doubt that they have provided the cornerstones of a comforting historical orthodoxy. This should not be surprising. Although there are serious drawbacks to the application of any theory to the investigation of imperial history, there remains an appealing logic for establishing a framework for the interplay of commerce and political power. Increasingly sensitive to the need for democratic popularity, governments in London eased the progress of the merchant classes by negotiating commercial treaties and reciprocity agreements which removed restraints wherever possible, and sought to enshrine free trade as the axiom of a stable international order. When diplomacy stumbled, the navy was often at hand to act as its 'cutting edge'[9] – as Palmerston's awesome rhetoric seemed to make abundantly plain. Speaking of such weak but nonetheless independent nations as China, Portugal and those of South America, he prescribed 'a dressing every eight or ten years to keep them in order'. 'They care little for words,' he ruled, 'and they must not only see the stick but actually feel it on their shoulders.'[10]

Yet detailed study of the British in La Plata poses a profound challenge to these conventional canons of imperial history. Like another recent study,[11] it calls into question earlier assumptions that large areas of Africa and the Middle East, China and Latin America can readily be consigned to the grey and loosely defined area of Britain's informal empire. On close investigation, the intervention in La Plata shows the degree to which British economic interests were themselves divided and government policy vacillating or contradictory. The intervention offers some evidence of metropolitan governments in Europe supporting and extending commerce; it offers far more evidence of governments acting according to quite different rationales. For governments to coordinate their actions with the needs of economic expansion implies a perception of interest and a measure of control, both of which demonstrably were lacking.

After his interviews with Aberdeen in November 1843, Florencio Varela formed the clear impression that 'England, such is my conviction, does not know its own interests.'[12] In a sense he was right. The men of state in London had but a hazy understanding of what precisely constituted the important trading ties with La Plata to which consuls and merchants so frequently referred. Aberdeen thought that 'our commerce with Montevideo is rapidly increasing and is very much more considerable than with Buenos Aires.'[13] Palmerston, by contrast, expressed his belief that 'England has at least as great if not a greater interest in Buenos Aires than in Montevideo.'[14] At the Foreign Office there was a general wariness, too, of association with men of material ambition; traders were usually regarded as unscrupulous individuals who sought to direct diplomacy to their own advantage. Howden's assessment of the British community in Montevideo would have raised few eyebrows and was in line with the prejudice of many in the diplomatic service.'Unprincipled villains calling themselves British merchants,' was how he described them in August 1847. They were 'but mere speculators in war, disturbance, and foreign domination,' he warned the Foreign Office, who were 'powerful in England from having much of the Press under their orders and in their pay.'[15]

This questionable identity, especially among metropolitan officials, with the cause of commerce was often matched by their uncertain control of local agents. It was common in the early nineteenth century for men on the spot to exercise considerable discretion both in determining and in implementing the national interest. Problems of communication and rivalries between civilian and naval officers on distant stations not infrequently hindered attempts to coordinate foreign policy. It was by no means unknown for force to be employed without approval. Lord Napier at Canton involved the navy in diplomacy contrary to his orders in 1834.[16] Consul John Beecroft was firmly reproached by the Foreign Secretary, Lord Granville, for his unauthorized seizure of Lagos in 1851.[17] Ouseley, who showed himself more than willing to debate the meaning of imprecise instructions, and even to disregard them when he saw fit, and who was both inclined and indeed required to work closely with his French colleague, may stand as a further example of how individual initiative could compromise a government at home.

Ouseley himself, of course, claimed that the problem lay with his political masters, who did not know their own minds. When censured for his excesses he consistently responded that he did no more than execute a policy agreed by the British and French governments before he sailed from Europe. Ouseley felt that he was made a scapegoat for all that had gone wrong; even a year after his recall from Montevideo he still complained of the 'harsh official treatment that I have experienced, and also the great loss and injury that I sustain in my private interests.'[18] His public career was ruined and he was denied the half salary for which he had asked after 30 years in the diplomatic service. Only years later was there any softening of official attitudes. Ouseley was knighted in 1852. In 1853 Aberdeen conceded to the then Foreign Secretary, Lord Clarendon, that though Ouseley had fallen foul of Clarendon's predecessors, on reflection it had not been Ouseley's fault.[19]

Aberdeen's candour, however, serves only to obscure the issue of liability for mistakes that were made: it does not exonerate Ouseley. Ouseley had faced criticism in La Plata from the Hoods, Howden, Herbert and some of the junior naval officers, who all accused him of forsaking his role as mediator and involving Britain as a belligerent in war. Critics certainly saw Ouseley as a man who had broken from the diplomatic leash and as one who had proved susceptible to the pressures put upon him. Foremost among these, of course, was his assertive French colleague. One irate Liverpool merchant told Palmerston in 1846 what was common knowledge at Montevideo: that 'Mr. Ouseley is too weak a man to oppose the views of Baron Deffaudis.'[20] Ouseley's detractors also alleged that he had allowed Deffaudis to wreck the peace mission of T.S. Hood. In short, he had naively fallen in with French political ambitions in the region while believing simply that he was following instructions to cooperate with his French counterpart.

The second pressure to which Ouseley allegedly succumbed was that from the British community at Montevideo, whose intrigues and distortions were intended to bolster enthusiasm for naval action. By early 1847 Palmerston was convinced that all the accusations against Ouseley were justified – in particular the manner in which the blockade had degenerated into a revenue-raising exercise for the Montevidean Customs House, and as a means thereby of providing surety for those merchants who had lent money to the Uruguayan government. For their part, the merchant body in Montevideo long harboured a grudge that the armed intervention had been ended and their interests abandoned by the British government. In 1851 Gore told Palmerston how Lennon-Hunt had felt obliged to withdraw himself from English society in the city on account of 'the abusive language that was invariably used against Your Lordship'.[21] In 1852 Frederick Bruce reminded the Foreign Office how for the past ten years the loan jobbers and contractors had been the only group which had benefited from the way in which the finances of Uruguay had been conducted. He added frankly that 'they have done with the successive administrations what they liked.'[22]

Not only had Ouseley fallen prey to these vested interests but, it was said, he had also failed properly to represent to his superiors the character of the local regime. In his wish to portray the struggle at Montevideo as a gallant stand for national survival against the dark force of Argentine tyranny, Ouseley played down the enormous influence of both the foreign legions and foreign interests in perpetuating the war and in blocking any chance of reconciliation between Oribe and the defenders of the city. He also glossed over the true nature of much of Rivera's marauding in the interior, prior to the latter's final defeat in January 1847. Rivera's campaigns were totally dependent on French naval assistance and it was a misnomer to refer to him as the leader of a concerted indigenous force fighting for Uruguay's freedom. Finally, Ouseley had on occasion exaggerated British commercial interests in need of protection in order to justify some of the measures taken by the navy. At Colonia, tales of distressed British merchants in fear for their lives and property proved to have little foundation. There was no British property in the town at all. As for British subjects there, one of the naval officers found them 'a lazy indolent set', deserving nothing by way of succour from the British government.[23] Herbert and Martin Hood certainly believed Ouseley to be quite untrustworthy. Hood in particular was convinced that 'Ouseley is always trying to mislead me and get me into trouble and therefore I have to be extremely cautious with him.'[24]

Ouseley's conduct between 1845 and 1847 certainly merited many of the complaints made against him. His dispatches were indeed selective and sympathetic in their portrayal of the government in Montevideo. The extent of his subsidy of the Uruguayan war effort was only revealed after his departure. As for his call for troops to be sent from Europe and for a declaration of war against Rosas, his discussions in London and Paris before he left for South America, and indeed his written instructions, should have left him in no doubt that naval measures alone were contemplated. The expense involved, the risk of reversal and the complications and commitments which could also arise from military expeditions overseas, always weighed heavily with politicians in London who calculated, rightly, that Britain's strength lay in her naval prowess and technology and not in the unwavering superiority of her fighting men. Aberdeen had envisaged a blockade of Oribe's supply ports and naval patrols in the River Uruguay. The only measures which he had specifically authorized against Rosas were the occupation of Martín García and the blockade at Buenos Aires. Later, with talk of war, the landing of soldiers from two British regiments to defend Montevideo and news of the Paraná expedition, Aberdeen not unnaturally concluded that matters were getting out of hand. Commercial interests had long complained that hostilities in the region disrupted opportunities for trade; they complained louder, however, when the extension of the conflict disrupted trade even further. Ouseley had been sent to stop the war and to achieve an Argentine withdrawal. By assuming the role of combatant, he displayed a rashness which had done nothing to further the object of his mission.

Yet to cast Ouseley as the victim of conspiracies and pressures inside Montevideo was to underestimate his character. Like Purvis and Inglefield, Ouseley saw the war as a struggle by a small nation for its survival. Montevideo became for him, as for many in Europe, the 'new Troy' where constitutionalism and liberty made their stand in South America against the tide of military despotism. This conviction governed his relations with the British community in the city as well as with the native authorities. While traders and commercial men profited from financial speculation, they also served Ouseley's own, yet separate, purpose well. Their petitions in favour of armed intervention were sent to London as useful evidence of local support; their loans to the Montevidean government were the life blood of the city's valiant defence.

As for the individuals who composed the shaky structure of authority in Montevideo, Ouseley harboured few illusions. Although he believed their cause to be just, the government there had scarcely a greater claim to power *de jure* than it possessed *de facto*. 'In fact,' Ouseley conceded to Palmerston in 1847, 'no government strictly in conformity with the constitution now exists in the Banda Oriental.'[25] Years of war and siege had postponed the required elections for the presidency and Assembly and Suárez continued to be head of state in part because nothing else was possible. In matters of personal integrity, Ouseley was anything but naive. 'With one or two exceptions, no confidence is to be placed in any of the members of this government in the administration of financial affairs,' he lamented in March 1846. 'Even those who would scruple to commit dishonourable acts in private pecuniary transactions would not hesitate to avail themselves of any opportunity for misappropriation of public funds.'[26] Nonetheless it was crucial to keep an indigenous administration in office and thus to preserve a display of Uruguayan independence and, of course, the legitimacy of Montevideo as its upholder. At times that was bound to involve Ouseley in domestic conspiracy and in the Uruguayan government's financial distress.

Aberdeen's admission to Clarendon in 1853 that Ouseley's disgrace had been overly harsh raised, by implication, his own responsibility and, indeed, the issue of whether there had been any effective check on policy at all. The instructions of February 1845 gave a greater latitude for manoeuvre than either Aberdeen or Palmerston were prepared to acknowledge; in the Commons in 1846 Russell rightly remarked that Ouseley had been given 'a large authority'.[27] Ouseley and Deffaudis were emphatically told that the most important issue as far as their governments were concerned was the independence of Montevideo. They were reminded too that if an ultimatum was delivered to the government at Buenos Aires, then it must be adhered to and measures must be taken such as would force the Argentine army out of Uruguay. How this was best done was for local consideration with the naval commanders. The unforeseen, Aberdeen acknowledged, could never be provided for. Far from home, but fully aware of the views of his government, Ouseley was expected to exercise the authority placed in him as Minister Plenipotentiary.

Furthermore, the Foreign Office was wrong to claim that by carrying the war into the Argentine with the Paraná expedition, Ouseley had at once gone beyond the scope of anything contemplated at the outset. Aberdeen had drawn the line at naval measures, but that did not preclude the grand strategy for forcing the Paraná which Ouseley and Deffaudis devised. Aberdeen himself, in December 1844, had informed Cowley that a naval demonstration in the Plate might be extended to an occupation of its tributaries. In Paris, in January 1845, the conference which settled the policy of intervention also envisaged an occupation of the rivers Paraná and Uruguay if Rosas refused the offer of mediation. Even the instructions which Ouseley received in February 1845 touched upon Britain's hope of one day gaining rights of navigation to the tributaries of the Plate, and Aberdeen mused on what might follow 'if eventually we should be compelled to occupy those waters with a combined force'.[28] Ouseley did have grounds, then, for protesting that it was not his actions which contradicted instructions but that the instructions themselves were being altered.

Ouseley had grounds, too, for taking exception to the manner in which Aberdeen had devised the mission of Thomas Hood in 1846. At best Aberdeen showed a clumsy handling of two envoys whose inclinations and authority were bound to clash. Certainly Ouseley and Deffaudis were unwilling to work with Hood; in their defence, though, they were but little informed as to Hood's purpose. The secretive mode of his diplomacy at Buenos Aires and at the Cerrito only reinforced the widespread belief in Montevideo that Hood was a poor choice as an impartial mediator. This distrust was compounded when Hood would not, or could not, produce satisfactory credentials which entitled him to take generous concessions to Rosas. In fact, Aberdeen gave Hood differing instructions.[29] In the peace propositions which were shown to Ouseley and Deffaudis, the blockade of Buenos Aires was to be lifted only when the foreign legions in Montevideo had been disarmed and Argentine troops had withdrawn from Uruguayan territory. In another dispatch of the same date, Aberdeen suggested that the blockade should be lifted as soon as Rosas and Oribe had accepted the propositions and an armistice had been declared. Hood told Ouseley and Deffaudis that he carried a private letter from Aberdeen which allowed him to accept modifications to the original propositions, but, according to Ouseley, this was never produced. Aberdeen, in any case, should have anticipated that Ouseley and Deffaudis would assert that their official written instructions took priority. Ouseley insisted in September 1846 that, in breaking with Hood, he had done only that which Aberdeen's dispatches required. 'It is evident,' he confidently concluded, 'that Mr. Hood, whose instructions have only been verbally communicated to me, has misunderstood Your Lordship's wishes.'[30]

Aberdeen's carelessness over T.S. Hood's mission was indicative of a broader failing for which he and Guizot were to blame – the very limited thought which was devoted to La Plata once the intervention was under way. For both men the issue became a minor problem. Peel's government in London and that of Guizot in Paris both had serious political difficulties. Each had to survive crises of confidence and uncertain majorities in the elected chambers; each was confronted with domestic and foreign issues of more pressing concern. Unquestionably, Spanish affairs preoccupied Anglo-French diplomacy and were crucial to the deterioration in relations between the two countries after 1845. For the French, Algiers was an additional distraction. Guizot rarely mentioned South America in his interviews with Cowley. His occasional instructions to Deffaudis were often just translations of those of Aberdeen to Ouseley, largely because he had no time to write instructions of his own. In 1846 Guizot agreed to Thomas Hood's mission without adequate consideration. Hood was known to French diplomats as a Francophobe; the embassy in London had warned Guizot that his connections with Oribe and Rosas made him most unsuitable as a mediator in La Plata, the more so since he was to be entrusted with the task of representing French as well as British interests. Aberdeen's problems also grew in the course of 1845. By September, when he offered Peel his resignation, Aberdeen faced Cabinet colleagues who balked at his pro-French policy and who were eager to convince Peel that attention to the nation's defences was a more profitable expenditure of political energy and of the Treasury's resources. Thereafter Aberdeen was diverted by the issues of tariffs and Ireland, which increasingly divided the Tory party and which forced Peel to resign the government, albeit temporarily, in December 1845. In 1846 Irish famine and the repeal of the Corn Laws dominated politics in London and relegated news from the south Atlantic. There was never another gathering of British and French officials such as had occurred in Paris in January 1845 to review the progress of their policy.

This problem of inadequate coordination did not end with Aberdeen and Guizot. Despite Palmerston's obvious willingness to work with the French in ensuring a simultaneous withdrawal from La Plata after 1846, Guizot's struggle for survival, and then the events which followed the revolution in Paris in 1848, threw Anglo-French relations into considerable confusion. Political instability and administrative paralysis in fact characterized French government until after 1852. Normanby's contacts with the Foreign Ministry were perforce infrequent and usually futile. The aspirations of French nationals in Montevideo were a matter of great sensitivity in the elected Assembly; no government in France was strong enough to make the concessions necessary to gain a settlement with Rosas. On top of that, latent Anglophobia in Paris was fanned by diplomatic disputes about Rome in 1849 and Greece in 1850.

Beyond these difficulties of communication at the level of government, there was the recurring distrust between British and French agents abroad. However well-intentioned the spirit of *entente* may have been, such sentiments were not always to be found among political and naval officers in South America. Thomas and Martin Hood, Howden and Herbert were all distinctly wary of cooperation with the French and were concerned about the dangers posed by what they were sure were French colonial ambitions in Uruguay. Hudson accurately foretold that Howden's mission with Walewski would come to nothing due to French intrigue against it. Passing through Rio de Janeiro *en route* for the Plate in 1847, Howden had boasted that he would be back in Brazil in two months with his task of achieving peace completed. 'He may be back in less if he has nothing to do with the French,' Hudson wrote dismissively, 'and he will never be back if he is to be guided by their councils.'[31] Among the French in La Plata, as among the British, there were at times differing interpretations of policy between naval and diplomatic personnel. Moreover, French diplomats and consuls generally received fewer instructions than their British counterparts and acted more independently of government control. After 1847, of course, there was a marked bitterness at the way in which the British had unilaterally pulled out of the intervention. To add to these problems, Buenos Aires and Montevideo were focuses for diplomatic rumours. Mandeville cautioned Aberdeen as early as January 1843 that, from what he understood, the French were angling for a chance to resume their bid for influence in the region prorogued at the time of the Makau treaty in 1840. In July 1845 Ouseley was told confidentially by a junior French diplomat that although Louis-

Philippe did not want hostilities against Rosas, Deffaudis nonetheless was determined to bring them about. Deffaudis and Guizot were old political enemies, Ouseley's informant had continued. Deffaudis was anxious to damage Guizot's career, while Guizot had sent Deffaudis to Buenos Aires in order to get him as far from Paris as possible. Such stories were fostered and distorted by political and economic interest groups in both capitals in La Plata; it was, so Howden and Herbert believed, to just such a climate of misinformation and manipulation that Walewski had succumbed when he went ashore at Montevideo in 1847. Mandeville and de Lurde, Ouseley and Deffaudis, Howden and Walewski, and Gore and Gros were all required to work together. Ingrained suspicion and local circumstances, however, often made it impossible to do so, and even common instructions were by no means guaranteed common interpretation. As Howden assured Palmerston: 'it is perfectly impossible for anybody not on the spot to form an idea of the strange and anomalous state of things here.'[32]

* * *

Consideration of Ouseley's impulsiveness, of Aberdeen's shortcomings in the direction of policy, and of the problems inherent in Anglo-French cooperation in La Plata must be set within the wider question of whether European intervention was realistic. In this respect events in La Plata clearly illustrate the limits within which great powers in the nineteenth century could exercise their international persuasion. That Britain and France possessed the foremost economies and naval forces of the day was never in dispute; that their leverage upon societies or regimes as distant as those in La Plata, East Asia or West Africa was as great as some contemporaries believed, or as many historians have subsequently assumed, is, however, far less certain. Understandably, officials took the view that, by acting together, Britain and France could impose a settlement in an area where they had legitimate concerns. Success in China in 1842 was an obvious precedent for the British. Recent naval blockades by both the British and French against small states in the Americas had also produced satisfactory outcomes to the issues in dispute. Dale took it for granted in 1843 that 'one single *act* on the part of England and France would keep Oribe far from Montevideo'[33] and Ouseley eventually fell victim to this same mentality. Bitter at the way in which his use of the navy was disowned in London, he cited the naval action in the Far East. Rosas and his lackeys deserved no better treatment, he admonished Palmerston in December 1846: 'we ought to have treated them as we did China.'[34]

Ouseley's comparison has been echoed by historians of British expansion who, in the attempt to identify an informal empire of the mid-nineteenth century, have likewise seen similarities between Britain's standing in Latin America and on the China coast. In both spheres British commerce was preponderant but still shackled by indigenous restraints; in both, important coastal cities were exposed to naval attack. But there were also crucial differences which Ouseley should have realized made such operations as he applauded in China near impossible in South America. Off Canton, the British had enjoyed incomparable advantages. Despised as outsiders to an ancient civilization, they had merited no defensive preparations. Their intentions were misunderstood; their technology and methods of warfare were almost unknown. Success in these circumstances had been relatively easy.

In post-colonial America, however, the reaction to European powers could not have been more marked in contrast – nor indeed, in the Argentine, could the will to assert a fledgling sovereignty have been more determined. 'They think you come either to cheat or oppress them,' Howden pointed out to Palmerston. 'They are determined to believe that there exists in Europe one vast league against American independence.'[35] Most Argentines trusted to the tenets of their religion, the traditions of their independence struggle and the proud republicanism which had developed from it, and they instinctively resisted what they identified as the aggressive acquisitiveness of a secular Europe. Rosas and Oribe rallied their followers throughout La Plata with an emotive cry from the past and took their stand for a passing order of society. Their nations, they proclaimed, had not been freed from Spain in order that they might now succumb to the subtler foreign bondage of commercial liberalism as propounded by craven unitarians and by the foreign puppets who defended Montevideo. Ill-equipped in modern military skills as his forces undoubtedly were, Rosas knew nonetheless that strength lay in the vastness of his domain and its inhospitability to the intruder.

Aberdeen and Guizot had acknowledged this in 1844 when they affirmed that on no account would European troops be landed. Offshore and in the rivers, Britain and France held an obvious superiority. Rosas realized this, but, as he boldly assured Ouseley at their final interview in 1845, naval dominance would not be enough. Mercantile opinion would soon protest at any diplomatic rupture. Furthermore, many of the warships would find it impossible to manoeuvre close to land. And, Rosas continued, there would be anxiety about the safety of the large foreign community in Buenos Aires.

The style of Rosas' delivery was pure bravado; the essence of what he said, though, Ouseley knew to be true. Rosas was not vulnerable from the sea. Blockading several ports and hundreds of miles of coastline was a task beyond the forces at Ouseley's disposal. Blockade was useless anyway as a means of bringing the Argentine government to heel. Ouseley had expressed private doubts about its value initially, but once the rupture with Buenos Aires occurred in June 1845, its implementation became simply an extension of diplomacy. Howden looked back in 1847 on what he believed should have been obvious at the outset: 'The institution of a blockade was productive of no evil so great as converting what was only a theory into a proved fact, which affects all negotiation,' he lectured Palmerston. 'It was supposed that such an attempt at coercion might not be very efficient: it is now a notorious truth that foreign nations hurt nobody by it but themselves.'[36] Rosas fed his capital from the interior. Oribe was inconvenienced by the blockade at Buceo but at no time was he compelled to relax his siege of Montevideo. In retrospect it was widely conceded that an Argentine withdrawal from Uruguay could not be accomplished within the limits set for European intervention. In the end it was Urquiza and the Brazilians who settled the future of the Banda Oriental – four years after Britain had backed out of participating in the war and had decided instead on an accommodation with Rosas.

It was not only in the execution of policy that the British government displayed questionable judgment. Aberdeen also entered into the joint intervention for a confusing mixture of economic, political and even humanitarian considerations. This is critical in any debate on imperial expansion and in particular on the dynamic for informal empire in the mid-nineteenth century. Everyone who witnessed the fighting in the early 1840s was moved by the bloodshed, and Aberdeen was undoubtedly affected by the accounts from Mandeville, Dale and Purvis. In 1842 he had been sickened by what he read of Rosas' death squads on the streets of Buenos Aires and of the callousness with which the dictator had rid the city of opponents. In August he rebuked Mandeville for not having more made forceful diplomatic protests to try to stop the slaughter. In June 1843 Purvis demanded of the commanders of both armies at Montevideo that the practice of putting prisoners to death in cold blood should cease. Aberdeen very much approved of Purvis' interposition and of representations which Mandeville had made at Buenos Aires about the atrocities committed by Oribe's army in Uruguay. 'If war is carried on between these two states in a manner contrary to the usages of civilized nations,' he instructed Mandeville to remind Arana, 'it may be necessary for Great Britain, in conjunction with France, to put an end to proceedings so disgraceful and revolting to humanity.'[37] Humanitarian concern to stop a bloody and, for Aberdeen, senseless conflict in a region long familiar to the British may not fit easily into any model for nineteenth-century expansion. Such sentiments expressed by Aberdeen and by officials in La Plata require, nonetheless, some consideration of a preparedness to intervene for reasons which transcend the normal concepts of national economic or strategic self-interest.

At the same time, of course, Aberdeen was mindful of Britain's commercial presence in La Plata. Much of the advice which he received from there was couched in stirring language about the role which these lands might play in Britain's manufacturing prosperity. It was bound to be noticed when Rosas closed the rivers Paraná or Uruguay to foreign vessels. In doing so, he highlighted the desirability of placing rights of navigation on an internationally recognized basis. Rosas' actions also confirmed many agents in their sympathy for the more cosmopolitan politics of Montevideo. Dale, for one, pressed strongly for direct intervention in the war. 'Re-establish peace, and support Montevideo against the grasping tyranny of the Buenos Airean despot,' he implored, 'and the preponderating influence of Great Britain in this republic will insure immense advantages to our merchants.' If Montevideo was lost to commercial freedom, he predicted, then 'we may bid goodbye to these countries as a mart for the manufactures of our over-producing millions at home.'[38] The commercial associations and trading houses which petitioned the government had the same message, to which, on occasion, Aberdeen did seem to be amenable. 'Our trade with Montevideo is very important,' he conceded in December 1844, 'and it is through the liberal policy of that republic that we may hope for its extension in South America.'[39] After 1845 Ouseley, too, laboured this point. He assured his government that the expenses incurred by war in the Argentine would be amply recovered by the great trade with Bolivia, the interior of Brazil and the inland states of the Confederation which would develop once the tributaries of the Plate were securely opened to foreign shipping. Even after his recall, Ouseley clung to the conviction that the intervention could and should have served as a chance to establish British trade on a more certain basis.

Even those who were at odds with Ouseley's robust approach to extending British enterprise were at least conscious of how any French territorial foothold in South America might restrict the opportunities for trade. For that reason Howden assured Palmerston in July 1847 that he would do all in his power to persuade the government in Montevideo to accept an accommodation with Oribe and to allow the latter to enter the city. Restoring Oribe to power was 'the best means of completely annihilating French influence here,' Howden concluded. 'If I succeed in this the whole river is ours.'[40] Howden did acknowledge, somewhat grudgingly, that trade mattered since, clearly, Britain's claim to a legitimate voice in the region rested largely with her status as 'the great commercial power in these waters.'[41] But it did not follow that the Foreign Office was constantly influenced by advice arriving from interested parties. Indeed, in 1843 Varela was struck by the official indifference shown in London towards the states of La Plata. 'The fact is that there does not exist here the interest for these countries which we would think,' he reported to the Foreign Ministry in Montevideo. 'Little attention is paid to them; they are not known; they are not appreciated therefore.' Men in London were preoccupied with major international affairs and were not disposed to waste their time worrying about events in South America. 'Do not find it strange then (I at least do not find it strange),' he cautioned, 'that ideas which seem most clear to us are not accepted here, nor are understood.'[42] Varela's conclusions, based on his own experience, do nothing to enhance the view that British governments, in practice, cared greatly for the benefit of trade and finance. They give little credence, thereby, to the historical judgment that Uruguay in the nineteenth century demonstrates that informal empire was both British policy and Latin American reality.[43]

In truth, Britain's intervention had but a tenuous relationship with economic matters and grew more directly from the political problems which arose from the conflict between Uruguay and the Argentine states. Mandeville's efforts to mediate in the war predated the chorus of grievances from the mercantile lobby. He made diplomatic representations and offered Britain's help in finding a settlement in 1839 and again in 1841. After August 1842, there were joint offers of mediation from the British and French governments – six months before Oribe crossed the River Uruguay and laid siege to Montevideo. In December 1842 Mandeville and de Lurde formally demanded an armistice and an Argentine troop withdrawal from Uruguay. This was done without instruction from the Foreign Office but, henceforth, as Aberdeen was aware, it constituted a diplomatic stance from which there was no honourable retraction. The government's concern to restore peace to the region developed at least as much from Britain's past involvement in its politics as from any anxiety for her future trade. As a party to the creation of the Banda Oriental in 1828, Britain claimed a right to intervene in circumstances where the nation's sovereignty was threatened. Preserving status in the international community, and an apprehension that national interests elsewhere might otherwise be jeopardized, required that a great power did not renege on its commitments. As Aberdeen confirmed in 1845, Uruguay was 'a state, the independence of which Great Britain is virtually bound to uphold.'[44] In 1846 Aberdeen assured the House of Lords that Uruguay 'was created under our mediation, and therefore it was impossible for us to be indifferent to its destruction.'[45]

For so long as the British government was persuaded after 1842 that a victory for Oribe was synonymous with an Argentine conquest of Uruguay, the possibility of armed intervention was a matter for serious deliberation. Aberdeen's judgment in February 1845 was clear: the army of Buenos Aires was engaged in a war in Uruguay and 'the object of that war is to place the domestic government of Montevideo in hands other than those to which the consent of the state has entrusted it. This alone,' he concluded, 'might justify the interposition of a Power under whose mediation the independence of Montevideo was established.'[46]

It was, however, on precisely this point of Uruguayan integrity that Aberdeen believed he had been misled, not only by commercial opinion but, more significantly, by his own diplomatic and consular subordinates. After December 1845, and now informed by Thomas Hood, Aberdeen was more willing to view the fighting in Uruguay as a civil war and not simply as an Argentine invasion. Palmerston and Howden shared this assessment, believing that even Oribe's return to power would not imperil the nation's sovereignty so long as Rosas thereafter withdrew his forces, having fulfilled his commitment to an ally of long standing. This was the sticking point in all negotiations.

It was essential, Palmerston reminded Howden, that all parties put their signatures to a clear recognition of the sovereignty of Uruguay. 'It is of importance that a record of the acknowledgement of such independence, which has been the constant object of the efforts of Great Britain and France,' he insisted, 'should formally result from the act which terminates the war.'[47] Palmerston paid no heed to traders' petitions which urged an unconditional end to the intervention. Such weighty matters as Britain's diplomatic standing and the need to coordinate policy with the French were not to be compromised by commercial expediency. Those who persisted in demanding peace at once, and at any price, in La Plata were invariably brushed away, being told merely that Her Majesty's Government afforded the matter its constant attention.

The predominance of political over commercial considerations was nowhere more expressly spelt out than in Ouseley's instructions. Aberdeen did not deny that the Plate and its tributaries were the key to the penetration of the continent by British enterprise. To open these rivers to unhindered foreign trade was an advantage for which the government would certainly press. But, Aberdeen stressed, 'in the opinion of Her Majesty's Government it is desirable to keep the one great purpose which they have in view as distinct from, and as little encumbered with, other considerations as possible.' The great purpose, he had already explained, was to preserve the independence of Uruguay. Placing rights of foreign navigation on a secure footing 'does not appear to have any necessary connection with the differences between the two republics, the adjustment of which is our first object.' 'You will do well,' Aberdeen concluded, 'not to introduce it as an essential point of negotiation.'[48]

The intervention was also guided throughout by a further political factor – Britain's relations with the French. Here again, politicians in London can be shown to have acted in a manner and for reasons which took little account of commercial advantage. Even at the time, suspicions were voiced that Aberdeen and Guizot had determined their policy because it was an opportunity to show that their *entente cordiale* could produce a tangible reward. Guizot's critics derided any cooperation with the British on the grounds that it could only mean a deference to British interests. Intervention in La Plata, where France could act as an equal partner, provided an escape from this line of attack. In May 1845 Louis-Philippe spoke enthusiastically of the spirit of cooperation between the British and French governments and of how this augured well for the resolution of other diplomatic problems. As a man of conciliatory disposition, Aberdeen certainly shared such sentiments.

In the recrimination which followed failure, it was perhaps only natural that each side should impute responsibility for it to the other. Guizot and Deffaudis insisted that France had only agreed to act with Britain in response to Aberdeen's overture in 1844. In February 1847 Louis-Philippe addressed Howden in indignant tones about the recent shift in British policy. The King now hated the whole business and, he added, 'we went there to please the English government.' Etiquette required that Howden did not dispute the recollections of a monarch; in a letter to Palmerston written immediately afterwards, however, Howden did put his own view on record. 'I certainly had never before suspected that the French intervention in the river Plate was to please the English government,' he protested. 'I had always believed implicitly that Lord Aberdeen had been somewhat reluctantly forced into this matter: partly by the interested merchants of Liverpool, and still more by his somewhat exhuberant desire to do what might be agreeable to the French government.'[49] But more than two years after the event, Palmerston did not care where the blame lay. He regretted only what he identified as Aberdeen's years of failure at the Foreign Office. 'I am afraid that Aberdeen's system of making himself under-secretary to Guizot has been injurious to British interests all over the world,' he informed Russell in December 1846.[50] As for the escapade in South America: 'I have never been able quite to make out whether Guizot led Aberdeen, or Aberdeen led Guizot into the Plata scrape.'[51] Having designated it a folly, Palmerston wanted only to organize a dignified retreat.

Discomforted as British governments were by much of what took place in La Plata in the 1840s, and unable as both the British and French governments were to effect a peace settlement on acceptable terms, the intervention undoubtedly was significant. Mandeville's insistence on an Argentine withdrawal in 1842 provided a clear marker that an assault by Oribe on Montevideo would not be allowed to proceed unchallenged. Dale, from inside the city, wrote emphatically that this impromptu but inspired diplomacy had been its salvation. Purvis' subsequent interference with the movements of the Argentine navy, and his demand for guarantees from Oribe as to the safety of foreign nationals inside Montevideo, deterred an early assault and gave the foreign legions time to organize. It was certainly the view in Buenos Aires that only the unauthorized behaviour of Purvis and Mandeville had denied Oribe a swift success – as Arana made plain to Moreno in November 1843.[52] Ouseley held the opinion that he had saved Montevideo again in 1845. Without a tinge of humility, he told Aberdeen in April 1846 that 'Montevideo was, it must be recollected, reduced to the last stage of weakness before the arrival of Baron Deffaudis and myself. Without the materials for carrying on the war – credit and ammunition exhausted – scarcely a hope existed of preventing the fall of Montevideo into the hands of Rosas.'[53] Although they could not force Rosas to abandon his campaign in Uruguay, the British and French had played a vital role in thwarting an Argentine victory.

The British also learnt a valuable lesson from the experience of the 1840s: that influence in South America was not readily attainable by the coordination of diplomacy and naval power. In the decades which followed, Britain's relationship with La Plata was transformed as the economy of the region was drawn ever more into the orbit of industrial Europe and as British investment poured in to finance an infrastructure of railways, telegraphs, tramways, docks, banking services and public utilities. British capital and trade were dominant in the River Plate republics until the early decades of the twentieth century. Uruguay had attracted £10 million of British investment by 1875 and £40 million by 1900; Argentina had drawn in £23 million by 1875 and £189 million by the end of the century. British money and British ranchers tamed the Pampas in the 1870s and 1880s. By the 1890's railway networks, wire fencing, agricultural technology and the techniques of canning and refrigeration had opened the markets of Britain and the world to the meat and arable produce of both the Platine states. After 1881 British exports to the region grew at a rate far greater than that of Britain's total export trade. The late nineteenth century thus brought the peace and prosperity which the British had wanted in La Plata. Their armed intervention in its politics had become by then an irksome memory from a distant epoch.

Notes

Introduction

1. J. Gallagher and R. Robinson, 'The Imperialism of Free Trade', *Economic History Review*, vi (1953). Some of the responses to their work have been brought together in recent collections. See in particular W.R. Louis (ed), *Imperialism* (London, 1976). Other compendiums which focus on the issues raised by Gallagher and Robinson include C.C. Eldridge (ed), *British Imperialism in the Nineteenth Century* (London, 1984); and A.G.L. Shaw (ed), *Great Britain and the Colonies 1815–1865* (London, 1970).

   The literature on nineteenth-century imperialism includes the following recent works which also bring together themes and controversies in convenient format: W. Baumgart, *Imperialism: The Idea and Reality of British and French Colonial Expansion 1880–1914* (Oxford, 1982); and W.J. Mommsen, *Theories of Imperialism* (New York, 1980). Older though still useful collections include R. Owen and B. Sutcliffe (eds), *Studies in the Theory of Imperialism* (London, 1972); and K.E. Boulding and T. Mukerjee (eds), *Economic Imperialism* (Ann Arbor, 1972). D.K. Fieldhouse, *The Theory of Capitalist Imperialism* (London, 1967) remains a good introduction to this field of enquiry. Fieldhouse's *Economics and Empire 1830–1914* (London, 1973) and R. Hyam, *Britain's Imperial Century 1815–1914: a Study of Empire and Expansion* (London, 1976) are valuable textbooks.

2. In addition to the references which Gallagher and Robinson made to Latin America there have been specific studies which set Britain's relationship with parts of the continent in this context – including both the Platine republics. See P. Winn, 'British Informal Empire in Uruguay in the Nineteenth Century', *Past and Present* (1976); and H.S. Ferns, 'Britain's Informal Empire in Argentina, 1806–1914', *Past and Present* (1953). There is a comparable study of Britain's contact with Peru in W.M. Mathew, 'The Imperialism of Free Trade: Peru, 1820–70', *Economic History Review*, xxi (1968).

Chapter 1

1. British policy towards Spanish America before and during the years of independence is discussed in J. Lynch, 'British policy and Spanish America, 1783–1808', *Journal of Latin American Studies*, i (1969), pp 1–30; W.W. Kaufmann, *British policy and the Independence of Latin America, 1804–1828* (New Haven, 1951); J. Street, 'Lord Strangford and Río de la Plata, 1808–1815', *Hispanic American Historical Review*, xxxiii (1953), pp 477–510; J.C.J. Metford, 'The Recognition by Great Britain of the United Provinces

of Río de la Plata', *Bulletin of Hispanic Studies*, xxix (1952), pp 201–24.
2. There is an account of this in J.W. Fortescue, *A History of the British Army* (London, 1910), vol V, chapters 10, 12 and 13. See also A. Pereira, *La Invasion Inglesa en el Río de la Plata* (Montevideo, 1877); M.G. Mulhall, *The English in South America* (Buenos Aires, 1878), pp 92–127; R. Levene, *A History of Argentina* (New York, 1937), pp 192–202.
3. These figures are from H.S. Ferns, *Britain and Argentina in the Nineteenth Century* (Oxford, 1960), p 59. The economic and political history of the Argentine states in the early nineteenth century is covered in D. Rock, *Argentina 1516–1982* (London, 1986).
4. No national census was conducted until 1869. The British diplomatic agent at Buenos Aires in 1824 estimated the population of the United Provinces to be 600,000. He thought that the state of Buenos Aires contained 170,000 inhabitants. R.A. Humphreys (ed), *British Consular Reports on the Trade and Politics of Latin America 1824–1826* (London, 1940), pp 16–17. J. Lynch, in *Argentine Dictator: Juan Manuel de Rosas 1829–1852* (Oxford, 1981), pp 92–3, cites the more conservative figure of 118,646 as the population of the state of Buenos Aires in 1822, rising to 142,957 in 1836.
5. Ferns, *Britain and Argentina*, pp 68 and 76. The British merchant body in Buenos Aires is also discussed in E.J. Pratt, 'Anglo–American Commercial and Political Rivalry on the Plata, 1820–1830', *Hispanic American Historical Review*, xi (1931), pp 302–35. See also Lynch, *Argentine Dictator*, pp 248–9.
6. Figures for British exports are succinctly discussed in Lynch, *Argentine Dictator*, p 255, and Ferns, *Britain and Argentina*, p 133. A more detailed study of British activity is in H.S. Ferns, 'Beginnings of British Investment in Argentina', *Economic History Review*, iv (1951–2), pp 341–52. See also D.C.M. Platt, *Latin America and British Trade 1806–1914* (London, 1972).
7. Kaufmann, *British policy and the Independence of Latin America*, p 176. Most of these commercial houses had correspondents in Rio de Janeiro and Montevideo. Between them, Kaufmann concludes, they controlled almost the entire export and import trade of Buenos Aires.
8. There is a large bibliography covering the life of Juan Manuel de Rosas (1793–1877), in particular Lynch, *Argentine Dictator*, and J. Lynch, *Caudillos in Spanish America 1800–1850* (Oxford, 1992), pp 241–74. Notable works of Argentine scholarship include Enrique Arana, *Rosas y la Política Exterior* (Buenos Aires, 1954); Julio Irazusta, *Vida Política de Juan Manuel de Rosas: a través de su correspondencia* (Buenos Aires, 1961); Emilio Ravignani, *Rosas: Interpretación real y moderna* (Buenos Aires, 1970).
9. The figure of 70,000 as the population of the city of Buenos Aires is cited in J.F. Cady, *Foreign Intervention in the Rio de La Plata 1838–1850* (London, 1929), p 4. The British legation compiled its own estimate of population throughout the Confederation based upon official Argentine publications, which was recorded in Mandeville to Palmerston, 20 March 1841, Public Record Office, London, F.O. 6/78.
10. The broad perspective of British policy in the nineteenth century is discussed in D.C.M. Platt, 'British Diplomacy in Latin America since the Emancipation', *Inter-American Economic Affairs*, xxi (1967); and J. Smith,

'New World Diplomacy: a reappraisal of British policy towards Latin America, 1823–1850', *Inter-American Economic Affairs*, xxxii (1978).
11. Griffiths to Bidwell, private, 23 September 1840, F.O. 6/76.
12. Quoted in Lynch, *Argentine Dictator*, p 177.
13. Southern to Palmerston, private, 18 October 1848, F.O. 6/139.
14. The diplomat was William Harris, who is quoted in Lynch, *Argentine Dictator*, p 293. Earlier United States representatives had felt equally frustrated by the priority given to British political opinion and commercial enterprise. See Pratt, 'Anglo-American Political Rivalry'; and J.F. Rippy, *Rivalry of the United States and Great Britain over Latin America 1808–1830* (Baltimore, 1929).
15. Felipe Arana (1786–1865) was Minister for Foreign Affairs from April 1835 until February 1852 and Deputy Governor of Buenos Aires after 1840. He was largely dismissed by contemporaries, and subsequently by many historians, as merely a mouthpiece for Rosas and lacking any ability or courage to confront Rosas with a contrary opinion on any issue. However, Adolfo Saldías in his *Historia de la Confederación Agentina* (Buenos Aires, 1911), vol IV, pp 314–15, regards Arana as an important prop to Rosas' regime. See also P.C.M. Braconnay, *La Legion Francesa en la Defensa de Montevideo* (Montevideo, 1943), p 201; and Lynch, *Argentine Dictator*, p 172. There is a useful outline of Felipe Arana's career in Enrique Arana, *Rosas y la Política Exterior*, vol I, pp 407–20.
16. Mandeville to Arana, 16 January 1838, enclosed in Mandeville to Palmerston, 16 January 1838, F.O. 6/63.
17. Mandeville to Palmerston, 3 January 1838, F.O. 6/63. There were discussions in 1844 about waiving all claim to the Falklands if the British would cancel outstanding Argentine debt, but no progress was made. Argentine documents relating to the proposal are reproduced and discussed in Irazusta, *Vida Politica*, vol IV, pp 221–33.
18. These figures are from Eduardo Acevedo, *Anales Históricos del Uruguay* (Montevideo, 1933), vol II, p 191. M.G. and E.T. Mulhall in their *Handbook of the River Plate Republics* (London, 1875), p 310, refer to an estimate of 60,000 as the population of Uruguay in 1826. Isidoro De-María in *Hombres Notables de la República Oriental del Uruguay* (Montevideo, 1939), vol I, p 137, cites figures of 74,000 and 128,371 as the Uruguayan population in 1830 and 1835 respectively. Such rapid expansion owed much to immigration. Braconnay in *La Legion Francesa*, p 19, claims that 33,600 migrants entered the country between 1836 and 1842, half of whom were from the Basque region of France. The warfare prevalent in Uruguay after 1842 reversed these trends. Acevedo in *Anales Históricos*, vol II, p 191, cites the census of Montevideo taken in October 1843 which revealed a reduced population in the city of 31,189, of whom only 11,431 were Uruguayan nationals. The remainder were French (5324), Italians (4205), Spaniards (3406), Argentines (2553), freed African slaves (1344), Portuguese (659), British (606) and Brazilians (492).
19. *Parliamentary Accounts and Papers*, 1837–8, vol XLVII, pp 393–8.
20. W. Page (ed), *Commerce and Industry: tables of statistics for the British Empire from 1815* (London, 1919), p 70.

Chapter 2

1. The main biographies of Fructuoso Rivera (1778–1854) are A. Lepro, *Fructuoso Rivera* (Montevideo, 1945); T. Manacorda, *Fructuoso Rivera* (Madrid, 1933); José Antuña, *Un Caudillo: El General Fructuoso Rivera* (Madrid, 1948); and De-María, *Hombres Notables*. There is also a good sketch in Raul M. Bustamante, *Estampas* (Montevideo, 1942).
2. The life of Manuel Oribe (1792–1857) is covered in Aquiles B. Oribe, *Manuel Oribe* (Montevideo, 1913); Julio Vignale, *Oribe* (Montevideo, 1942); and Lorenzo Carnelli, *Oribe y su epoca* (Montevideo, 1959). His character and career are also touched on in Braconnay, *La Legion Francesa*, pp 9–10; Juan Pivel-Devoto, *Historia de la Republica Oriental del Uruguay 1830–1930* (Montevideo, 1945), pp 77–8; and G.G. Selgas, *La Eleccion Presidencial de Don Manuel Oribe* (Montevideo, 1935). Political rivalry in the Banda Oriental in the 1830s is most authoritatively dealt with by Juan Pivel-Devoto in volume II of *Historia de los Partidos y de las Ideas Politicas en el Uruguay* (Montevideo, 1956).
3. The most recent investigation of this episode is in I.W. Morgan, *Anglo-French Confrontation and Co-operation in Spanish America, 1836–1848* (University of London, PhD thesis, 1975). See also Cady, *Foreign Intervention*; Gabriel Puentes, *La intervencion francesa en el Río de la Plata* (Buenos Aires, 1958); and Néstor S. Colli, *La Política francesa en el Río de la Plata: Rosas y el bloqueo de 1838–1840* (Buenos Aires, 1963).
4. This engagement is described in R. Levene, *Historia de la Nacion Argentina* (Buenos Aires, 1950), vol VII, part 2, p 235; and Teodoro Caillet-Bois, *Historia naval Argentina* (Buenos Aires, 1944), pp 396–9.
5. The career of José María Paz (1791–1854) is well covered in his *Memorias Póstumas* (Buenos Aires, 1930); and the biography by Juan Terán, *José María Paz* (Buenos Aires, 1936).
6. Quoted in R. Bullen, *Palmerston, Guizot and the collapse of the Entente Cordiale* (London, 1974), p 7.
7. Quoted in M.E. Chamberlain, *Lord Aberdeen* (London, 1983), p 306. There are other studies of Aberdeen's conduct of foreign policy by A.B. Cunningham, 'Peel, Aberdeen and the Entente Cordiale', *Bulletin of the Institute of Historical Research*, xxx (1957); E. Jones-Parry, 'A Review of the relations between Guizot and Lord Aberdeen 1840–1852', *History*, xxiii (1938–9); W.D. Jones, *The American Problem in British Diplomacy, 1841–1861* (London, 1974); and W.D. Jones, *Lord Aberdeen and the Americas* (University of Georgia Press, Athens, GA, 1958).
8. Aberdeen to Cowley, 22 July 1842, *Papers of the Earl of Aberdeen*, British Library, London, Add. mss. 43129.
9. D. Johnson, 'The Foreign Policy of Guizot 1840–1848', *University of Birmingham Historical Journal*, vi (1957); and D. Johnson, *Guizot: Aspects of French History 1787–1874* (London, 1963).
10. Lynch, *Argentine Dictator*, p 256.
11. Morgan, *Anglo–French Confrontation*, pp 121, 137 and 230; and Acevedo, *Anales Históricos*, vol II, p 255.
12. See Morgan, *Anglo–French Confrontation*; and W.S. Robertson, 'French Intervention in Mexico in 1838', *Hispanic American Historical Review*, xxiv

(1944), pp 222–52.
13. Aberdeen to Mandeville, 12 March 1842, F.O. 6/82.
14. Mandeville to Aberdeen, 3 August 1842, F.O. 6/84.
15. Aberdeen to Mandeville, 7 December 1842, F.O. 6/82.
16. Mandeville to Aberdeen, 18 December 1842, F.O. 6/84.
17. Aberdeen to Mandeville, 5 April 1843, F.O. 6/87.
18. Hood to Palmerston, 26 August 1839, F.O. 51/15.
19. The task of defending Montevideo was given to General José Paz, who was appointed by the Uruguayan government to the post of Commander of the Army of Reserve on 12 December 1842. Details of Paz's preparations are given in J. Pivel-Devoto, *Historia de la Republica Oriental del Uruguay*, pp 109–11; and in César Diaz, *Memorias Inéditas* (Buenos Aires, 1878), pp 108–11. The generous testiments to Paz as one of the saviours of Uruguay in 1843 are recorded in Terán *José María Paz*, pp 121–2. See also Setembrino Pereda, *Los Extranjeros en la Guerra Grande* (Montevideo, 1904), p 106; and L.M. Torterolo, *Vida de Melchor Pacheco y Obes* (Montevideo, 1920), p 233.
20. Joaquín Suárez (1781–1868) was elected both President of the Senate and Vice-President of Uruguay in 1842. In the latter role he performed many of the presidential functions since the President, Rivera, was either disinterested or else away conducting military campaigns. See De-María *Hombres Notables*, vol III; and Lepro, *Fructuoso Rivera*, pp 348–54.
21. Purvis to Admiralty, 24 February 1843, Public Record Office, London, ADM 1/5531 Cap. p 115.
22. The text of Oribe's declaration is reproduced and discussed in Acevedo, *Anales Históricos*, vol II, pp 124–5.
23. Memorandum by Purvis enclosed in Admiralty to Foreign Office, 22 July 1844, F.O. 51/32.
24. Dale to Aberdeen, 25 April 1843, F.O. 51/22.

Chapter 3

1. Irazusta, *Vida Politica*, vol V, p 21.
2. William Brown (1777–1857) was born in Ireland and entered the armed service of the Argentine republic in 1814. His career is covered in Caillet-Bois, *Historia naval Argentina;* and Mulhall, *The English in South America*.
3. Sarratea to Arana, 26 March 1843, and Moreno to Arana, 23 April 1843, Irazusta, *Vida Politica*, vol IV, pp 67 and 69; also de Angelis to Guido, 14 July 1843, Irazusta, *Vida Politica*, vol IV, p146.
4. Admiral's Journal, 17 February 1843, ADM 50/215. Details of Purvis' interference with the Argentine squadron during its blockade of Montevideo are given in Hector R. Ratto, *Los Comodoros Británicos de Estacion en el Plata, 1810–1852* (Buenos Aires, 1945), pp 137–41.
5. Dale to Aberdeen, 23 February 1843, F.O. 51/22.
6. Canning to Dale, 30 May 1843, F.O. 51/22.
7. Admiral's Journal, 9 April 1843, ADM 50/215.
8. Purvis to Admiralty, 19 May 1844, enclosed in Admiralty to Foreign Office, 2 August 1844, F.O. 6/99.
9. Foreign Office to Admiralty, 3 July 1843, F.O. 51/25.

10. Aberdeen to Mandeville, 1 August 1843, F.O. 6/87.
11. Aberdeen to Ellauri, 12 August 1842, J. Ellauri, *Correspondencia diplomática del doctor José Ellauri 1839–1844* (Montevideo, 1919), p 310. The terms offered by the British government in 1842 were little changed from the original proposals. The 1842 treaty was similar to the Anglo-Argentine treaty of 1825. See Mulhall, *The English in South America*, p 566.
12. Mandeville to Vidal, private, 26 October 1842. To Mandeville's embarrassment, his private correspondence with the Montevidean government was published in the *Britannia and Montevidean Reporter* in March 1844. Dale tried unsuccessfully to stop the publication, a copy of which was enclosed in Dale to Bidwell, private, dated March 1844, F.O. 51/30.
13. Vázquez to Mandeville, 10 March 1843, enclosed in Admiralty to Foreign Office, 19 August 1843, F.O. 51/25.
14. Mandeville to Vidal, private, 2 September 1842, enclosed in Dale to Bidwell, private, dated March 1844, F.O. 51/30.
15. Aberdeen to Vázquez, 31 August 1843, F.O. 51/24.
16. Mandeville to Vidal, private, 12 January 1843, enclosed in Dale to Bidwell, private, dated March 1844, F.O. 51/30.
17. Aberdeen to Mandeville, 3 May 1843, F.O. 6/87.
18. Ellauri to Vázquez, 17 May 1843, Ellauri, *Correspondencia diplomática*, p 83.
19. Ellauri to Vázquez, 10 July 1843, Ellauri, *Correspondencia diplomática*, pp 89–90.
20. The British Merchants and Residents in Montevideo to Ouseley, 9 May 1846, Foreign Office, Confidential Print, 260.
21. Dale to Bidwell, private, 31 October 1842, F.O. 51/20.
22. Canning to Sandon, 1 August 1843, F.O. 6/93.
23. Enclosures in Peel to Aberdeen, 30 November 1843, F.O. 6/93.

Chapter 4

1. Aberdeen to Peel, 25 November 1843, *Papers of Sir Robert Peel*, British Library, London, Add. mss. 40454.
2. Peel to Aberdeen, 26 November 1843, *Peel Papers*, Add. mss. 40454.
3. Florencio Varela (1807–1848) was an Argentine exile in Montevideo. He was a gifted poet and journalist and on his return to Montevideo became one of the main propagandists of the government, founding his own paper, the *Comercio del Plata*, which published its first edition on 1 October 1845. There is a biography by Leoncio Gianello, *Florencio Varela* (Buenos Aires, 1948); and a study of his career as a journalist between 1845 and 1848 by Felix Weinberg (ed), *Florencio Varela y el Comercio del Plata* (Bahía Blanca, 1970).
4. Varela to Magariños, 3 January 1844, quoted in Mateo Magariños de Mello, *La Misión de Florencio Varela a Londres 1843–4* (Montevideo, 1944), p 287.
5. This correspondence in 1842 is quoted in Chamberlain, *Lord Aberdeen*, pp 353–4, and discussed further in Morgan, *Anglo- French Confrontation*, pp 236–9 and 367–8.

NOTES 213

6. *Papers of Lord Cowley*, Diary 1843, Public Record Office, London, F.O. 519/73.
7. Aberdeen to Peel, 27 November 1843, *Peel Papers*, Add. mss. 40454.
8. Dale to Bidwell, private, 15 January 1844, F.O. 51/30.
9. See Morgan, *Anglo–French Confrontation*, p 257. There were further criticisms of Guizot's failure to defend the French community and French interests in Montevideo on 31 May and later on 31 August 1844. See Cady, *Foreign Intervention*, p 120. Extracts from the speeches made by Thiers, and the defence of the government made by Makau, are reproduced in Acevedo, *Anales Históricos*, vol II, pp 261–3; and in Braconnay, *La Legion Francesa*, pp 217–22.
10. Foreign Office to The Mexican and South American Association, 27 May 1844, F.O. 6/99.
11. Aberdeen to Mandeville, 2 November 1844, *Aberdeen Papers*, Add. mss. 43126.
12. Ellauri to Vázquez, 1 September 1844, Ellauri, *Correspondencia diplomática*, p 97.
13. Quoted in Chamberlain, *Lord Aberdeen*, p 361.
14. Hamilton to Aberdeen, 18 July 1843, F.O. 13/196.
15. Brazilian diplomacy in 1843 is examined in Mateo Magariños de Mello, *La Politica Exterior del Imperio del Brasil y las Intervenciones Extranjeras en el Río de la Plata* in Instituto 'Gonzalo Fernandez de Oviedo', *Miscelanea Americanista* (Madrid, 1952), vol III, pp 465–530.
16. Hamilton to Aberdeen, 27 July 1844, F.O. 13/213.
17. Hamilton to Aberdeen, private, 24 August 1844, F.O. 13/213.
18. Aberdeen to Hamilton, 4 December 1844, F.O. 13/209; and Aberdeen to Hamilton, 4 December 1844, *Aberdeen Papers*, Add. mss. 43124.
19. Aberdeen to Hamilton, 4 December 1844, *Aberdeen Papers*, Add. mss. 43124.
20. Aberdeen to Cowley, 17 December 1844, F.O. 27/691.
21. Memorandum by Ouseley, 12 December 1844, enclosed in Ouseley to Ward, 23 December 1844, F.O. 6/96.
22. Ouseley to Aberdeen, 10 January 1845, F.O. 6/103.
23. The influence of Louis-Philippe, Desages and Makau on Guizot's thinking is discussed in Morgan, *Anglo–French Confrontation*, pp 24–9. Makau's doubts about an armed intervention were not overcome in the course of argument. On 4 March 1845 Guizot wrote to Makau in an effort to reassure him. This letter is reproduced in Arana, *Rosas y la Política exterior*, vol I, p 312.
24. Cowley to Aberdeen, 17 January 1845, F.O. 27/720.
25. The difficulty of securing an anti-slave trade treaty is investigated in L. Bethell, *The Abolition of the Brazilian Slave Trade: Britain, Brazil and the slave trade question 1807–1869* (Cambridge, 1970). The failure of D'Abrantes' mission to Europe is analysed, and much of his correspondence is cited and discussed, in Magariños de Mello, *La Politica Exterior del Imperio del Brasil*, pp 501–18.
26. Aberdeen to Turner, 21 February 1845, F.O. 505/17.
27. Deffaudis' character and career are discussed in Morgan, *Anglo–French Confrontation*, especially pp 87, 95 and 104. The United States envoy at Buenos Aires described Deffaudis as 'unscrupulous, energetic and

crafty'. Harris to Buchanan, 15 July 1847, in William R. Manning (ed), *Diplomatic Correspondence of the United States: Inter-American Affairs 1831–1860* (Washington, 1932), vol I (Argentina), p 436.
28. Cowley to Aberdeen, 3 and 24 March 1845, F.O. 27/722.
29. Aberdeen to Cowley, 20 February 1845,*Parliamentary Accounts and Papers*, 1846, vol LII.

Chapter 5

1. Ouseley to Canning, private, 27 April 1845, F.O. 6/103.
2. Ouseley to Aberdeen, 21 May 1845, F.O. 6/103.
3. The coincidence of British and American interests is explained in D.C.M. Platt, 'British Diplomacy in Latin America since Emancipation', *Inter-American Economic Affairs*, xxi (1967).
4. The history of relations between the two nations is covered in Harold F. Peterson, *Argentina and the United States 1810–1960* (New York, 1964).
5. Rosas' stalling tactics, and also his conviction that any blockade of Buenos Aires would be ineffective, are explained by Irazusta in *Vida Politica*, vol V, pp 7–8.
6. Turner made no secret of his support for the authorities in Montevideo. Florencio Varela had met Turner in London in February 1844 and reported that Turner was sympathetic to the Uruguayan cause. Varela to Vázquez, 6 February 1844, quoted in Magariños de Mello, *La Misión de Florencio Varela a Londres 1843–4*, p 257.
7. Turner to Aberdeen, 4 July 1845, F.O. 505/16.
8. Ouseley to Aberdeen, private, 26 June 1845, F.O. 6/103.
9. Memorandum by Ouseley, 5 July 1845, enclosed in Ouseley to Aberdeen, 5 July 1845, F.O. 6/104.
10. Ouseley to Canning, private, 27 April 1845, F.O. 6/103.
11. Ouseley to Aberdeen, private, 26 June 1845, F.O. 6/103.
12. Ouseley to Inglefield, 30 June 1845, and Inglefield to Ouseley, 2 July 1845, enclosed in Inglefield to Aberdeen, private, 9 July 1845, F.O. 6/108.
13. Memorandum by Ouseley, 5 July 1845, enclosed in Ouseley to Aberdeen, 5 July 1845, F.O. 6/104.
14. Inglefield to Hamilton, private, 10 July 1845, ADM 1/5549 Qa.180.
15. Log of HMS *Comus*, 2 August 1845, ADM 53/2252. There is an account of the seizure of Brown's squadron drawn from Argentine sources in Ratto, *Los Comodoros Británicos*, pp 161–9.
16. Ouseley to Aberdeen, 13 August 1845, F.O. 6/104.
17. Journal of HMS *Frolic*, 2 May 1845, *Papers of Admiral Sir Leopold McClintock*, National Maritime Museum, Greenwich, MCL/7/m.s. 58/024. There is also a description of the defences of Colonia in Eduardo Moreno, *Aspectos de la Guerra Grande 1847–1851* (Montevideo, 1925), pp 87–8 and a plan on p 90.
18. Hotham to Inglefield, 8 September 1845, *Papers of Sir Charles Hotham*, University Library, Hull, DD HO 10/7. Also log of HMS *Satellite*, 30 and 31 August 1845, ADM 53/3183; Log of HMS *Dolphin*, 30 and 31 August 1845, ADM 53/2373; Log of HMS *Firebrand*, 31 August 1845, ADM 53/2535; Log of HMS *Philomel*, 31 August 1845, ADM 53/1025; Log of HMS *Gorgon*,

5 September 1845, ADM 53/2562.
19. Ouseley to Aberdeen, 9 September 1845, *Aberdeen Papers*, Add. mss. 43127.
20. Ouseley to Aberdeen, private, 27 October 1845, F.O. 6/105.
21. Ouseley to Aberdeen, private, 30 October 1845, F.O. 6/105.
22. Ouseley to Aberdeen, private, 26 November 1845, F.O. 6/106.
23. Guido to Arana, 15 April 1845, and Guido to Garrigos, 1 May 1845, Irazusta, *Vida Politica*, vol IV, pp 313–15 and 337.
24. Aberdeen's interview with McLane is recorded in McLane to Buchanan, 3 October 1845, Manning, *Diplomatic Correspondence of the United States: Inter-American Affairs 1831–1860* (Washington, 1936), vol VII (Great Britain), pp 271–3.
25. Quoted in Peterson, *Argentina and the US*, p 137.
26. Aberdeen to Ouseley, 8 October 1845, *Aberdeen Papers*, Add. mss. 43127.
27. Aberdeen to Ouseley, 17 November 1845, F.O. 6/102.
28. Aberdeen to Ouseley, 3 December 1845, *Aberdeen Papers*, Add. mss. 43127.
29. Aberdeen to Ouseley, 27 December 1845, *Aberdeen Papers*, Add. mss. 43127.
30. Aberdeen to Ouseley, 3 December 1845, *Aberdeen Papers*, Add. mss. 43127.
31. Aberdeen to Peel, 28 December 1845, *Peel Papers*, Add. mss. 40455.
32. Aberdeen to Ouseley, 3 December 1845, *Aberdeen Papers*, Add. mss. 43127.
33. Aberdeen to Ouseley, 27 December 1845, *Aberdeen Papers*, Add. mss. 43127.
34. Aberdeen to Peel, 28 December 1845, *Peel Papers*, Add. mss. 40455.
35. Aberdeen to Ouseley, 27 December 1845, *Aberdeen Papers*, Add. mss. 43127.

Chapter 6

1. The Paraná was reopened on 1 August 1844. However, in December 1844 Corrientes and Paraguay signed a convention by which, much to Rosas' fury, a member state of the Confederation implicitly recognized Paraguay's sovereignty. In retaliation, Rosas closed the Paraná to shipping destined for Corrientes and Paraguay on 8 January 1845. See Irazusta, *Vida Politica*, vol IV, p 299; and Beatriz Bosch, *Los Tratados de Alcaraz* (Buenos Aires, 1955), p 46.
2. Memorandum by Ouseley, 9 October 1845, enclosed in Inglefield to Admiralty, 30 October 1845, ADM 1/5549 Qa.247.
3. Ouseley to Aberdeen, 12 October 1845, F.O. 6/105.
4. Hotham included information from the Paraná in correspondence to members of his family. This information was recorded by his sister, Anne Barlow, in an undated letter preserved in the *Hotham Papers*, DD HO 10/47.
5. Log of HMS *Gorgon*, 20 November 1845, ADM 53/2562.
6. The difficulties of supplying the batteries are explained in Irazusta, *Vida Politica*, vol V, pp 12 and 53; E. Ramirez-Juarez, *Conflictos Diplomaticos y militares en el Rio de la Plata 1842–1845* (Buenos Aires, 1938), pp 101–50 and 161–8; and Ratto, *Los Comodoros Británicos*, pp 173–82. The engagement at Obligado is described in Caillet-Bois, *Historia naval Argentina*, pp 423–8; and Ramirez-Juarez, *Conflictos Diplomaticos y militares*, pp 171–84.
7. 145 marines and 180 seamen were landed. Hotham to Inglefield, 23 November 1845, *Hotham Papers*, DD HO 10/7; and log of HMS *Gorgon*, 20 November 1845, ADM 53/2562.

8. Hotham to Inglefield, 25 June 1846, *Hotham Papers*, DD HO 10/7. See also Santiago Moritan, *Mansilla: su memoria inedita (Buenos Aires, 1945)*.
9. Documents from the early decades of the nineteenth century are reproduced in B.V. Peña, *Paraguay–Argentina Correspondencia diplomática 1810–1840* (Buenos Aires, 1945). Carlos López formally declared Paraguay a sovereign state on 25 November 1842. See Emilio Ravignani (ed), *Asambleas Constituyentes Argentinas* (Buenos Aires, 1939), vol VI, part 2, pp 1120–21. Rosas was never prepared to concede Paraguayan sovereignty, since to do so would have both encouraged secessionism within the Confederation and also undermined his insistence that the Paraná was an inland waterway of the Confederation subject solely to Argentine jurisdiction. See Irazusta, *Vida Politica*, vol IV, pp 117–31; and Levene, *Historia de la Nacion Argentina*, vol VII, part 2, pp 329–35. Paraguayan sovereignty was recognized at Buenos Aires after the overthrow of Rosas in 1852. See Ravignani (ed), *Asambleas Constituyentes*, vol VI, part 2, pp 1122–3.
10. Hotham to Inglefield, 31 January 1846, *Hotham Papers*, DD HO 10/7.
11. Hotham to Inglefield, 2 January 1846, *Hotham Papers*, DD HO 10/7.
12. Log of HMS *Melampus*, 8–24 December 1845, ADM 51/3630; and Inglefield to Admiralty, 19 January 1846, ADM 1/5560 Qa.50.
13. Ouseley to Aberdeen, 24 January 1846, *Aberdeen Papers*, Add. mss. 43127.
14. Ouseley to Aberdeen, 31 January 1846, F.O. 6/115.
15. The paper dollar of Buenos Aires was distinct from the metal-based dollar (peso) which was the common currency of the region and had a sterling value of about 4 shillings, i.e. about 5 dollars to 1 pound. The paper dollar was the product of Rosas' wish to expand the money supply, particularly after 1837, which led naturally to inflation and a swift collapse in its value. See Humphreys (ed), *British Consular reports*, p xxi; and W. Hadfield, *Brazil and the River Plate in 1868* (London, 1869), p 231. Rosas' finances and the fate of the paper dollar are explained in M. Burgin, *The Economic aspects of Argentine Federalism 1820–1852* (New York, 1946), pp 184–217.
16. Lucas to Aberdeen, 2 March 1846, F.O. 6/128; and Lucas to Aberdeen, 22 April 1846, F.O. 6/129. A different set of figures is given in Lynch, *Argentine Dictator*, p 285; and in Morgan, *Anglo–French Confrontation*, p 332. According to these, British exports to Buenos Aires had stood at £700,000 in 1840 and £989,000 in 1841 but were reduced to £592,279 in 1845 and then collapsed to £187,481 in 1846.
17. Aberdeen to Ouseley, 15 January 1846, *Aberdeen Papers*, Add. mss. 43127.
18. Aberdeen to Ouseley, 4 February 1846, *Aberdeen Papers*, Add. mss. 43127.
19. Aberdeen to Ouseley, 4 February 1846, F.O. 6/114.
20. Aberdeen to Ouseley, 4 March 1846, *Aberdeen Papers*, Add. mss. 43127.
21. Aberdeen to Cowley, 23 January 1846, F.O. 27/745.
22. Hansard (Lords), LXXXIII, 19 February 1846.
23. Hansard (Commons), LXXXIV, 23 March 1846.
24. Haddington to Ellenborough, 1846, *Papers of Lord Ellenborough*, PRO, London, PRO 30/12/34/6.
25. Gladstone to Ellenborough, 20 April 1846, *Ellenborough Papers*, PRO, 30/12/5/1.

26. Wellington to Ellenborough, 3 March 1846, *Ellenborough Papers*, PRO, 30/12/5/1.
27. Ellenborough to Wellington, 11 June 1846, *Ellenborough Papers*, PRO, 30/12/5/1.
28. Ellenborough to Peel, 23 February 1846, *Ellenborough Papers*, PRO, 30/12/4/29.
29. Memorandum by Ellenborough, 24 May 1846, *Ellenborough Papers*, PRO, 30/12/5/1.
30. Somerset to Graham, 20 May 1846, enclosed in Graham to Ellenborough, 20 May 1846, *Ellenborough Papers*, PRO, 30/12/5/1.
31. Turner to Aberdeen, 26 November 1845, F.O. 51/37.
32. Turner to Aberdeen, 13 August 1845, F.O. 51/37.
33. Turner to Aberdeen, 26 November 1845, F.O. 51/37.
34. Saldías, *Historia de la Confederación Argentina*, vol IV, pp 246 and 424–5.
35. Torterolo *Vida de Melchor Pacheco y Obes*, pp 122–3.
36. Turner to Aberdeen, 18 April 1846, F.O. 51/40.
37. Aberdeen to Ouseley, 8 April 1846, *Aberdeen Papers*, Add. mss. 43127.
38. Aberdeen to Ouseley, 2 July 1846, F.O. 6/114.
39. Aberdeen to Ouseley, 2 July 1846, *Aberdeen Papers*, Add. mss. 43127.
40. Aberdeen to Ellenborough, 19 June 1846, *Ellenborough Papers*, PRO, 30/12/34/7.
41. Log of HMS *Alecto*, 10 February 1846, ADM 53/2057; and L.B. MacKinnon, *Steam Warfare in the Paraná* (London, 1848), vol I, pp 217–24. Log of HMS *Lizard*, 21 April 1846, ADM 53/2787; Log of HMS *Harpy*, 11 May 1846, ADM 53/2681; Hotham to Inglefield, 30 May 1846, *Hotham Papers*, DD HO 10/7.
42. Hotham to Inglefield, 7 June 1846, *Hotham Papers*, DD HO 10/7.
43. Letter by Barlow, undated, *Hotham Papers*, DD HO 10/47. Caillet-Bois covers events at San Lorenzo in *Historia naval Argentina*, pp 432–4. See also Irazusta, *Vida Politica*, vol V, pp 156–7. MacKinnon, who commanded the rocket brigade on the island, gives an account of the action in *Steam Warfare in the Paraná*, vol II, pp 17–38. See also P.H. Colomb, *Memoirs of Admiral Sir Astley Cooper Key* (London, 1898), p 115.

Chapter 7

1. Aberdeen to Hood, 19 May 1846, F.O. 6/125.
2. Burgin, *The Economic aspects of Argentine Federalism*, pp 185 and 195.
3. Alvear to Guido, 31 December 1845, quoted in Irazusta, *Vida Politica*, vol V, p 108. Details of international reaction are given in Aquiles Oribe, *Manuel Oribe*, vol I, pp 201–4; and Irazusta, *Vida Politica*, vol V, pp 180–219.
4. Buchanan to Brent, 30 March 1846, in Manning, *Diplomatic Correspondence of the United States*, vol I, p 31.
5. Guido to Lozano, 22 December 1845, quoted in Irazusta, *Vida Politica*, vol V, p 102.
6. That Rosas knew this before Hood even left England is plain from Moreno to Alvear, 2 May 1846, quoted in Irazusta, *Vida Politica*, vol V, p 115.

7. Such ideas are succinctly explained in J. Pivel-Devoto, *Historia de la Republica Oriental del Uruguay*, pp 52–3.
8. The career of Justo José de Urquiza (1801–1870) is fully covered in Beatriz Bosch, *Urquiza y su tiempo* (Buenos Aires, 1971); and Comisión Nacional del Homenaje, *Urquiza: El juicio de la posteridad* (Buenos Aires, 1921).
9. Details of Paz's military campaign against Entre Rios in the early months of 1846 are given in Irazusta, *Vida Politica*, vol V, pp 145–8; and Terán, *José María Paz*, pp 126–33.
10. Ouseley to Aberdeen, 6 June 1846, F.O. 6/119. There is also a reference to the meetings with Ouseley in Castro to Urquiza, 12 September 1846, reproduced in Bosch, *Los Tratados de Alcaraz*, p xiii.
11. Hood to Ouseley, 9 July 1846, enclosed in Ouseley to Aberdeen, private, 9 August 1846, F.O. 6/121.
12. Hood to Aberdeen, 13 August 1846, F.O. 6/125.
13. Braconnay, *La Legion Francesa*, p 244. In 1844, when the port had been blockaded by the Argentine squadron, only three merchant ships had left Montevideo. The improvement in commerce in 1845 and 1846 had therefore been very noticeable. The customs receipts at the port, which had amounted to 40,000 dollars in August 1845, were running at 200,000 dollars every month by mid-1846.
14. Ouseley to Aberdeen, private, 9 August 1846, F.O. 6/121.
15. Hood to Aberdeen, private, 24 July 1846, F.O. 6/125.
16. Hood to Addington, private, 25 July 1846, F.O. 6/125.
17. Hood to Aberdeen, 26 August 1846, *Aberdeen Papers*, Add. mss. 43126. This assessment was shared by L.B. MacKinnon of HMS *Alecto*, who was in Montevideo in August 1846. See his *Steam Warfare in the Paraná*, vol II, pp 95–6. The United States chargé d'affaires likewise observed that the members of the Montevidean government 'are the merest puppets, moved by the will and the hands of the British and French Ministers'. Harris to Buchanan, 14 July 1846, in Manning, *Diplomatic Correspondence of the United States*, vol I, p 369.
18. Aberdeen to Hood, 19 May 1846, F.O. 6/125.
19. Hope to Hamilton, 5 December 1845, ADM 1/5579 Cap. H.115.
20. Inglefield to Admiralty, 12 May 1846, ADM 1/5560.
21. Foreign Office to Admiralty, 11 August 1846, F.O. 6/130.
22. Hood to Aberdeen, 26 August 1846, *Aberdeen Papers*, Add. mss. 43126.
23. Hood to Aberdeen, 26 August 1846, F.O. 6/125.
24. Hood to Palmerston, 13 September 1846, F.O. 6/125.
25. Ouseley to Palmerston, private, 11 September 1846, F.O. 6/122.
26. Ouseley to Palmerston, private, 12 September 1846, F.O. 6/122.
27. Hotham to Hamilton, end of August/beginning of September 1846, *Hotham Papers*, DD HO 10/8.
28. Ouseley to Palmerston, private, 12 September 1846, F.O. 6/122.
29. Ouseley to Aberdeen, 4 September 1846, F.O. 6/122.
30. Hotham to Hamilton, end of August/beginning of September 1846, *Hotham Papers*, DD HO 10/8.
31. Hotham to Auckland, 29 September 1846, *Hotham Papers*, DD HO 10/8.
32. Inglefield to Admiralty, 4 September 1846, enclosed in Admiralty to

Foreign Office, 16 November 1846, F.O. 6/131.
33. Ouseley to Aberdeen, 4 September 1846, F.O. 6/122.

Chapter 8

1. The involvement of British merchants in Montevideo with government funding is summarized in their petition to Ouseley, 9 May 1846, F.O. Confidential Print 260. The Uruguayan government's measures to raise money during the war are discussed in Acevedo, *Anales Históricos*, vol II, pp 214–29.
2. Herbert had spent time in Buenos Aires earlier in his career and undoubtedly was well disposed towards Rosas. This is plain from his letter to Rosas, 17 May 1840, and another to Manuelita Rosas, 13 October 1846, reproduced in A. Saldías, *Papeles de Rozas* (La Plata, 1904), vol I, pp 170–2 and 238. There is a sketch of Herbert's career and of his time in the River Plate in Ratto, *Los Comodoros Británicos*, pp 185–216.
3. Ouseley to Palmerston, 26 October 1846, F.O. 6/123.
4. Ouseley to Palmerston, private, 27 November 1846, F.O. 6/124.
5. Hood to Ouseley, 7 December 1846, enclosed in Hood to Palmerston, 28 December 1846, F.O. 51/41.
6. Hood to Bidwell, private, 28 December 1846, F.O. 51/42.
7. Martin Hood to T.S. Hood, 29 January 1847, enclosed in Hood to Stanley, 30 March 1847, F.O. 6/136.
8. Nicholson to Palmerston, 14 January 1847, F.O. 6/136.
9. Auckland to Hotham, 16 November 1846, *Hotham Papers*, DD HO 10/2.
10. Palmerston to Normanby, 29 January 1847, quoted in Morgan, *Anglo-French Confrontation*, p 341.
11. Normanby to Russell, 23 August 1846, *Papers of Lord John Russell*, PRO, London, PRO, 30/22/5B.
12. Aberdeen to Russell, 17 November 1846, *Russell Papers*, PRO, 30/22/5E.
13. Russell to Jarnac, 26 October 1846, *Russell Papers*, PRO, 30/22/5D.

Chapter 9

1. Bosch, *Los Tratados de Alcaraz*, p 44.
2. This was also the prediction of the United States envoy. Harris to Buchanan, 11 May 1847, in Manning, *Diplomatic Correspondence of the United States*, vol I, p 414.
3. Ouseley to Herbert, 6 April 1847, ADM 1/5575 Qa.182.
4. Herbert to Ouseley, 22 March 1847, enclosed in Howden to Palmerston, 14 July 1847, F.O. 6/134.
5. Howden to Palmerston, 26 May 1847, F.O. 6/133.
6. Howden to Palmerston, private, 25 April 1847, F.O. 6/133. Walewski was the son of Maria Walewska and Napoleon Bonaparte. His earlier career included military experience and then a phase of literary and theatrical work as a comedy playwright. Walewski spoke near perfect English, but unfortunately no Spanish. Jacques Duprey, *Un fils de Napoleon I dans les Pays de la Plata, sous la Dictature de Juan Manuel de Rosas: La mis-*

220   WAR, DIPLOMACY AND INFORMAL EMPIRE

sion du Comte Alexandre Colonna Walewski en Argentine et en Uruguay (1847) (Montevideo, 1937) is a useful biography which, pp 155–212, quotes much of Walewski's correspondence with both Guizot and Howden during July and August 1847. Irazusta in *Vida Politica*, vol V, pp 314–15, sums up Howden and Walewski as 'two spoilt little boys'.

7. Howden to Palmerston, 23 May 1847, F.O. 6/133.
8. Howden to Palmerston, 3 June 1847, F.O. 6/133.
9. Howden to Palmerston, 5 June 1847, F.O. 6/133.
10. Howden to Palmerston, 16 June 1847, F.O. 6/133.
11. Howden to Palmerston, 16 June 1847, F.O. 6/133.
12. Howden to Walewski, 5 July 1847, enclosed in Howden to Palmerston, 15 July 1847, F.O. 6/134.
13. Howden to Walewski, 13 July 1847, enclosed in Howden to Palmerston, 15 July 1847, F.O. 6/134.
14. Howden to Palmerston, 15 July 1847, F.O. 6/134.
15. Howden to Palmerston, private, 25 July 1847, F.O. 6/134.
16. Howden to Palmerston, 15 July 1847, F.O. 6/134.
17. In 1847 Rivera wrote to Howden complaining that Montevideo was under French influence 'and at the will of Garibaldi'. Quoted in Aquiles Oribe, *Manuel Oribe*, vol I, p 331. For a biographical sketch of Jean Thiébaut (1790–1851) see Duprey, *Un fils de Napoléon I dans les Pays de la Plata*, pp 275–306.
18. Howden to Palmerston, 15 July 1847, F.O. 6/134. L.B. MacKinnon had formed the same impression in August 1846: see his *Steam Warfare in the Paraná*, vol II, pp 96–7.
19. Howden to Palmerston, 15 July 1847, *Papers of Lord Palmerston*, Historical Manuscripts Commission, London, GC/HO 895–907.
20. Howden to Walewski, 14 July 1847, enclosed in Howden to Palmerston, 12 November 1847, F.O. 13/245.
21. Howden to Palmerston, 20 July 1847, F.O. 6/134.
22. Howden to Palmerston, 15 July 1847, *Palmerston Papers*, GC/HO 895–907.
23. Howden to Palmerston, private, 25 July 1847, F.O. 6/134; and Howden to Campbell, 20 August 1847, *Palmerston Papers*, GC/HO 895–907.
24. Memorandum by Ouseley, 7 June 1847, enclosed in Hood to Palmerston, 9 June 1847, F.O. 51/46.
25. Howden to Hood, 16 June 1847, enclosed in Hood to Palmerston, 18 June 1847, F.O. 51/46.
26. Howden to Aberdeen, 25 July 1847, *Aberdeen Papers*, Add. mss. 43124.
27. Palmerston to Howden, 2 October 1847, *Palmerston Papers*, GC/HO 949–69.
28. Normanby to Russell, 18 September 1847, *Russell Papers*, PRO 30/22/6F.
29. Wood to Russell, 19 September 1847 and 7 October 1847, *Russell Papers*, PRO 30/22/6F.
30. Palmerston to Normanby, 8 October 1847, F.O. 27/776.
31. Normanby to Russell, 18 September 1847, *Russell Papers*, PRO 30/22/6F.

Chapter 10

1. Hood to Palmerston, 12 August 1847, F.O. 51/46. Hood's account of

events was largely confirmed by William Harris in a dispatch to Washington reproduced in Manning, *Diplomatic Correspondence of the United States*, vol I, p 445.
2. The *Nacional* was published between 1838 and its closure in July 1846. The *Courrier de la Plata* appeared between 1846 and 20 August 1848, when its publication was suspended by the government in Montevideo. It reappeared under the name *Sentinelle de la Plata* between September 1848 and February 1849 before reverting to its original title. The *Conservador* was produced for only a few months between November 1847 and its final edition on 3 August 1848. A survey of the Montevidean Press exists in Antonio Zinny, *Historia de la Prensa Periódica de la República Oriental del Uruguay 1807–1852* (Buenos Aires, 1883). There is also a brief sketch in Eduardo Acevedo, *Manual de Historia Uruguaya: Después de Artigas* (Montevideo, 1942), pp 143–5. The history of the *Courrier de la Plata* is outlined in a letter from Herrera y Obes to Ellauri, 17 October 1849, reproduced in *Correspondencia del doctor Manuel Herrera y Obes: Diplomacia de la Defensa de Montevideo* (Buenos Aires, 1913), vol II, pp 152–3.
3. The dispatches written by Devoize to Guizot in August and September 1847 are quoted in Braconnay, *La Legion Francesa*, p 156.
4. The correspondence between Urquiza and Madariaga and between Arana and Urquiza is reproduced in Ravignani (ed), *Asambleas Constituyentes Argentinas*, vol VI, part 2, pp 421–34.
5. Palmerston to Gore, 18 December 1847, F.O. 51/51.
6. Guizot to Devoize, enclosed in Palmerston to Gore, 18 December 1847, F.O. 51/51.
7. Gore to Palmerston, 14 April 1848, F.O. 51/54.
8. Hood to Bidwell, private, 14 April 1848, F.O. 6/140.
9. Hood to Bidwell, private, 22 April 1848, F.O. 6/140.
10. Hood to Gore, 31 March 1848, F.O. 505/31A.
11. This is established by Saldías in *Historia de la Confederación Argentina*, vol V, pp 98–105; by Arana in *Rosas y la Política exterior*, vol I, pp 395–6; and by Levene in *Historia de la Nacion Argentina*, vol VII, part 2, pp 264–6. The 'allied' negotiating position was made clear to Oribe in Arana to Villademoros, 17 May 1848, quoted in Irazusta, *Vida Politica*, vol V, pp 421–3. See also Acevedo, *Anales Históricos*, vol II, pp 296–7. It is the opinion of most Argentine and Uruguayan historians who have written about these events that Rosas made a fatal miscalculation in obliging Oribe to break with the two commissioners, who were really conceding everything that Oribe wanted. In addition see Enrique Olivera, *Evolución y Apogeo de la Diplomacia Uruguaya 1828–1948* (Montevideo, 1984), p 60.
12. Gore to Gros, 25 May 1848, enclosed in Gore to Palmerston, 16 June 1848, F.O. 51/54.
13. Gore to Palmerston, 16 June 1848, F.O. 51/54.

Chapter 11
1. Gore to Palmerston, private, 22 August 1848, F.O. 51/55.
2. Palmerston to Normanby, 12 July 1848, F.O. 27/799.

222 WAR, DIPLOMACY AND INFORMAL EMPIRE

3. Southern to Palmerston, private, 14 October 1848, F.O. 6/139.
4. Southern to Palmerston, private, 14 October 1848, F.O. 6/139.
5. Southern to Palmerston, private, 14 October 1848, F.O. 6/139.
6. Southern to Palmerston, 17 December 1848, F.O. 6/139.
7. Howden to Palmerston, 23 May 1847, F.O. 6/133.
8. Southern to Palmerston, 21 November 1848, F.O. 6/139.
9. Southern to Palmerston, 24 November 1848, F.O. 6/139.
10. O'Brien to Palmerston, 7 November 1848, F.O. 51/60.
11. Palmerston to O'Brien, 13 November 1848, F.O. 51/60. Palmerston's response to O'Brien caused such offence that Herrera contemplated suspending Gore's exequatur as Consul-General in Montevideo, though subsequently he realized that his government was in no position to take this step. Herrera resigned himself henceforth to his belief that Palmerston 'is but the echo of Rosas and the people of the Cerrito'. Herrera to Le Long, 22 March 1849, Herrera, *Correspondencia*, vol II, p 54.
12. Palmerston to Gore, 15 November 1848, F.O. 51/56.
13. Southern to Palmerston, 14 January 1849, F.O. 6/143.
14. Southern to Gore, 20 February 1849, enclosed in Gore to Palmerston, 5 March 1849, F.O. 51/62.
15. Southern to Palmerston, 6 March 1849, F.O. 6/143.
16. Southern to Palmerston, 6 March 1849, F.O. 6/143.
17. Palmerston to Normanby, 20 April 1849, F.O. 27/835.
18. Palmerston to Normanby, 20 April 1849, F.O. 27/835.
19. Palmerston to Southern, 21 April 1849, F.O. 6/142.
20. Gore to Palmerston, private, 9 April 1849, F.O. 51/62.
21. Gore to Palmerston, 28 April 1849, *Palmerston Papers*, GC/GO 54–60.
22. Russell to Palmerston, 13 April 1849, *Russell Papers*, PRO 30/22/7F.
23. Normanby to Palmerston, 9 July 1849, F.O. 27/846.
24. The text of the Arana-Southern convention is printed in the *Registro Oficial de la República Argentina 1810–1873* (Buenos Aires, 1880), vol II, p 466. The British conceded the point on which the negotiations of Howden and Walewski had foundered in 1847. The Paraná River was recognized as an interior waterway of the Argentine Confederation subject solely to its laws and regulations; then, for the River Uruguay, the original Argentine wording was adopted: 'lo mismo que la del Río Uruguay en commún con el Estado Oriental'. Correspondence between Rosas and Arana relating to the negotiations which preceded the convention is reproduced in José Muñoz-Azpiri, *Rosas frente al imperio ingles: historia intima de un triunfo argentino* (Buenos Aires, 1960). In the long run, the form of words relating to the two rivers mattered little. Freedom of navigation on both was granted by the Constituent Congress which met in Santa Fé in 1853 to endorse an international agreement negotiated by the new regime in the Argentine Confederation.

Chapter 12

1. Minute by Palmerston, 30 November 1849, on Normanby to Palmerston, 29 November 1849, F.O. 27/848.

2. Normanby to Palmerston, 28 January 1850, F.O. 27/868.
3. Southern to Palmerston, private, 13 December 1849, F.O. 6/145.
4. The text of this agreement is reproduced in *Registro Oficial de la República Argentina*, vol II, p 468. Le Predour, like Southern in the British agreement of 24 November 1849, now conceded the status of the rivers Paraná and Uruguay.
5. Gore to Palmerston, private, 14 September 1850, F.O. 51/66.
6. Southern to Palmerston, 10 September 1850, F.O. 6/151. The rivalry between Rosas and Urquiza is discussed in Lynch, *Argentine Dictator*, pp 314–16; and in Acevedo, *Anales Históricos*, vol II, pp 334–5.
7. Hudson to Palmerston, private, 12 January 1847, F.O. 13/248.
8. Hudson to Palmerston, private, 13 May 1850, F.O. 13/275.
9. Hudson to Palmerston, private, 9 September 1850, F.O. 13/275.
10. 'War is now certain', the Uruguayan Minister at Rio de Janeiro wrote to his government, 'and, I repeat, perhaps sooner than we think.' Lamas to Herrera, 27 September 1850, Herrera, *Correspondencia*, vol III, p 108.
11. Palmerston to Normanby, 20 December 1850, F.O. 27/867.
12. Urquiza's declaration of 1 May 1851 is reproduced in *Registro Oficial de la República Argentina*, vol II, p 471. See also Urquiza to Rosas, 1 May 1851, reproduced in Ravignani (ed), *Asambleas Constituyentes Argentinas*, vol VI, part 2, pp 998–9. The league between Entre Rios, Brazil and the government in Montevideo was signed on 29 May 1851. Corrientes declared against Rosas on 21 May 1851, although it did not formally sign the pact with Entre Rios, Brazil and Uruguay until 21 November. *Registro Oficial de la República Argentina*, vol II, pp 472 and 475.
13. The career of Eugenio Garzón (1796–1851) is covered in Eugenio Garzón, *La Tragedia del Plata* (Montevideo, 1937); and his early years in Telmo Manacorda, *El General Eugenio Garzón* (Montevideo, 1931). See also Alfredo Lepro, *Años de Forja: Venancio Flores* (Montevideo, 1962), p 19; and Olivera, *Evolución y Apogeo de la Diplomacia Uruguaya*, p 60. The best biographical sketch is in De-María, *Hombres Notables*, vol II, pp 161–78.
14. Gore to Palmerston, 5 September 1851, F.O. 51/71.
15. Southern to Palmerston, 2 October 1851, F.O. 6/160.
16. Southern to Reynolds, 2 October 1851, enclosed in Southern to Palmerston, 2 October 1851, F.O. 6/160.
17. Southern to Palmerston, 2 November 1851, F.O. 6/160.
18. Gore to Palmerston, private, 4 January 1852, F.O. 6/167.
19. Gore's estimate is lower than that given in Bosch, *Urquiza y su tiempo*, p 208. According to Bosch, Urquiza commanded over 28,000 soldiers: 10,350 Entre Reans, 5260 Correntinos, 4249 captured Buenos Aireans, 1970 Uruguayans and 4020 Brazilians. Lynch in *Argentine Dictator*, p 330, mentions 24,000 men with Urquiza and as many as 23,000 in the army of Rosas.
20. The treaty was signed at Rio de Janeiro on 12 October 1851. Its terms are discussed in Acevedo, *Anales Históricos*, vol II, pp 344–7. See also Olivera, *Evolución y Apogeo de la Diplomacia Uruguaya*, p 66, who comments on the modifications to that treaty which were made in March 1852.
21. Bruce to Malmesbury, private, 4 August 1852, F.O. 51/76.

22. Lennon-Hunt to Russell, 6 March 1853, F.O. 51/78. The eclipse of the *caudillo* in Uruguayan politics is discussed by Acevedo in *Anales Históricos*, vol II, pp 346–7.

Chapter 13

1. Auckland to Hotham, 16 June 1847, *Hotham Papers*, DD HO 10/2.
2. Hood to Bidwell, private, 15 June 1848, F.O. 6/140.
3. Memorandum by Howden, December 1848, F.O. 6/141.
4. Hood to Bidwell, private, 21 January 1849, F.O. 6/146.
5. Hood to Palmerston, private, 23 February 1850, F.O. 6/153.
6. Herrera to Ellauri, 22 May 1850, Herrera, *Correspondencia*, vol II, pp 286–7.
7. Lennon-Hunt to Russell, 7 March 1853, F.O. 51/78.
8. Ellauri to Herrera, 9 July 1851, Herrera, *Correspondencia*, vol III, p 303.
9. G.S. Graham, *The China Station: War and Diplomacy 1830–1860* (Oxford, 1978), p 408.
10. Quoted in C.J. Bartlett, *Great Britain and Sea Power 1815–1853* (Oxford, 1963), pp 261–2.
11. Martin Lynn, 'The "Imperialism of Free Trade" and the Case of West Africa c.1830–c.1870', *Journal of Imperial and Commonwealth History*, xv (1986), pp 22–40.
12. Florencio Varela, *Auto-Biografía* (Montevideo, 1848), p 34.
13. Aberdeen to Peel, 25 November 1843, *Peel Papers*, Add. mss. 40454.
14. Palmerston to Howden, 11 February 1847, *Palmerston Papers*, GC/HO 949–69.
15. Howden to Campbell, 20 August 1847, *Palmerston Papers*, GC/HO 895–907. Sir John Davis, as Superintendent of Trade and Governor of Hong Kong, expressed similar sentiments in 1844: 'I am not the first who has been compelled to remark that it is more difficult to deal with our own countrymen at Canton than with the Chinese government.' Quoted in P. Lowe, *Britain in the Far East: a survey from 1819 to the present* (London, 1981), p 17.
16. P. Lowe, *Britain in the Far East*, p 11.
17. Lynn, 'Imperialism of Free Trade', p 27.
18. Ouseley to Palmerston, private, 22 June 1848, F.O. 51/60.
19. Aberdeen to Clarendon, 23 February 1853. See Chamberlain, *Lord Aberdeen*, p 370.
20. Nicholson to Palmerston, 6 November 1846, F.O. 6/131.
21. Gore to Palmerston, private, 3 December 1851, F.O. 6/160.
22. Bruce to Alston, private, 4 June 1852, F.O. 51/75.
23. Proctor to Hood, private, 27 December 1846, F.O. 505/25.
24. M. Hood to T.S. Hood, private, 29 January 1847, F.O. 6/136.
25. Ouseley to Palmerston, 29 April 1847, F.O. 51/50.
26. Ouseley to Aberdeen, 29 March 1846, F.O. 6/116.
27. *Hansard* (Commons), vol LXXXIV, 23 March 1846.
28. Aberdeen to Ouseley, 20 February 1845, *Parliamentary Accounts and Papers*, 1846, vol LII.
29. Comparable instances of Aberdeen's administrative shortcomings are discussed in Chamberlain, *Lord Aberdeen*, pp 317–37.

30. Ouseley to Aberdeen, 4 September 1846, F.O. 6/122.
31. Hudson to Forster, private, 4 May 1847, F.O. 13/249.
32. Howden to Palmerston, 26 May 1847, F.O. 6/133.
33. Dale to Bidwell, private, 20 January 1843, F.O. 51/22.
34. Memorandum by Ouseley, enclosed in Ouseley to Palmerston, private, 27 November 1846, F.O. 6/124.
35. Howden to Palmerston, 26 May 1847, F.O. 6/133.
36. L.B. MacKinnon formed the same opinion from his observations when HMS *Alecto* took Thomas Hood to Buenos Aires in September 1846. See his *Steam Warfare in the Paraná*, vol II, p 99.
37. Aberdeen to Mandeville, 8 November 1843, F.O. 6/87.
38. Dale to Bidwell, private, 27 June 1843, F.O. 51/22.
39. Aberdeen to Hamilton, 4 December 1844, *Aberdeen Papers*, Add. mss. 43124.
40. Howden to Palmerston, 3 July 1847, *Palmerston Papers*, GC/HO 895–907.
41. Howden to Palmerston, 20 July 1847, F.O. 6/134.
42. Varela to Magariños, 5 December 1843, quoted in M. Magariños de Mello, *La Misión de Florencio Varela a Londres 1843–4*, p 283. Irazusta makes the same point in *Vida Politica*, vol V, p 31.
43. Winn, 'British Informal Empire', p 100.
44. Aberdeen to Ouseley, 20 February 1845, *Parliamentary Accounts and Papers*, 1846, vol LII.
45. *Hansard* (Lords) lxxxiii, 19 February 1846. A later Foreign Secretary, Lord Malmesbury, used much the same language in confidential dispatches when he considered the possible threat to Uruguay from Brazil's occupation of Montevideo. Malmesbury told Southern, now at Rio de Janeiro, that he must make the point firmly to the Brazilian government that the British would accept no compromise on Uruguayan sovereignty and that any plans entertained in Rio for putting in an administration at Montevideo sympathetic to Brazil should be dropped at once. Uruguay was created under British mediation in 1828, Malmesbury continued, and interference in the nation's domestic affairs would justify the intervention of the mediating power. Malmesbury to Southern, 1 May 1852, F.O. 13/291.
46. Aberdeen to Ouseley, 20 February 1845, *Parliamentary Accounts and Papers*, 1846, vol LII.
47. Palmerston to Howden, 22 March 1847, F.O. 6/132.
48. Aberdeen to Ouseley, 20 February 1845, *Parliamentary Accounts and Papers*, 1846, vol LII.
49. Howden to Palmerston, 8 February 1847, *Palmerston Papers*, GC/HO 877–894.
50. Palmerston to Russell, 8 December 1846, *Russell Papers*, PRO 30/22/5F.
51. Palmerston to Howden, 11 February 1847, *Palmerston Papers*, GC/HO 949–69.
52. Arana to Moreno, 20 November 1843, quoted in Irazusta, *Vida Politica*, vol IV, p 109. See also the correspondence cited on p 57. Irazusta concludes that, without European interference on behalf of the defenders of Montevideo in 1843, the efforts of its inhabitants to organize resistance would have been worthless. Saldías, in *Historia de la Confederación Argentina*, vol IV, pp 75–7, takes much the same line. Oribe's plan was to take

Montevideo not by a military assault but as the result of successful conspiracy and defections to his cause under the pressures of blockade and hunger. Oribe and Rosas never anticipated that the British and French agents in La Plata would actively obstruct this plan or that Purvis would have the effect of stiffening the will of the inhabitants of the capital to defy them. The judgment of Argentine historians thus supports that of the Liverpool merchant, John Nicholson, who complained in 1844 that 'the protraction of the war is almost entirely owing to the interference of Commodore Purvis'. Nicholson to Aberdeen, 4 March 1844, F.O. 51/32.
53. Ouseley to Aberdeen, 16 April 1846, F.O. 6/117.

Bibliography
Unpublished Material

1. Official Papers

FOREIGN OFFICE RECORDS *(Public Record Office, London)*
General Correspondence Series:
F.O. 6/ Argentina
F.O. 13/ Brazil
F.O. 27/ France
F.O. 59/ and 118/ Paraguay
F.O. 51/ Uruguay

Embassy and Consular:
F.O. 146/
F.O. 505/

ADMIRALTY RECORDS *(Public Record Office, London)*
Correspondence Series:
ADM 1/
ADM 2/

Admirals' Journals:
ADM 50/

Ships' Logs:
ADM 51/
ADM 53/

2. Private Collections

(a) In the Public Record Office, London
Colchester Papers	PRO 30/9
Cowley Papers	F.O. 519/
Ellenborough Papers	PRO 30/12
Howden Papers	PRO 323/3
Russell Papers	PRO 30/22

(b) In the British Library, London

Aberdeen Papers	Add. mss.
Peel Papers	Add. mss.

(c) In the National Maritime Museum, Greenwich

Papers of Rear Admiral Charles John Austen	AUS/
Papers of Admiral Sir Francis William Austen	AUS/
Papers of Admiral Sir Edward Codrington	COD/
Papers of Admiral Sir Henry John Codrington	COD/
Papers of Admiral Sir Leopold McClintock	MCL/
Papers relating to the service of Admiral Edward Tatham	RUSI/

(d) At the Historical Manuscripts Commission, London

Palmerston Papers   General Correspondence series (GC/)

(e) In the University Library, Hull

Papers of Sir Charles Hotham   DD HO/

Published Material

1. Documentary Sources

Correspondencia diplomática del doctor José Ellauri 1839–1844 (Montevideo, 1919)

Correspondencia del doctor Manuel Herrera y Obes: Diplomacia de la defensa de Montevideo
Volume I   (Montevideo, 1901)
Volume II   (Buenos Aires, 1913)
Volume III (Buenos Aires, 1915)

Foot, M.R.D. and **Matthew, H.C.G.** (eds), *The Gladstone Diaries*
Volume III 1840–1847 (Oxford, 1974)
Foreign Office, Confidential Print
(Number 260)

Guillemot, E., *Affaires de la Plata: Extrait de la Correspondance de M. Eugène Guillemot pendant sa mission dans L'Amérique du Sud* (Paris, 1849)
Hansard (Parliamentary Debates)

Humphreys, R.A. (ed), *British Consular Reports on the trade and politics of Latin America 1824–1826* (London, 1940)
Intervention Anglo-Française dans Le Rio de la Plata. Missions de M.M. Deffaudis et Walewski: Documents Destinés aux Chambres (Paris, 1848)

Manning, W.R. (ed), *Diplomatic Correspondence of the United States: Inter-American Affairs 1831–1860*

Volume I: Argentina (Washington, 1932)
Volume VII: Great Britain (Washington, 1936)
Parliamentary Accounts and Papers

Peña, B.V. (ed), *Paraguay-Argentina: Correspondencia diplomática 1810–1840* (Buenos Aires, 1945)
Registro Oficial de la República Argentina 1810–1873
Volume II: 1822–1852 (Buenos Aires, 1880)

Saldías, A. (ed), *Papeles de Rozas* Volumes I and II (La Plata, 1904)
The Times

Webster, C.K. (ed), *Britain and the Independence of Latin America 1812–1830* Volumes I and II (London, 1938)

2. Secondary Sources

Acevedo, E., *Anales Históricos del Uruguay* (Montevideo, 1933)

——— *Manual de Historia Uruguaya: Después de Artigas* (Montevideo, 1942)

Adams, E.D., *British Interests and Activities in Texas 1838–1846* (Baltimore, 1910)

Allison, J.M.S., *Thiers and the French Monarchy* (London, 1926)

Antuña, J.G., *Un Caudillo: El General Fructuoso Rivera* (Madrid, 1948)

Arana, E., *Rosas y la Política Exterior* (Buenos Aires, 1954)

Baldwin, J.R., 'England and the French seizure of the Society islands', *Journal of Modern History*, X (1938)

Bandi, G., *Anita Garibaldi* (Florence, 1932)

Bartlett, C.J., *Great Britain and Sea Power 1815–1853* (Oxford, 1963)

Baumgart, W., *Imperialism: the Idea and Reality of British and French Colonial Expansion 1880–1914* (Oxford, 1982)

Beasley, W.G., *Great Britain and the Opening of Japan 1834–1858* (London, 1951)

Bethell, L., *The Abolition of the Brazilian Slave Trade: Britain, Brazil and the slave trade question 1807–1869* (Cambridge, 1970)

——— (ed), *Spanish America after Independence c.1820–c.1870* (Cambridge,1987)

Bosch, B., *Los Tratados de Alcaraz* (Buenos Aires, 1955)

——— *Urquiza y su tiempo* (Buenos Aires, 1971)

Boulding, K.E. and **Mukerjee, T.** (eds), *Economic Imperialism* (Ann Arbor, 1972)

Bourne, K., *Palmerston: the early years 1784–1841* (London, 1982)

Braconnay, P.C.M., *La Legion Francesa en la Defensa de Montevideo* (Montevideo, 1943)

Brossard, A., *Considérations historiques et politiques sur les Républiques de la Plata* (Paris, 1850)

Brown, L., *The Board of Trade and the Free-Trade Movement 1830–1842* (Oxford, 1958)

Bullen, R., *Palmerston, Guizot and the collapse of the Entente Cordiale* (London, 1974)

Burgin, M., *The Economic aspects of Argentine Federalism 1820–1852* (New York, 1946)

Bury, J.P.T. and **Tombs, R.P.,** *Thiers 1797–1877: a political life* (London, 1986)

Bustamante, J.L., *Los Cinco Errores Capitales de el Intervencion Anglo-Francesa en la Plata* (Montevideo, 1849)

Bustamante, R.M., *Estampas* (Montevideo, 1942)

——— *Juan Maria Perez 1790–1845* (Montevideo, 1945)

Cady, J.F., *Foreign Intervention in the Rio de la Plata 1838–1850* (London, 1929)

Caillet-Bois, J., *Lucio Victorio Mansilla: una excursion a los Indios Ranqueles* (Buenos Aires, 1947)

Caillet-Bois, T., *Historia naval Argentina* (Buenos Aires, 1944)

Carnelli, L., *Oribe y su epoca* (Montevideo, 1959)

Chamberlain, M.E., *Lord Aberdeen* (London, 1983)

——— *Lord Palmerston* (London, 1987)

Colli, N.S., *La Política francesa en el Río de la Plata: Rosas y el Bloqueo de 1838–1840* (Buenos Aires, 1963)

Colomb, P.H., *Memoirs of Admiral Sir Astley Cooper Key* (London, 1898)

Comisión de Homenaje al General Juan O'Brien, *Repatriacion de los Restos del General Juan O'Brien* (Buenos Aires, 1938)

Comisión Nacional Del Homenaje, *Urquiza: El juicio de la posteridad* (Buenos Aires, 1921)

Cunningham, A.B., 'Peel, Aberdeen and the Entente Cordiale', *Bulletin of the Institute of Historical Research*, xxx (1957)

Dean, B., 'British Informal Empire: the case of China', *Journal of Commonwealth and Comparative Politics*, xiv (1976)

Deffaudis, A., *Questions Diplomatiques et particulièrement des Travaux et de l'Organisation du Ministère des Affaires Étrangères* (Paris, 1849)

De-María, I., *Anales de la Defensa de Montevideo 1842–1851* (Montevideo, 1883–7)

——— *Hombres Notables de la Republica Oriental del Uruguay* (Montevideo, 1939)

Diaz, A., *Historia politica y Militar de las Repúblicas del Plata 1828–1866* (Montevideo, 1877–8)

Diaz, C., *Memorias Inéditas* (Buenos Aires, 1878)

Dike, K.O., *Trade and Politics in the Niger Delta 1830–1885* (Oxford, 1956)

Duprey, J., *Un fils de Napoleon I dans les Pays de la Plata, sous la Dictature de Juan Manuel de Rosas: La mission du Comte Alexandre Colonna Walewski en Argentine et en Uruguay (1847)* (Montevideo, 1937)

Eldridge, C. (ed), *British Imperialism in the Nineteenth Century* (London, 1984)

Fabietti, E., *Garibaldi* (Italy, 1930)

Fairbank, J.K., *Trade and Diplomacy on the China Coast: the opening of the Treaty Ports 1842–1854* (Stanford, 1953)

Ferns, H.S., 'Investment and Trade between Britain and Argentina in the nineteenth century', *Economic History Review* iii (1950–1)

——— 'Beginnings of British Investment in Argentina', *Economic History Review*, iv (1951–2)

——— 'Britain's Informal Empire in Argentina, 1806–1914', *Past and Present*, iv (1953)

——— *Britain and Argentina in the Nineteenth Century* (Oxford, 1960)

——— *Argentina* (London, 1969)

Fieldhouse, D.K., *The Theory of Capitalist Imperialism* (London, 1967)

——— *Economics and Empire 1830–1914* (London, 1973)

Finch, M.H.J., *A Political Economy of Uruguay since 1870* (London, 1981)

Flournoy, F.R., *British policy towards Morocco in the Age of Palmerston* (London, 1935)

Fortescue, J.W., *A History of the British Army* (London, 1910)

Fox, G., *Britain and Japan 1858–1883* (Oxford, 1969)

Freitas, N., *Garibaldi en América* (Buenos Aires, 1946)

Gallagher, J. and **Robinson, R.,** 'The Imperialism of Free Trade', *Economic History Review*, vi (1953)

Garibaldi, G., *Autobiography* (London, 1889)

Garzón, E., *La Tragedia del Plata* (Montevideo, 1937)

Gash, N., *Peel* (London, 1976)

Gianello, L., *Florencio Varela* (Buenos Aires, 1948)

Graham, G.S., *The China Station: War and Diplomacy 1830–1860* (Oxford, 1978)

Graham, G.S. and **Humphreys, R.A.** (eds), *The Navy and South America 1807–1823* (London, 1962)

Hadfield, W., *Brazil, the River Plate, and the Falkland Islands* (London, 1854)

────────── *Brazil and the River Plate in 1868* (London, 1869)

Hibbert, C., *Garibaldi and his enemies* (London, 1965)

Hopkins, A.G., 'Economic Imperialism in West Africa: Lagos, 1880–92', *Economic History Review*, xxi (1968)

Hyam, R., *Britain's Imperial Century 1815–1914: A study of Empire and Expansion* (London, 1976)

Ibarguren, C., *Vida del Tirano Rosas* (Buenos Aires, 1930)

Imlah, A.H., *Lord Ellenborough* (Harvard, 1939)

Irazusta, J., *Vida Politica de Juan Manuel de Rosas: a través de su correspondencia*, Volume IV: *La intriga internacional anti-Argentina* (Buenos Aires, 1950), and Volume V: *La agresion Anglo-Francesa* (Buenos Aires, 1961)

Johnson, D., 'The foreign policy of Guizot 1840–1848', *University of Birmingham Historical Journal*, vi (1957)

────────── *Guizot: Aspects of French History 1787–1874* (London, 1963)

Jones, W.D., *Lord Aberdeen and the Americas* (University of Georgia Press, Athens, 1958)

────────── 'The Argentine British Colony in the time of Rosas', *Hispanic American Historical Review* xl (1960)

────────── *The American Problem in British Diplomacy, 1841–1861* (London, 1974)

Jones-Parry, E., 'A Review of the relations between Guizot and Lord Aberdeen 1840–1852', *History*, xxiii (1938–9)

Kaufmann, W.W., *British Policy and the Independence of Latin America, 1804–1828* (New Haven, 1951)

Key, A.C., *A narrative of the recovery of HMS Gorgon: Stranded in the bay of Montevideo, May 10 1844* (London, 1847)

Kiernan, V.G., 'Britain's first contacts with Paraguay', *Atlante*, iii (1955)

Larg, D., *Giuseppe Garibaldi* (London, 1934)

Lepro, A., *Fructuoso Rivera* (Montevideo, 1945)

────────── *Años de Forja: Venancio Flores* (Montevideo, 1962)

Levene, R., *A History of Argentina* (New York, 1937)

———— *Historia de la Nacion Argentina* Volume VII: *Rosas y su época* (Buenos Aires, 1950)

Lewis, C.M., *British Railways in Argentina 1857–1914* (London, 1983)

Louis, W.R. (ed), *Imperialism* (London, 1976)

Loveman, B., *Chile* (New York, 1979)

Lowe, P., *Britain in the Far East: a survey from 1819 to the present* (London, 1981)

Lynch, J., 'British policy and Spanish America, 1783–1808', *Journal of Latin American Studies*, i (1969)

———— *The Spanish American Revolutions 1808–1826* (London, 1973)

———— *Argentine Dictator: Juan Manuel de Rosas 1829–1852* (Oxford, 1981)

———— *Caudillos in Spanish America 1800–1850* (Oxford, 1992)

Lynn, M., 'The "Imperialism of Free Trade" and the Case of West Africa c.1830–c.1870', *Journal of Imperial and Commonwealth History*, xv (1986)

MacKinnon, L.B., *Steam Warfare in the Paraná* (London, 1848)

McLean, D., 'Finance and "Informal Empire" before the First World War', *Economic History Review*, xxix (1976)

———— 'The Greek revolution and the Anglo-French entente 1843–4', *English Historical Review*, xcvi (1981)

Mack-Smith, D., *Garibaldi* (London, 1957)

Magariños de Mello, M., *La Misión de Florencio Varela a Londres 1843–4* (Montevideo, 1944)

———— *La Politica Exterior del Imperio del Brasil y las Intervenciones Extranjeras en el Rio de la Plata (Antecedentes de la Misión Ouseley-Deffaudis)* in Instituto 'Gonzalo Fernandez de Oviedo', *Miscelanea Americanista*, iii (Madrid, 1952)

Manacorda, T., *El General Eugenio Garzón* (Montevideo, 1931)

———— *Fructuoso Rivera* (Madrid, 1933)

Manchester, A.K., *British Preeminence in Brazil: its rise and decline* (Chapel Hill, 1933)

Markham, C., *Life of Admiral Sir Leopold McClintock* (London, 1909)

Mathew, W.M., 'The Imperialism of Free Trade: Peru, 1820–70', *Economic History Review*, xxi (1968)

Metford, J.C.J., 'The Recognition by Great Britain of the United Provinces of Río de la Plata', *Bulletin of Hispanic Studies*, xxix (1952)
Mission de M. Ouseley et du Baron Deffaudis a Rio de la Plata (Paris, 1846)

Mitre, B., *Un Episodio Troyano: recuerdos del sitio grande de Montevideo* in G. Garibaldi, *Garibaldi en América* (Buenos Aires, 1888)

Mommsen, W.J., *Theories of Imperialism* (New York, 1980)

Mommsen, W.J. and **Osterhammel, J.** (eds), *Imperialism and After* (London, 1986)

Moreno, E., *Aspectos de la Guerra Grande 1847–1851* (Montevideo, 1925)

Morgan, I.W., *Anglo-French Confrontation and Co-operation in Spanish America, 1836–1848* (University of London, PhD thesis, 1975)

Moritan, S., *Mansilla: su memoria inedita* (Buenos Aires, 1945)

Mulhall, M.G., *The English in South America* (Buenos Aires, 1878)

Mulhall, M.G. and **Mulhall, E.T.,** *Handbook of the River Plate Republics* (London, 1875)

Muñoz-Azpiri, J.L., *Rosas frente al imperio ingles: historia intima de un triunfo argentino* (Buenos Aires, 1960)

Olivera, E.A., *Evolución y Apogeo de la Diplomacia Uruguaya 1828–1948* (Montevideo, 1984)

Oribe, A.B., *Manuel Oribe* (Montevideo, 1913)

Owen R. and **Sutcliffe, B.** (eds), *Studies in the Theory of Imperialism* (London, 1972)

Page, W. (ed), *Commerce and Industry: tables of statistics for the British Empire from 1815* (London, 1919)

Palomeque, A., *Estudios Históricos de la Diplomacia de la Defensa de Montevideo* (Montevideo, 1898)

——— *El General Rivera y La campaña de Misiones (1828)* (Buenos Aires, 1914)

——— *Asambleas Legislativas del Uruguay 1850–1863* (Barcelona, 1915)

Paz, J.M., *Memorias Póstumas* (Buenos Aires, 1930)

Pendle, G., *Paraguay* (London, 1956)

——— *Uruguay* (Oxford, 1965)

Pereda, S.E., *Los Extranjeros en la Guerra Grande* (Montevideo, 1904)

——— *Garibaldi en el Uruguay* (Montevideo, 1914–16)

Pereira, A.N., *La Invasion Inglesa en el Rio de la Plata* (Montevideo, 1877)

Peterson, H.F., *Argentina and the United States 1810–1960* (New York, 1964)

Pivel-Devoto, J.E., *Historia de la Republica Oriental del Uruguay 1830–1930* (Montevideo, 1945)

——— *Historia de los Partidos y de las Ideas Politicas en el Uruguay* (Montevideo, 1956)

Platt, D.C.M., 'British Diplomacy in Latin America since the Emancipation', *Inter-American Economic Affairs*, xxi (1967)

─────────── *Finance, Trade, and Politics in British Foreign Policy 1815–1914* (Oxford, 1968)

─────────── *Latin America and British Trade 1806–1914* (London, 1972)

─────────── (ed), *Business Imperialism 1840–1930* (Oxford, 1977)

Pomer, L., *Conflictos en la Cuenca del Plata en el siglo XIX* (Buenos Aires, 1984)

Pratt, E.J., 'Anglo-American Commercial and Political Rivalry on the Plata, 1820–1830', *Hispanic American Historical Review*, xi (1931)

Puentes, G.A., *La Intervencion Francesa en el Rio de la Plata* (Buenos Aires, 1958)

Puryear, V.J., *International Economics and Diplomacy in the Near East: a study of British Commercial Policy in the Levant 1834–1853* (London, 1935)

Quesada, E., *La Epoca de Rosas* (Buenos Aires, 1926)

Ramirez-Juarez, E., *Conflictos Diplomaticos y Militares en el Rio de la Plata 1842–1845* (Buenos Aires, 1938)

Ratto, H.R., *Los Comodoros Británicos de Estacion en el Plata (1810–1852)* (Buenos Aires, 1945)

─────────── (ed), *Memorias del Almirante Guillermo Brown sobre las Operaciones Navales de la Escuadra Argentina de 1814 a 1828* (Buenos Aires, 1956)

Ravignani, E., *Rosas: Interpretación real y moderna* (Buenos Aires, 1970)

─────────── (ed), *Asambleas Constituyentes Argentinas* Volume VI (Buenos Aires, 1939)

Redford, A., *Manchester Merchants and Foreign Trade 1794–1858* (Manchester, 1934)

Reeves, J.S., *American Diplomacy under Tyler and Polk* (Baltimore, 1907)

Rippy, J.F., *Rivalry of the United States and Great Britain over Latin America 1808–1830* (Baltimore, 1929)

Robertson, W.S., 'Foreign Estimates of the Argentine Dictator, Juan Manuel de Rosas', *Hispanic American Historical Review*, x (1930)

─────────── 'French Intervention in Mexico in 1838', *Hispanic American Historical Review*, xxiv (1944)

Robinson, R. and **Gallagher, J.,** *Africa and the Victorians: the official mind of Imperialism* (London, 1961)

Rock, D., *Argentina 1516–1982* (London, 1986)

Ruiz-Moreno, I., *Historia de las Relaciones Exteriores Argentinas (1810–1955)* (Buenos Aires, 1961)

Sacerdote, G., *La Vita di Giuseppe Garibaldi* (Milan, 1933)

Saldías, A., *Historia de la Confederación Argentina* (Buenos Aires, 1911)

Seckinger, R., *The Brazilian Monarchy and the South American Republics 1822–1831* (Baton Rouge, 1984)

Selgas, G.G., *La Eleccion Presidencial de Don Manuel Oribe* (Montevideo, 1935)

Shaw, A.G.L. (ed), *Great Britain and the Colonies 1815–1865* (London, 1970)

Smith, J., 'New World Diplomacy: a reappraisal of British policy toward Latin America, 1823–1850', *Inter-American Economic Affairs*, xxxii (1978)

Sosa, J.M., *Lavalleja y Oribe* (Montevideo, 1902)

Southgate, D., *The Most English Minister: the policies and politics of Palmerston* (London, 1966)

Street, J., 'Lord Strangford and Río de la Plata, 1808–1815', *Hispanic American Historical Review*, xxxiii (1953)

──────── *Artigas and the Emancipation of Uruguay* (Cambridge, 1959)

Terán, J.B., *José María Paz 1791–1854* (Buenos Aires, 1936)

Torterolo, L.M., *Vida de Melchor Pacheco y Obes* (Montevideo, 1920)

Van Alstyne, R.W., 'The Central American policy of Lord Palmerston, 1846–1848', *Hispanic American Historical Review*, xvi (1936)

Varela, F., *Auto-Biografía* (Montevideo, 1848)

Vignale, J.C., *Oribe* (Montevideo, 1942)

Ward, J.M., *British policy in the South Pacific 1786–1893* (Sydney, 1948)

Weinberg, F. (ed), *Florencio Varela y el Comercio del Plata* (Bahía Blanca, 1970)

Williams, J.B., *British Commercial Policy and Trade Expansion 1750–1850* (Oxford, 1972)

Williamson, E., *The Penguin History of Latin America* (London, 1992)

Winn, P., 'British Informal Empire in Uruguay in the Nineteenth Century', *Past and Present*, 73 (1976)

Zinny, A., *Historia de la Prensa Periódica de la República Oriental del Uruguay 1807–1852* (Buenos Aires, 1883)

Index

45th regiment, 83, 87, 91, 92, 95, 103, 105
73rd regiment, 86, 91, 92, 95, 103, 105

Aberdeen, Earl of, 26, 27, 28, 29, 32, 33, 34, 35, 41, 42, 46, 47, 48, 49, 50, 51, 52, 53, 55, 56, 60, 63, 64, 67, 70, 71, 73, 76, 77, 78, 79, 80, 81, 86, 87, 88, 89, 90, 92, 93, 96, 97, 98, 99, 105, 106, 107, 108, 110, 111, 112, 116, 122, 124, 125, 191, 193, 194, 195, 196, 197, 198, 199, 200, 201, 203, 204, 205;
health of, 30
D'Abrantes, Count, 59, 61, 62, 63
HMS *Alfred*, 39, 43
Algeria, 31
de Alvear, Carlos, 68, 102
Anglo-Argentine Treaty (1825), 9, 20, 40, 160, 162
Anglo-French fleet, 46, 57, 59, 75, 104, 105, 144
Anglo-French relations, 28, 29, 30, 41, 51, 52, 63, 64, 86, 114, 118, 125, 127, 138, 143, 148, 150, 166, 169, 170, 172, 175, 177, 188, 196, 197, 204, 205
Arana, Felipe, 15, 24, 25, 26, 32, 33, 35, 39, 40, 41, 43, 67, 68, 70, 72, 77, 105, 106, 112, 122, 127, 131, 132, 133, 134, 135, 136, 137, 161, 162, 170, 183, 201, 206
Argentine Confederation, 7, 11, 17, 18, 21, 24, 25, 26, 33, 34, 35, 36, 39, 40, 43, 44, 47, 57, 67, 69, 70, 72, 73, 81, 82, 83, 84, 85, 93, 97, 99, 102, 103, 117, 118, 122, 127, 128, 129, 131, 132, 134, 135, 136, 138, 148, 151, 154, 156, 160, 162, 165, 170, 171, 172, 175, 177, 180, 182, 185, 192, 199, 202, 206;
peace restored with Britain, 171;
relations with Brazil, 180

Artigas, José, 10, 11,
Association of Mexican and South American Merchants, 48
Auckland, Earl of, 123, 188
Austria, 29, 126, 169

Banda Oriental *see* Uruguay
Beaumont, Lord, 90
Beecroft, John, 191
Bolivia, 7, 202
Brazil, 11, 16, 19, 20, 37, 57, 58, 59, 60, 62, 66, 75, 95, 102, 135, 154, 175, 177, 179, 180, 182, 183, 184, 186, 187, 197, 202;
neutrality of, 179;
relations with Britain, 178
Brent, William, 68, 77, 102
Britain, 1, 20, 34, 39, 40, 41, 42, 47, 58, 59, 60, 61, 62, 63, 66, 67, 76, 80, 81, 87, 88, 94, 95, 96, 101, 102, 105, 106, 109, 119, 124, 128, 132, 134, 135, 136, 137, 144, 152, 155, 159, 160, 168, 177, 181, 182, 187, 188, 198, 199, 201, 202, 203, 204, 205;
commercial interests in La Plata, 80, 96, 201, 206;
diminished credibility of, 189;
diplomacy of, 3;
economic interests, 10, 190;
exports from, 6, 8, 9, 17, 87, 118, 123, 167, 206;
intervention policy of, 49–65;
limits of authority, 2;
navy *see* Royal Navy;
neutrality of, 45, 46, 52, 67, 97;
occupation of Falkland Islands, 15;
offer of mediation, 25, 26;
peace restored with Argentine Confederation, 171;
policy before 1836, 5;
relations with Brazil, 178;
treaty with Uruguay, 45 *see also*

Anglo-French fleet *and* Anglo-French relations
British residents, pressed into service, 120
Brooke, James, 92
Brown, Admiral William, 40, 41, 43, 69, 72, 73
Bruce, Frederick, 187, 192
Buceo, blockade of, 44
Buchanan, James, 77, 102, 138
Buenos Aires: blockade of, 22, 23, 31, 36, 70, 73, 74, 75, 80, 102, 106, 110, 111, 113, 122, 128, 129, 131, 137, 140, 141, 157, 188, 195 (threatened, 20; lifting of, 161);
British nationals in, 9, 10, 14, 59, 70;
economic boom in, 167;
French nationals in, 70;
growth of, 13;
labour shortage in, 24;
terror in, 14

China, 189, 198;
British in, 199
Clarendon, Lord, 157, 191, 194
Colchester, Lord, 90
Colonia, 139, 192;
battle at, 74;
fall of, 158
HMS *Comus*, 73
Confederation of the United Provinces of the River Plate, 12
Corrientes state, 22, 24, 26, 27, 34, 54, 58, 76, 82, 85, 88, 99, 103, 104, 122, 129, 131, 148, 178, 182, 184
Cowley, Lord, 52, 62 63, 64, 89, 195, 196

Dale, John, 37, 38, 39, 42, 46, 47, 53, 120, 200, 205
Deffaudis, Baron Anton, 64, 66, 69, 70, 71, 72, 73, 75, 77, 78, 81, 82, 86, 88, 89, 90, 91, 93, 96, 97, 98, 101, 103, 106, 107, 108, 109, 110, 111, 112, 113, 114, 116, 118, 121, 123, 124, 129, 137, 141, 147, 168, 191, 194, 195, 196, 198, 205, 206
Desages, Emile, 61
Devoize, Consul-General, 148, 151, 154

HMS *Eagle*, 72
Echagüe, General Pascual, 22, 23, 26
Egypt, 29
Ellauri José, 47, 50, 56, 189

Ellenborough, Lord, 91, 92
entente cordiale, 28, 56, 124, 125, 146, 147, 197, 204
Entre Rios, 76, 103, 104, 122, 131, 148, 176, 177, 178, 182, 184;
invasion threatened, 85, 86;
plunder in, 26

Falkland Islands, 75, 155;
occupied by Britain, 15
France, 16, 17, 20, 22, 23, 28, 39, 41, 42, 46, 47, 51, 58, 59, 60, 61, 62, 66, 67, 70, 76, 80, 81, 88, 89, 90, 92, 94, 95, 96, 101, 102, 105, 106, 109, 120, 122, 123, 124, 126, 128, 132, 134, 135, 136, 137, 139, 140, 143, 144, 147, 148, 152, 154, 155, 158, 159, 160, 162, 164, 168, 174, 176, 177, 181, 184, 186, 187, 198, 199, 202, 204, 205;
British distrust of, 27, 51, 114, 170, 197;
intervention policy of, 49–65, 119;
navy of, 21, 22, 33, 35, 72, 73, 74, 78, 83, 84, 94, 99, 106, 111, 121, 138, 139, 145, 147, 150, 151, 161, 167, 183, 192;
recalls London ambassador, 175;
revolution in, 158, 197;
withdrawal from Morocco, 56 *see also* Anglo-French fleet *and* Anglo-French relations

Garibaldi, Giuseppe, 37, 141, 153
Garzón, Eugenio, 182, 186
Gladstone, William, 91
Gore, Captain Robert, 149, 150, 151, 152, 153, 155, 156, 157, 160, 163, 164, 166, 167, 168, 171, 174, 175, 183, 184, 185, 192, 198
Granville, Lord, 191
Greco–Turkish War, 51
Greece, 52, 56
Grenfell, Admiral John, 181
Gros, Baron Jean Battiste Louis, 149, 150, 152, 155, 156, 157, 158, 163, 170, 198
Guido, General Tomás, 66, 77, 102, 103, 178, 180
Guillemot, Eugène, 164, 166
Guizot, François, 30, 32, 51, 52, 53, 54, 55, 56, 59, 60, 61, 62, 63, 78, 79, 88, 89, 96, 98, 108, 123, 124, 125,

INDEX

126, 127, 140, 144, 146, 148, 149, 154, 169, 196, 197, 198, 199, 204, 205

Haddington, Lord, 90
Hamilton, Hamilton Charles, 57, 58, 75
Harris, William, 138
Herbert, Sir Thomas, 119, 122, 130, 134, 137, 141, 151, 158, 161, 191, 193, 197, 198
Herrera y Obes, Manuel, 152, 153, 189
Hervey, Lord William, 125
de la Hitte, General, 172, 173, 176
Hood, Martin, 120, 121, 143, 147, 153, 154, 155, 157, 162, 188, 191, 193, 197 (takes up consular post, 167)
Hood, Thomas Samuel, 17, 35, 98, 109, 115, 120, 121, 122, 126, 128, 129, 132, 133, 141, 149, 154, 155, 160, 162, 164, 165, 166, 191, 195, 196, 197, 203;
    mission to La Plata, 101–17
Hotham, Charles, 83, 84, 85, 86, 96, 99, 100, 114, 115, 123
Howden, Lord, 126, 127, 147, 149, 160, 171, 190, 191, 197, 198, 199, 202, 203, 204;
    diplomatic activity of, 128–46
Hudson, James, 164, 178, 179, 180, 181, 182, 197

India, 92
Inglefield, Samuel, 69, 70, 71, 72, 73, 84, 85, 90, 92, 95, 97 105, 108, 111, 114, 115, 116, 119, 121, 193
Ireland, 98
Isabella, Queen, 52, 125, 149
Italy, 149, 169

Jacuhy, Baron, 179, 180

Lainé, Admiral, 53, 54, 72, 105, 111
La Plata: economy of, 10;
    exports of, 6;
    viceroyalty created, 6
Lavalle, General Juan, 12, 20, 21, 22, 23, 24;
    killed, 26
legions, foreign, 37, 38, 54, 65, 107, 119, 139, 141, 143, 153, 154, 167, 168, 174, 192;
    disarming of, 54, 106, 175, 176, 180, 181, 195

Lennon-Hunt, George, 186, 187, 189, 192
Le Predour, Joseph, 142, 151, 160, 164, 165, 166, 167, 168, 170, 172, 173, 174, 175, 176, 180, 181, 182
de Lhuys, Drougn, 169
López, General Carlos, 85, 86
Louis-Philippe, 32, 52, 56, 61, 125, 126, 169, 198, 204, 205
Louisa, Infanta, 52, 125
de Lurde, Comte Alexandre, 33, 35, 39, 40, 43, 61, 62, 198, 203

de Madariaga, Joaquín, 104, 122, 129, 148
Magariños, Francisco, 95
de Makau, Baron René Armand, 23–4, 51, 61, 62, 197
Maldonado: fall of, 139;
    port closed, 44
Mandeville, John, 22, 23, 24, 25, 26, 32, 33, 34, 35, 39, 40, 41, 42, 43, 44, 45, 46, 47, 48, 54, 55, 66, 198, 200, 201, 202, 203, 205, 206
Mazorca society, 13
Mehemet Ali, 29
Mexican and South American Association, 55
Mexico, 31, 63, 138
migration: British, 9;
    European, 186;
    French, 9, 16;
    Italian, 9, 16;
    Spanish, 16
Montevideo, 37, 95, 153;
    as merchant centre, 16;
    Basque presence in, 35, 37;
    blockade of, 21, 37, 39, 40, 44, 47, 64, 65, 68, 70, 71, 72, 80, 115, 123, 134, 137, 142, 144, 145, 192, 200, 203 (lifting of, 183);
    British interests in, 50, 190;
    British merchants in, 118, 142, 190;
    British nationals in, 31, 37, 161, 192;
    danger of bombardment of, 69;
    defence of, 22, 36, 41, 80, 93, 94, 97, 115, 130, 139, 151, 158, 167, 186, 188, 193, 194, 199;
    economy of, 186;
    fall of (in 1814, 10; in 1817, 11);
    foreign nationals in, 42, 43, 53, 97, 118, 141, 205 (disarming of, 110, 134, 150);
    French nationals in, 31, 37, 38, 53, 54, 114, 126, 153, 176, 187;

garrison at, 65, 67, 86, 128, 129 133, 163, 180, 182;
growth of, 19;
Italians in, 53;
liberation of, 172–87;
martial law declared, 95;
proposal of surrender, 139, 140, 189;
threat of attack on, 75
Montpensier, Duke, 125
Moreno, Manuel, 41, 79, 159, 206
Morgan, John, 181
Muñoz, Francisco, 96

Napier, Lord, 191
Napoleon, Louis, 164, 169, 172
New Zealand, annexation of, 92
Normanby, 124, 125, 126, 144, 145, 146, 166, 168, 169, 170, 172, 173, 176, 181, 197

O'Brien, John, 162, 163
Oribe, General Manuel, 19–21, 24, 25, 32 34, 35, 36, 37, 38, 39, 42, 43, 44, 50, 55, 57, 60, 65, 68, 69, 71, 72, 75, 78, 80, 81, 86, 88, 93, 97, 101, 102, 104, 105, 106, 107, 108, 109, 113, 114, 115, 120, 122, 128, 130, 132, 133, 134, 135, 137, 139, 140, 141, 142, 146, 147, 148, 150, 151, 152, 153, 154, 155, 156, 158, 160, 163, 167, 168, 171, 173, 174, 175, 176, 178, 179, 181, 182, 183, 192, 195, 198, 199, 200, 201, 202, 203, 205, 206;
problem of recognition as president of Uruguay, 79, 107, 110, 132, 136, 152, 165, 166, 172;
surrender of, 183, 186
Ouseley, William Gore, 55, 60, 61, 62, 63, 64, 66–81, 82, 85, 86, 87, 89, 90, 92, 93, 95, 96, 97, 98, 99, 100, 101, 102, 103, 105, 106, 107, 108, 109, 110, 111, 112, 113, 114, 115, 116, 117, 129, 130, 142, 143, 149, 162, 168, 191, 192, 193, 194, 195, 196, 197, 198, 200, 201, 202, 204, 206;
role in continuation of war, 118–27

Palmerston, Lord, 21, 23, 24, 25, 27, 28, 29, 31, 32, 90, 98, 110, 111, 112, 113, 114, 116, 119, 121, 122, 123, 125, 126, 127, 133, 137, 138, 140, 142, 143, 144, 145, 146, 158, 159, 161, 162, 163, 164, 166, 168, 170, 175, 176, 178, 179, 180, 181, 182, 185, 188, 189, 191, 192, 194, 197, 198, 199, 200, 202, 204, 205;
and search for settlement, 147–57
Pampas, culture of, 7
Paraguay, 7, 84, 85, 86, 88, 103
Paraná river, 195, 201;
clearing of, 76, 185;
closure of, 8, 25, 70, 182;
expedition into, 81, 82–100;
fortifications of, 83, 99;
rescue of stranded ships, 82;
status as waterway, 156, 165
Paysandu, surrender of, 121, 122
Paz, José María, 26, 27, 58, 76, 85, 86, 104
Peel, Sir Robert, 27, 29, 30, 48, 49, 50, 51, 52, 53, 56, 58, 79, 81, 90, 92, 124, 196;
resignation of, 98
Plate river, importance of, 5–18;
imposition of customs dues, 12
Polk, James, 77, 102, 103, 138
Portugal, 10, 11;
civil war in, 28, 149
Prussia, 29
Purvis, Commodore John, 36, 39, 40, 41, 42, 43, 44, 45, 48, 54, 193, 200, 201, 205, 206

Republicano warship, 83, 84
Reynolds, Admiral Barrington, 173, 183
Rivera, General Fructuoso, 19–22, 24, 25, 26, 27, 36, 37, 54, 71, 95, 105, 120, 121, 192;
defeat of, 34, 35, 65, 129;
military expedition of, 101;
opposition to Rosas, 21
de Rosas, General Juan Manuel, 12, 13–15, 20, 25, 27, 33, 35, 37, 41, 45, 46, 50, 55, 57, 58, 59, 60, 61, 64, 67, 68, 70, 74, 75, 76, 77, 79, 80, 81, 93, 97, 98, 101, 102, 103, 105, 106, 107, 109, 110, 112, 113, 115, 116, 117, 119, 122, 128, 129, 130, 131, 132, 133, 134, 135, 137, 138, 141, 146, 150, 154, 155, 156, 157, 158, 159, 160, 161, 162, 163, 164, 165, 167, 170, 172, 173, 174, 175, 176, 177, 178, 180, 182, 183, 184, 185, 186, 188, 189, 198, 199, 200, 206;
army routed, 185;

INDEX 241

opposition to, 16, 24, 85, 86, 147, 148;
  question of war with, 96;
  reign of terror, 13, 14, 200;
  relations with Britain, 15
Rosas, Manuelita, 14, 72, 133, 185
Royal Navy, 3, 17, 35, 39, 68, 72, 73, 74, 83, 84, 94, 97, 99, 106, 111, 121, 129, 138, 139, 145, 150, 151, 175, 189, 198
Russell, Lord John, 124, 125, 144, 146, 169, 194, 205
Russia, 28, 29

slave trade, suppression of, 63, 178
slaves, emancipation of, 11, 36
Southern, Henry, 157, 158, 159, 160, 161, 162, 163, 164, 165, 167, 168, 170, 171, 172, 173, 175, 176, 180, 183, 184
Spain, 5, 10, 89, 102, 125, 126, 148, 169, 196;
  civil war in, 28, 36;
  fragmentation of empire, 7
Spanish marriage issue, 169
Suárez, Joaquín, 36, 95, 140, 147, 152, 158, 194
Switzerland, civil war in, 149

Tahiti: British consul arrested, 56, 61;
  Queen of, 55
Tangiers, bombardment of, 56
Texas, independence of, 63
Thiébaut, Jean, 141, 154, 174
Thiers, Adolphe, 30, 153
Tréhouart, Captain François-Thomas, 83, 84, 99
Turkey, 29

Turner, Adolphus, 54, 58, 64, 65, 67, 69, 95, 120

United States of America (USA), 15, 29, 67, 68, 70, 77, 92, 102, 103, 138, 175
de Urquiza, Justo José, 104, 105, 122, 129, 148, 176, 177, 182, 183, 184, 185, 200
Uruguay, 11, 15, 17, 26, 32, 34, 35, 37, 39, 43, 49, 50, 67, 71, 74, 79, 81, 82, 88, 90, 93, 94, 95, 101, 102, 103, 106, 113, 114, 118, 119, 122, 127, 128, 130, 132, 134, 136, 139, 143, 144, 145, 151, 153, 155, 156, 158, 162, 172, 174, 176, 178, 183, 184, 192, 197, 202, 206;
  invasion of, 19–38;
  relations with Britain, 45, 189;
  sovereignty of, 135, 170, 182, 187, 203, 204 *see also* Oribe, problem of recognition
Uruguay river, 195, 201;
  clearing of, 73;
  closure of, 25, 70;
  status as waterway, 136, 138, 156

Varela, Florencio, 50, 51, 190, 202
Vázquez, Santiago, 45, 47, 56, 96
Vidal, Francisco, 45, 46, 47
Vuelta del Obligado, action at, 83–5, 99, 100, 111

Walewski, Comte Colonna, 127, 160, 197, 198;
  diplomatic activity of, 128–46
Wellington, Duke of, 90, 91
Whitelocke, General John, 6
Wood, Sir Charles, 145

www.ingramcontent.com/pod-product-compliance
Lightning Source LLC
Chambersburg PA
CBHW072147290426
44111CB00012B/1998